ETHICAL AND LEGAL ISSUES IN COUNSELING CHILDREN AND ADOLESCENTS

Edited by Teri Ann Sartor, Bill McHenry, and Jim McHenry

Routledge
Taylor & Francis Group

NEW YORK AND LONDON

First published 2017
by Routledge
711 Third Avenue, New York, NY 10017

and by Routledge
2 Park Square, Milton Park, Abingdon, Oxon, OX14 4RN

Routledge is an imprint of the Taylor & Francis Group, an informa business

© 2017 Taylor & Francis

Library of Congress Cataloging-in-Publication Data
Names: Sartor, Teri Ann, author. | McHenry, Bill, 1971– author. |
    McHenry, Jim, 1937– author.
Title: Ethical and legal issues in counseling children and adolescents /
    by Teri Ann Sartor, Bill McHenry and Jim McHenry.
Description: New York, NY : Routledge, 2016. | Includes bibliographical
    references and index.
Identifiers: LCCN 2015050396 | ISBN 9781138947993 (hardback : alk. paper) |
    ISBN 9781138948006 (pbk. : alk. paper) | ISBN 9781315660714 (ebook)
Subjects: LCSH: Counselors—Professional ethics. | Counseling—Law and
    legislation. | Children—Counseling of—Moral and ethical aspects. |
    Teenagers—Counseling of—Moral and ethical aspects.
Classification: LCC BF636.67 .S27 2016 | DDC 174/.91583—dc23
LC record available at http://lccn.loc.gov/2015050396

ISBN: 978-1-138-94799-3 (hbk)
ISBN: 978-1-138-94800-6 (pbk)
ISBN: 978-1-315-66071-4 (ebk)

Typeset in Adobe Caslon
by Apex CoVantage, LLC

ETHICAL AND LEGAL ISSUES IN COUNSELING CHILDREN AND ADOLESCENTS

Ethical and Legal Issues in Counseling Children and Adolescents provides counselors and other professionals with clinical cases and accurate, up-to-date information on both ethical standards and case law. Chapters take a comprehensive, developmental approach to legal and ethical decision making when counseling children and adolescents, one that presents each chapter topic from the perspective of an adult and then explores accommodations important to children and adolescents. The book is a vital resource for faculty who recognize the limited scope with which other texts cover the topic and for practitioners looking to better understand the legal and ethical concerns around working with young people.

Teri Ann Sartor, PhD, LPC-S, NCC, CHST, is an assistant professor of counseling at Texas A&M University–Texarkana.

Bill McHenry, PhD, LPC, NCC, is dean of graduate studies and research and associate professor of counseling at Texas A&M University–Texarkana. He has coauthored four books, including *What Therapists Say and Why They Say It* and *A Counselor's Introduction to Neuroscience*.

Jim McHenry, EdD, NCC, LPC, CRC, is professor emeritus at Edinboro University of Pennsylvania. He has coauthored three books, including *What Therapists Say and Why They Say It* and *A Counselor's Introduction to Neuroscience*.

This book is dedicated to the mental health professionals who serve the substantial needs of their child and adolescent clients, to the children and adolescents who deserve the best professional care that our field can offer, and to those professionals who came before us in the fields of counseling children and adolescents as well as legal and ethical issues in counseling—upon whom our work is built.

CONTENTS

ABOUT THE AUTHORS

Dr. Teri Ann Sartor, PhD, LPC-S, NCC, CHST, is an assistant professor of counseling at Texas A&M University–Texarkana. Prior to becoming a counselor educator, she worked as a child and adolescent counselor with juvenile justice, children's advocacy, foster care, and as a private practitioner. Her areas of specialty include counseling children and adolescents, expressive arts, and trauma counseling.

Dr. Bill McHenry, PhD, LPC, NCC, is the dean of graduate studies and research and associate professor of counseling at Texas A&M University–Texarkana. Prior to taking this post, he was a counselor educator for over a decade. His areas of specialty include skills development, counseling teens, expressive arts, substance abuse counseling, grief and loss, and neurocounseling. He has coauthored 18 peer-reviewed journal articles and four books.

Dr. Jim McHenry, EdD, NCC, LPC, CRC, is professor emeritus at Edinboro University of Pennsylvania. He was a public school teacher (5 years), a guidance counselor (3 years), and a professor of counselor education (32 years). Both NBCC certified (retired) and CRC certified (retired), he directed for many years both a CORE accredited graduate rehabilitation counseling program and a university program for disadvantaged college students, sometimes concurrently. He has authored and coauthored numerous journal articles and three books.

CONTRIBUTING AUTHORS

As authors, we recognize our individual knowledge and collective awareness of effective, professional, and both ethical and legal counseling of children and adolescents. Inherent in analyzing what we know are those areas (provided in this book as contributed chapters) for which we felt other voices with more specific training, education, and professional experience would better serve readers. Therefore, we wrote/edited this book from that particular perspective and are pleased to offer you what we consider the best of both worlds.

The contributing authors have focused their efforts on providing up-to-date information related to their specific chapter topic. Assuredly, you will find their efforts meaningful and chock-full of useful and timely information. We are very thankful for their much-needed additions.

However, a significant disclaimer is required here. None of us—your primary authors or contributing authors—offer this book or our work within as a final, definitive statement on any particular case you may be working or will work in the future. As we will reiterate throughout this text, legal and ethical decisions should be made in concert with literature, consultation, and at times legal advice from attorneys who specialize in this area.

Amir Abbassi, PhD, is a Licensed Professional Counselor–Supervisor and a Licensed Marriage and Family Therapist–Supervisor. Dr. Abbassi completed his doctorate degree at the University of North Texas and is an associate professor of counseling at a CACREP accredited institution. Dr. Abbassi's clinical background includes working with children, adolescents, adults, couples, and families. He is a former president of the Texas Association of Marriage and Family Counselors and is a clinical member of the American Association of Marriage and Family Therapy.

S. Dean Aslinia, PhD, is a Licensed Professional Counselor, a National Certified Counselor, and an approved counselor supervisor by the Board of Examiners for Professional Counselors in the State of Texas. Dr. Aslinia's educational background includes a bachelor's and master's degree in psychology from the University of Houston, and a second master's and doctoral degree from Texas A&M University–Commerce. Dr. Aslinia's clinical background includes working with children, adolescents, adults, couples, and families. Dr. Aslinia is also a graduate faculty member and counselor educator teaching courses ranging from clinical skills to ethics and legal issues. He is the past president of the Texas Association of Marriage and Family Counselors and currently serves on the board of directors of the Texas Counseling Association.

Laurel Clement, JD, LPC, is a mother who happens to do a few other things on the side. At this time, she is in private practice as an attorney. She is also a Licensed Professional Counselor. Her practice consists of Family Law, Special Education cases, and representing therapists. Laurel has spent too much time and money attending school. She received a bachelor's degree from Austin College in Sherman. Her two majors were business and sociology. Laurel received a master of arts degree from the University of Texas at Arlington in criminal justice. Laurel received a doctor of jurisprudence from Baylor University. After passing the bar exam, Laurel was licensed as an attorney in November 1989. Laurel received a master of arts degree from Amberton University in 1997. She was licensed by the Texas Board of Examiners of Professional Counselors in 1998. Recently, she returned to school at A&M–Commerce, taking counseling classes in the PhD program. Laurel has one son, four dogs, and plenty of Wedgwood china.

Salene J. Cowher, PhD, NCC, LPC, has devoted over 35 years to working within the helping professions. Currently in part-time private practice, specializing in treatment of trauma, Dr. Cowher has been awarded emeritus status as a graduate professor from Edinboro University of Pennsylvania. During her tenure at Edinboro, Dr. Cowher served three terms as department chair in counseling and provided leadership for CACREP, CORE, NCATE, and Middle States accreditations. Additionally, she has held certification from Pennsylvania as a secondary school counselor and as a secondary English teacher.

The author of more than 25 articles and reviews, Dr. Cowher has also written and coauthored two books and several grants, and she serves on a local CASA (Court-Appointed Special Advocate) board. She also regularly provides legislative advocacy for ACA, NBCC, and IAIE (International Alliance for Invitational Education) and has been a frequent keynote speaker and presenter for numerous organizations and professional groups. Most importantly, she is a proud wife, mother, and grandmother. Dr. Cowher resides in Cambridge Springs, Pennsylvania.

Andrea Davis is a board-certified Art Therapist–Supervisor and, Licensed Professional Counselor–Supervisor. She specializes in art therapy with clients who have experienced trauma, loss, foster/adopt, and medical issues. She earned a BA in psychology at the University of Dallas and has an MA in humanistic psychology from the University of West Georgia. Andrea finished her postgraduate work at the Art Therapy Institute and University of Dallas.

Andrea has dedicated herself to advancing the profession of art therapy. She was the first art therapist at Cook Children's Hospital, which led to the development of a creative arts program in the hospital. She has served as the local conference chairperson for the American Art Therapy Association. She has served on the board of the North Texas Art Therapy Association as president. Andrea ardently supports community projects to educate the public about the role of the art therapist. She has published and appeared on Art of Living Cable TV and NPR-Texas Standard, showcasing the benefits of art therapy in mental health care. Currently, she is working at Children's Medical Center, Dallas Psychiatric Inpatient and Outpatient Units, and in private practice.

Darren E. Dobrinski, PhD, NCSP, is an associate professor of psychology in the Department of Addiction Studies, Psychology, and Social Work. Having taught at Minot State University for the past 9 years at the undergraduate and graduate levels, Dobrinski is currently the program and clinical director of the school psychology graduate program. His area of interest is autism spectrum disorders, rural school psychology, and behavioral disorders. He serves on the governor-appointed North Dakota Autism Task Force. His current research includes role and function of rural school psychologists, blending technology with interdisciplinary autism clinics, and decreasing off-task behavior in children using direct verbal praise statements. Dobrinski completed his undergraduate work at Concordia College, Moorhead, and went on to complete his master's and doctoral degrees in school psychology at the University of South Dakota–Vermillion.

Stephanie S. J. Drcar, PhD, is a visiting assistant professor at Cleveland State University within the counseling, administration, supervision, and adult learning department. She received her PhD from the University of Akron, and her research interests center on the intersection of gender, oppression, and sexual violence. Clinically, she is a generalist and enjoys working with college student populations regarding developmental concerns and engaging in outreach within college campus communities.

Joseph R. Engler, PhD, NCSP, currently serves as an assistant professor in the school psychology program at Minot State University. Dr. Engler received his PhD from the University of South Dakota and BA from Minot State University. Prior to his appointment at Minot State University, Dr. Engler was the director of school psychology at Fort Hays State University and previously practiced as a school psychologist for the Tooele County School District in Tooele, Utah. His research interests and publications include cognitive assessment, academic interventions, motivation, and increasing parental involvement.

Trigg A. Even, PhD, LPC-S, NCC, is a counselor educator in school and clinical mental health counseling. In private practice, he works primarily with children, adolescents, and their families and provides counseling supervision with interns in both school and community settings. His research and scholarship interests include counselor ethics, supervision, counselor professional self-efficacy, and applications of postmodern, constructivist counseling models to school and clinical mental health counseling. He has published in the *Journal of Counseling and Development*, the *Journal of Individual Psychology*, and *Counseling Today* and has presented to numerous regional, state, and national conferences.

M. Sarfaraz Khan, MD, is a board-certified adult psychiatrist and a child and adolescent psychiatrist. Dr. Khan has focused on many different areas of psychiatry and is well versed in working with children and adolescents. Dr. Khan is a member of the American Academy of Child and Adolescent Psychiatry and the American Psychiatric Association. For the past 3 years, Dr. Khan has worked closely with Dr. Aslinia and Dr. Abbassi in a collaborative mental health practice focusing on providing children and adolescents the best mental health treatment possible.

Kathryn C. MacCluskie, PhD, is a professor of counselor education at Cleveland State University where she has taught since 1994. Her degree in counseling psychology from West Virginia University paved the way for her subsequent areas of expertise as an individual therapist with adolescents and adults and in psychological assessment. She also specializes in teaching students basic and advanced clinical skills with emphases on self-awareness and personal growth as components of clinical training. Her passions in life, outside of her professional activities, are her husband and family, skiing, cycling, yoga, and engaging with nature in all forms, especially animals and gardening.

Cyndi Matthews, PhD, is a counselor educator, researcher, Licensed Professional Counselor–Supervisor, and National Certified Counselor working with diversity, multicultural, and social justice issues in the areas of marriage and family relationships and personal/individual counseling. She is currently the president of the Texas Association for Marriage and Family Counselors and past senator for Texas Counselors for Social Justice. Dr. Cyndi, as she is called by her students, is currently the program coordinator of the University of North Texas at Dallas Counseling Program, the clinical director of the

UNT Dallas Community Counseling Center, and a counseling lecturer at UNT Dallas. She has taught various courses in counseling, including couples and family therapy, multicultural counseling, career counseling, developmental processes through the lifetime, professional ethics, crisis intervention, human sexuality, and clinical courses such as practicum, beginning skills, and internship. Dr. Matthews's private practice specializes in lesbian, gay, bisexual, and transgendered issues/gender identity; depression/anxiety/stress; addiction; religious abuse and cult recovery; post-traumatic stress disorder; sexual, emotional, and physical abuse; anger management; domestic violence; sex therapy; premarital counseling; communication skills; and relationship effectiveness.

Brian Peterson, chief deputy of Somervell County, started his law enforcement career in 1997. He has held several positions with the Johnson County Sheriff's Office, including sergeant in the patrol division; lieutenant over the support services division (communications, warrants, and transport); and a detective assigned to Crimes Against Children, which includes major physical abuse and sexual assaults. He was previously assigned to a multicounty Major Case Investigation Team. Brian has also served with the City of Roanoke Police Department as a detective working cases ranging from thefts to homicides and the multiagency missing child/child abduction response team. Brian has state certifications as a Crisis Negotiator, Peace Officer Instructor, and Firearms Instructor, and has a state license in forensic hypnosis. Brian has an Advanced Peace Officer Certification. He is a 2002 graduate of the School of Police Supervision from the Southwestern Law Enforcement Institute of the Southwestern Legal Foundation.

Don Redmond, PhD, is an assistant professor of counseling at Mercer and director of the Center for the Study of Narrative at Penfield College of Mercer University. He has 20 years of human service experience, including counseling and administrative roles with Hillside Hospital in Atlanta and the Fresh Air Fund in New York—both of which serve at-risk youth. Dr. Redmond developed an interest in narrative theory and positive psychology while working with these and other vulnerable populations. He received his bachelor's degree in political science and master of science in rehabilitation counseling from University of North Carolina–Chapel Hill and his doctorate in counselor education from the University of Virginia.

Darnell L. Robinson earned his master's degree in school counseling from Kent State University. He has over 15 years in public education working with students from elementary to high school in classroom and administrative roles. Darnell is also a proud veteran of the United States Army (Aviation Regiment). He enjoys learning and helping others actualize their full potential, as well as volunteering with wounded veterans.

PREFACE

Fifty-two years ago, as this sentence is written, I (Jim) emerged as a freshly flushed master-in-counseling graduate of the Pennsylvania State University. The graduate program there was first rate (though significantly shorter than that of today). I had passed all the course work in areas like counseling and assessment; this education, coupled with my 5 years of teaching experience, rendered me duly certified in the field. However, looking back over that full half century, I now realize that during those years, guidance counselors were actually in the process of inventing and evolving their professional roles; as counselors are wont to say, we were "in the process of becoming." This inventing and evolving was also occurring in every other field of counseling and therapy. Many of these creators did a commendable job with the tools they had been given. Still, one area where graduates of the 1960s had been shortchanged was in the area of *ethics*. I have no recollection of any course work dealing directly, specifically with this aspect. Maybe the faculty felt that simply choosing candidates who appeared to be nice, bright people who generally exhibited positive moral values was enough. Or possibly they reasoned that the ethical aspects of practice would somehow, osmotically, be filtered in through the required course work, equipping graduates to do the "right" thing.

Certainly, 1964 was a simpler time in America. Computers took the form of main frames filling entire buildings in places like Schenectady, New York. In fact, my public school system was using General Electric's main frame computer to schedule our students. But no one was walking around with them in their backpacks, and the Internet had yet to be invented. Telephones were relatively rare utilities, usually on desks, maybe on a wall, and located in specific offices. If I or the principal wanted to contact a teacher, either a student aide or the PA system might be used. The only person who had a phone on his wrist was Dick Tracy, who was in the daily comic pages. It was a different world.

Fast-forward to 2016, of course, and both *the world* and *the world of counseling and therapy* have changed. Geometrically. In many ways it is faster, ever more complex; sometimes more dangerous (drug use, for example) and sometimes more promising (the wealth of opportunities presented by the increased availability of knowledge). Positive possibilities are many, but accurate and effective personal navigation for our clients is, if anything, even more critical.

Counselors have learned to play significant roles in this process, although the clear and basic fact that we cannot live clients' lives for them is still absolutely unchanged. What we can do, however, is assist them as they chart their own paths. And in this navigation process, we now recognize the paramount need for ethics to be infused in and to permeate every fiber of our professional roles. Significantly then, in 2016 every professional organization in the field now clearly—*strongly*—recognizes the need to continually address this aspect of professional training in both formal training programs (e.g., MA programs, etc.) and in-service requirements.

MUDDY WATERS

Counselors work and function in a professional world filled with uncertainty. Daily, as the human experience and the uniqueness of our individual clients confront us, our practice forces us to consider multiple variables simultaneously. The term *gray area* is used often, and constantly having to function in such a world is challenging to all counselors, especially to those just beginning their careers.

For counselors working with children and adolescents, of course, even more variables may complicate decisions and therapeutic direction—the age of the client, for example. Fortunately, for our purposes, legal precedence has been developed that defines various youth designations (juvenile, non-adult, child, or adolescent), although such demarcations may vary in different political districts (e.g., states, etc.).

Further, there are gray areas related to age of adulthood that complicate the process of counseling. For example, consider a client who is 17 ¾ years old and lives in a state where the legal age is 18. Although she has been through significant abuse and neglect in her childhood, she has come out the other side well. She is seeing her counselor for "relationship" issues. She is still living with her mother (who abuses medications and demonstrates little to no parental care for her daughter). By law, her mother has the right to know about not only counseling services but also some of the general content. It makes sense by the letter of the law that mom can know such information, but does it make sense ethically and professionally to disclose anything to this particular mother? Here, then, is the core rationale for this book—an effort to highlight, elucidate, denote, and describe many of the variables associated with good ethical decision making for children and teens.

The *ACA Code of Ethics* identifies the agreed upon ethical mandates for counselors to use when working with children and adolescents. And, because it is the best resource counselors have available to them regarding the necessary guidelines for working professionally and from a place of doing no harm, these constructs should be studied and implemented by all counselors. Following are some of the sections of the American Counseling Association's (2014) *Code of Ethics* that specifically relate to children and adolescents.

A.2.d. Inability to Give Consent

When counseling minors, incapacitated adults, or other persons unable to give voluntary consent, counselors seek the assent of clients to services and include them in decision making as appropriate. Counselors recognize the need to balance the ethical rights of clients to make choices, their capacity to give consent or assent to receive services, and parental or familial legal rights and responsibilities to protect these clients and make decisions on their behalf.

A.8. Multiple Clients

When a counselor agrees to provide counseling services to two or more persons who have a relationship, the counselor clarifies at the outset which person or persons are clients and the nature of the relationships the counselor will have with each involved person. If it becomes apparent that the counselor may be called upon to perform potentially conflicting roles, the counselor will clarify, adjust, or withdraw from roles appropriately.

A.10.f. Receiving Gifts

Counselors understand the challenges of accepting gifts from clients and recognize that in some cultures, small gifts are a token of respect and gratitude. When determining whether to accept a gift from clients, counselors take into account the therapeutic relationship, the monetary value of the gift, the client's motivation for giving the gift, and the counselor's motivation for wanting to accept or decline the gift.

B.5.a. Responsibility to Clients

When counseling minor clients or adult clients who lack the capacity to give voluntary, informed consent, counselors protect the confidentiality of information received—in any medium—in the counseling relationship as specified by federal and state laws, written policies, and applicable ethical standards.

B.5.b. Responsibility to Parents and Legal Guardians

Counselors inform parents and legal guardians about the role of counselors and the confidential nature of the counseling relationship, consistent with current legal and custodial arrangements. Counselors are sensitive to the cultural diversity of families and respect the inherent rights and responsibilities of parents/guardians regarding the welfare of their children/charges according to law. Counselors work to establish, as appropriate, collaborative relationships with parents/guardians to best serve clients.

B.5.c. Release of Confidential Information

When counseling minor clients or adult clients who lack the capacity to give voluntary consent to release confidential information, counselors seek permission from an appropriate third party to disclose information. In such instances, counselors inform clients consistent with their level of understanding and take appropriate measures to safeguard client confidentiality.

> (Reprinted from *ACA Code of Ethics* [ACA, ©2014].
> American Counseling Association. Reprinted with permission.
> No further reproduction authorized without written
> permission from the American Counseling Association.)

Unfortunately, however, sometimes when we drill down into the details of individual cases we discover that ethical mandates seem to run counter to legal rules and best practices. For example, I (Bill) at the very beginning of my career as a counselor educator had a student in my practicum course who had an issue with a case. As the class was built, she was able to show the tape in class and get feedback from her peers and me as the supervisor.

The student counselor reported to us that she had been working with a 14-year-old client in school for some time, and she sensed the client was going to share a lot, perhaps even disclose something big during a particular session. Relying on her intuition, she was careful to remind the client of her (the counselor's) ethical obligation as a mandated reporter. The student counselor then played the tape.

The client told her that she had been seeing an "older" man and that she and her best friend, who was also seeing an older man, had engaged in the destruction of property. This destructive event was not the simple egging or toilet papering of a house. It was much more. She said that after they had all become high on marijuana, they decided to steal a car so they could go for a joy ride. One thing led to another, and by the end of the joy ride, they decided to destroy the vehicle by setting it on fire. So they did.

There were at minimum two *major* issues to recognize immediately in this case. The first is the fact that this client was possibly engaging in sexual activities with an adult (which would be defined in that state as illegal). Further, she had been involved in a crime that was a clear felony under state laws. So the question became—to whom do you report and what, if anything, needs to be reported.

Further complicating the issue, the client had basically confessed to breaking several laws *on tape*. And the student counselor was in possession of the tape. What should happen to the tape? (According to the class syllabus I used, once the tape had been reviewed by the supervisor or class, it was to be destroyed/erased.)

What would you have done? What is *right* and *ethical* in this case? And from a very pragmatic view, what guides your consideration in what is best for the client, keeping in mind, of course, that counselors work *first* from the perspective of what is best for the client. Client issues will present quandaries that we have never considered, ones never covered in our training. In this instance, I (Bill) was initially stumped by what I would do (or ask the student counselor to do) with the tape. Thank goodness, however, I had been trained to consider all of the legal and ethical mandates involved with a case and to consult often on difficult cases.

So, of course, the question is, what happened in this case? Initially, *nothing* happened. Recognize here that sometimes, *if time permits*, the very best decision you can make is to take time to consider all of the variables you can and consult with professionals who might aid you with the issue. In this case, the first person I consulted with was a much more seasoned counselor educator in the program. He provided veteran and sage advice—but it took him some time to arrive at anything definitive. The second person consulted was the school counselor (under whom the student counselor was doing her on-site practicum). She was also quite helpful in guiding the student through part of the process.

The following decisions were made: the tape was kept in my office, the client was encouraged to share her story with authorities (the police), and her case manager was informed of the relationship the client had.

So what was the outcome? It appeared clear after some time passed that the client had been crying for help when she disclosed to the student counselor. She readily shared her story with the police, and we felt that she had been actually practicing a test run with the student counselor. The older men had, in fact, been on the radar of the police for some time, and they were both arrested for the crime. Both the case manager and the school counselor became much more actively engaged with the client, and she started showing improvement. Once the client shared her story (which was nearly exact detail by detail with what was on the tape), the tape was destroyed.

Not all cases turn out so well for the client. And not all cases turn out so well for the counselor. The weight of this case was heavy on the student counselor, myself (Bill), and on those we consulted. However, as a team, we did the best we could to manage this legal and ethical conundrum.

Expect some loss of sleep as a counselor, especially at the beginning of your career. This work is rewarding and growth fostering, but it can be extraordinarily challenging at times. We sincerely hope this book provides guidance in your career as a professional counselor.

ACKNOWLEDGMENTS

I, Teri, would like to thank Bill and Jim for agreeing to pursue this project with me. I would also like to thank our contributing authors for including their thoughts and knowledge on key areas that influence how counselors effectively work with children and adolescents. Additionally, thanks to Kishon Daniels for his efforts in finding specific legal cases involving ethical violations related to counseling children and adolescents. Lastly, I would like to thank former clients, supervisors, supervisees/students, and colleagues who assisted me in developing my love for counseling children and adolescents, educating future counselors, and modeling ethical standards.

I, Bill, would like to thank you, Teri, for being such a dedicated and wonderful coauthor. I am so glad to have had the chance to learn so much from you in this process. Dad, once again, as with every book we coauthor, I am amazed by your skill, knowledge, and care in crafting our words into meaningful and poignant messages to the current and next generation of skilled therapists. I want to thank the former clients, supervisors, colleagues, and students who helped shape my deep and steadfast ethical and moral approach to working with people. I would also like to thank Jennie Miller for her effort, attention to detail, and skill in helping with this book.

I, Jim, also thank both of you, Teri and Bill, for the work put into this effort. I've seen the field of counseling grow exponentially over the years, in both scope and effectiveness, and thank all those pioneers and road builders for their immense contributions to our vibrant, growing, and ever-evolving profession.

INTRODUCTION TO THE UNIQUE LEGAL AND ETHICAL CHALLENGES WHEN COUNSELING CHILDREN AND ADOLESCENTS

Bill McHenry, Jim McHenry, and Teri Ann Sartor

WELCOME

While doing research for another book dealing with counseling children and adolescents, we were struck by the paucity of material available on ethical aspects of dealing with that particular age group. At best, there are only a few books that attempt to deal with the topic. This dearth of literature and the ever-growing focus of credentialing and licensing agencies to require coverage of ethical principles and practices inspired the volume you presently hold in your hands. Our aim is to help both beginning and advanced counselors deal more effectively and more ethically with today's children and youth.

Each of your authors has worked not only as a counselor with this age group, but also as a counselor educator charged with training counseling students in classes such as Counseling Children and Adolescents and Play Therapy. Additionally, we have also invited a number of author practitioners to share their expertise and experience from a diverse number of perspectives. We recognize, of course, that even with what we regard as an excellent team of writers in place, *no book* can provide definitive answers to the unique questions posed by difficult cases. Hopefully, however, this volume will help your efforts to become a more effective and ethical counselor.

WHAT WILL BE COVERED?

In Chapter 2, we will address some of the larger scale issues that counselors face when working with youth. Specifically, we will discuss *informed* consent, reporting abuse/neglect, handling subpoenas, and *an ethical decision making model.*

In Chapter 3, we will address some of the vital elements to the ethical decision making process inherent within the counselor such as *supervision/consultation, self-care, personal views on medications,* and *diversity issues.*

In Chapter 4, Dr. Trigg Even will cover the similarities and differences inherent in the two unique and distinct roles of clinical mental health counselors and professional school counselors. Understandably, the two roles have divergent ethical mandates and legal constructs in relation to *case notes, confidentiality,* and *the primary goal of the counselor.*

In Chapter 5, Dr. Don Redmond will cover the multitude of different legal, ethical, and professional issues in the area of residential treatment center care for children and adolescents. Inherent in working with this special population are topics such as *adolescent groups and social, emotional, and behavioral difficulties populations.* Specific attention is paid to the interaction between *residential treatment centers and the legal system.*

In Chapter 6, Dr. Cyndi Mathews will cover the potentially challenging issues that a counselor may face when working with lesbian, gay, bisexual, and transgendered children and adolescents. Topics in this chapter range from *confidentiality* to *self-harm/suicidal ideation.*

In Chapter 7, Art Therapist Andrea Davis will cover the legal and ethical issues that can occur when using expressive arts approaches with teens and children. This chapter discusses issues ranging from *competency* to *scope of practice* to *information "discovered"* through the use of approaches such as art, music, and bibliotherapy. Additionally, specific codes of ethics for these specialty areas will be referenced along with best practices.

In Chapter 8, Dr. Darren E. Dobrinski and Dr. Joseph R. Engler will cover the necessary and mandated rules and guidelines around the proctoring and interpretation of formal tests and assessments with this population. *Professional standards pertaining to intelligence tests, personality profiles, diagnostic tools, and projective techniques* will be covered.

In Chapter 9, Brian Peterson will cover the legal and ethical issues that surround reporting of abuse/neglect. This chapter will discuss the function and *role of the counselor* within investigations and the *overall investigation process* from the view of the investigator.

In Chapter 10, Drs. S. Dean Aslinia, Amir Abbassi, and M. Sarfaraz Khan will cover the inherent value of consulting with psychiatrists. In this chapter, issues such as *medications, diagnoses,* and *the medical model* will be reviewed.

In Chapter 11, Laurel Clement, JD, will cover the processes and procedures involved in providing courtroom testimony. Because the process can be overwhelming, taxing, and at times quite intimidating, this chapter will cover both pragmatic and specific examples of what to expect. Further, the author will address the ways to *serve your client throughout the legal process.*

In Chapter 12, Drs. Kathryn MacCluskie, Stephanie S. J. Drcar, and Darnell L. Robinson will discuss the role of technology as it pertains to legal and ethical professional conduct by counselors. Attention and details will cover *cybercounseling, data protection, asynchronous services*, and *current case law.*

In Chapter 13, Dr. Salene Cowher will address the resources counselors can use when faced with ethical and legal questions regarding their work with children and adolescents.

In Chapter 14, Dr. Teri Ann Sartor will address high-profile cases that have provided clear interpretations for counselors to understand when considering the legal interpretation of ethical and legal practices. Both historic and current cases will be reviewed in relation to *reporting abuse, confidentiality*, and *the release of case notes.*

WHAT IS *NOT* COVERED IN THIS BOOK

The work of a counselor is often done one-on-one, in the trenches as it were. As such, a practitioner's personal experiences and personal codes of moral behavior often come into play, both good and bad. Further complicating the work is the fact that there is also a seemingly endless array of possibilities open to a counselor as to how he or she chooses to work with the client. While these possibilities offer opportunity for both creativity and optimal growth, they also open the door to both interpretation and misinterpretation of ethical and legal mandates. Indeed, we have found some of our most challenged students and supervisees to be those who (for whatever reasons) failed to know, consider, or act in accordance with prescribed guidelines. For example, we have seen counselors try to justify their attempts to adopt clients (in spite of knowing our rules about keeping professional boundaries with our clients) because "no one else will care for them like me." One vital aspect here is that there is a major difference between using the appropriate resources (e.g., code of ethics, literature) to inform the ethical decision making process and simply using them to justify a preconceived decision the counselor (or you have) already made.

So indeed, whether you are new to the field or a veteran counselor, you need to fully recognize that issues the client brings to the table do not always lend themselves to quick and easy solutions. Our field does not have a specific method for treating *depression, anxiety, schizoaffective disorder*, and so on. So, too, our ethical and legal mandates and necessary constraints vary across different cases as the multitude of different variables complicates decisions. Counselors then must learn to deal with ambiguity being a significant aspect of their professional roles.

As a consequence, a counselor must understand that self-care is also a vital aspect of the professional and, indeed, ethical role. As a counselor, *you will* experience dissonance, a lack of clarity, and probably even the pain of real uncertainty related to some cases. And while we have already indicated some strategies that often help here—taking time to reflect on the issue rather than attempting the quick cure, consulting with other professionals, and so on—it is imperative that you develop your own strategies that will work best for you. Counselor self-care is extremely important. Personal attention to your approach and ways of working with clients are also ongoing and critical ingredients. Attending to these factors is your responsibility.

We are limited in what we can offer you in this book. We cannot simply transfer our hard-earned battle scars of knowledge, our mistakes, and the lessons we have learned from working with clients. Somehow, as with the many other aspects of the counseling profession, legal and ethical issues specific to children and adolescents require consistent study, maintenance of awareness, and a well-centered approach.

This is the profession you chose and the professional world in which you will hopefully succeed. Although we will address personal factors from *your* end, or at least the counselor's end, it is up to each and every counselor to persist and move toward the best ethical and legal decisions he or she can make to benefit clients. Awareness of self is most likely as important as knowing the rules that are to be followed.

WHY WE WROTE THIS BOOK

Variability and variety offer counselors great resources when working with clients. We wrote this book because we believe there is a gap in the literature that has caused therapists working with children and adolescents to often rely primarily on their own counsel when confronted with ethical and/or legal crossroads.

This book is an adjunct to professional practice, a supplement to the knowledge, awareness, and skills that counselors develop throughout their professional practice. Recognizing such, we are happy to share with you not only our voices and knowledge, but also those of many other professionals who have expertise in specific areas of practice. Our common, shared goal is to better arm you with information to more effectively serve the clients you work with. Therefore, in essence this book arrives in your hands to help those who come to you in need—the children and adolescents you serve.

ETHICS OF WORKING WITH CHILDREN, ADOLESCENTS, AND THEIR PARENTS

Teri Ann Sartor, Bill McHenry,
and Jim McHenry

At first blush, the ethics of working with children, adolescents, and their parents/guardians (the last two terms will be used interchangeably) can seem to be clear and straightforward. However, upon further investigation, this critical element to the therapeutic process can be quite complex. Truly, words like *challenging, multidimensional*, and *complicated* are a bit more accurate. In working with children and adolescents, counselors must remember not only their responsibility for the minor client but also their accountability to the guardian. This additional aspect adds a new dimension to legal and ethical issues. Because guardians are sometimes the ones requesting counseling, counselors need to be open to working with and consulting with parents on a regular basis. Furthermore, counselors should also be aware of the varied and various shades of gray that may be found within these various relationships. Often we find there is no singular, definitive answer, but rather multiple options with a myriad of outcomes.

As your basis, of course, you should refer to the *ACA Code of Ethics* (2014), as it will be referenced numerous times throughout this book. However, in considering ethical issues involved in working with children and adolescents and their guardians, specific ethical issues often emerge. Consequently, definitive answers and clear decisions on the unique characteristics of individual cases you *will* face may not be provided. Additionally, of course, you should also always consider consultation with other professional counselors, especially those you consider proficient, seasoned veterans who work with children and adolescents.

The very first place to start in all counseling relationships is the negotiation and clarification of the consent to treat.

CONSENT

With all counseling relationships consent is a critical part of the process. Because of difficulties that arise when working with children and adolescents, counselors need to ensure parents are informed from the outset of the *child's rights* and the *guardian's rights* within the counseling process. The informed consent document formally grants permission enabling treatment to occur among client(s) and counselor. This document delineates the counseling process and the relationship between the child/adolescent client and counselor as well as the parent/guardian and counselor. Beginning counselors are often confused or unaware of what is detailed in the informed consent document and how it should be explained to the client. We have found this process takes practice and knowledge of the value of taking the time to thoroughly explain the consent document. Even in cases and situations where children or adolescents cannot provide legally binding consent, it is still important to cover the facts and information about consent to treat.

Detailed within contents of the informed consent is the counselor's information to include, where applicable,

- professional name and place of business;
- contact information;
- professional licensure number, issuing state, and when obtained;
- professional certifications;
- education and training experience;
- explanation of the counseling process, types of counseling offered, and theoretical orientation to allow the client to know what to expect;
- risks associated with counseling;
- the state board contact information for filing a complaint (if necessary);
- child and parental/guardian rights;
- insurance and payment information;
- limits of confidentiality; and
- the name of the child or minor along with the names and signatures of the minor's guardian and counselor.

Clearly, this is a lot of information for an adult to consume in one sitting; much less for a child or teen to understand and absorb. A difference does exist, however, between simply getting the informed consent signed and actually *informing* the child/teen and his or her parent(s)/guardian(s). Because the cornerstone of counseling is based on trust, counselors should strive to obtain *consent* that really is *informed*. Actually, therapeutic value and rapport may be augmented when this process is done correctly. Conversely, of course, when the form is simply handed to a parent/guardian to sign without explanation, mistrust and/or disrespect may be felt on the part of the receiving party. Of course, at times, counselors may be working with parents/guardians who are either slow readers or illiterate. In such cases, without verbally explaining the document and the services/consent to provide services, such parents/guardians may be left in the position of expressing a potentially embarrassing issue or simply signing.

For counselors-in-training or interns, the supervisor's name and contact information must be included for the caregivers' reference. This is vital and professional because clients have the legal right to know all of the parties involved in the treatment process and, of course, the overall level of education and training of the primary counselor. As is the case with all consent forms, both the guardian and counselor should maintain a copy of the signed informed consent for their records. We have found it important to sometimes go back to the consent form to remind guardians of the services and, of course, to remind them of confidentiality. Having the informed consent document signed and discussed, with a formalized understanding clearly noted, allows for an easier transition back to it as needed throughout the counseling process. Parents/guardians may, in some cases, want to know the details of the sessions as the counselor and child/adolescent develop rapport and get into "deeper stuff." In some cases, it is simply out of care and interest in the child's welfare and "what is going on?" However, we have found in other cases the motivation to know the details may be out of fear of the child disclosing family secrets. Counselors need to recognize the requests for greater and greater details to be shared and then work appropriately with the parent/guardian on the parameters and boundaries as agreed upon in the informed consent document. In cases in which the child or minor client has guardians who are divorced, counselors must obtain a copy of the divorce decree. By obtaining a current copy of the divorce decree counselors are aware of who has specified rights in regard to seeking treatment for children. Additionally, the counselor's understanding of the divorce decree will allow the counselor to ensure she or he is following custody rules set forth. If a noncustodial guardian is seeking treatment for or information about counseling with a child/adolescent client and the counselor obliges, the counselor is liable and is at risk for a malpractice suit. This may seem obvious, but believe it or not malpractice suits have been brought against counselors providing treatment to children that was sought by a noncustodial guardian (Stein, 1990). We have found that in some cases, grandparents, aunts, and uncles believe they have the right to information or to provide consent to treat. Counselors can find themselves in difficult situations if they fail to fully understand who has rights and what rights they have in the process. Additionally, it is critical that counselors ask parents/guardians about the family system and who might be transporting the child to counseling. This discussion can reveal any potential issues with adults who may be in the inner circle of the family, but do not have legal access or rights to information.

In many cases, separated guardians are required to notify the other party or have an agreement to seek treatment for the minor. Because of rules set forth in the divorce decree, it is important for the counselor to have consent from both guardians if deemed necessary by a court of law.

Prior to the signing of the informed consent, counselors need to ensure older children/adolescent clients fully understand what counseling entails. When entering counseling relationships with minor clients, the discussion of child/adolescent confidentiality is one of extreme importance. Because guardians are the legal authority in seeking treatment, they may inquire frequently about what the child or adolescent client discloses. Oftentimes older children and adolescent clients are hesitant about the counseling process due to fear the counselor will "reveal all" to their parents or guardian. Few people want their secrets and issues presented to others without their consent. Discussion with all parties about the importance of trust and confidentiality in the counseling relationship at the beginning will assist in the process. From our experience, simply updating guardians is helpful, and it is best to include the client within the update process. Updates are generally broad and nonspecific. As a general practice, often the less you share, the better. The review of the informed consent is more for the parent/caregiver and adolescent. As a result of cognitive abilities, it is not necessary to review this information with very young children. It is, however, very good practice to encourage parents/guardians to refrain from quizzing or questioning their child about the content of the sessions. In many cases, especially with very young children, such requests are difficult to refuse, which may further complicate the therapeutic process. I (Teri) have found it helpful to provide parents of young children with additional information regarding the "dos and don'ts" before and after counseling sessions. While this may concern some parents, it is important to remember the therapeutic relationship is the best predictor of success in counseling, and trust is a necessity in the relationship.

The American Counseling Association (ACA) has identified one of its core ethical standards as being the counselor's awareness of the degree to which (if at all) the client is able to truly provide consent. This is a critical ethical mandate that not only clearly prescribes what the counselor is to do, but also the client's rights in the process. As can be seen in the following ethical standard, consent is not an either-or process; rather, counselors are mandated to work to the best of their ability to include the client in the consent process to the highest degree possible.

This standard further provides counselors with guidance related to the intersection between legal issues and consent for treatment. ACA has clearly noted here that although efforts need to be made to include all of the necessary parties in the consent process, in some instances, legal issues will prevent including some family members (parents/guardians) in the consent process.

A.2.d. Inability to Give Consent

When counseling minors, incapacitated adults, or other persons unable to give voluntary consent, counselors seek the assent of clients to services and include them in decision making as appropriate. Counselors recognize the need to balance the ethical rights of clients to make choices, their capacity to give consent or assent to receive services, and parental or familial legal rights and responsibilities to protect these clients and make decisions on their behalf.

ACA ethical guidelines further delineate the role and responsibilities of the counselor in regard to the maintenance of information from the counseling session and relationship. Although the parent/guardian is the provider of the *legal* consent, that does not preclude the counselor maintaining confidentiality. B.5.a below clearly describes the fact that minors *still* have the rights, privileges, and expectations of confidentiality. Importantly, this standard is often not fully described and articulated to parents/guardians, which can result in confusion and frustration on their part.

B.5.a. Responsibility to Clients

When counseling minor clients or adult clients who lack the capacity to give voluntary, informed consent, counselors protect the confidentiality of information received—in any medium—in the counseling relationship as specified by federal and state laws, written policies, and applicable ethical standards.

Although parents/guardians are not authorized to have detailed information from the sessions with minors, ACA does have clear language in the code of ethics that describes the counselor's responsibility to the parents/guardians. In standard B.5.b (below), counselors are mandated to educate the parents/guardians on not only the counseling process, but specifically, the bounds of confidentiality necessary in the counseling relationship with minors.

B.5.b. Responsibility to Parents and Legal Guardians

Counselors inform parents and legal guardians about the role of counselors and the confidential nature of the counseling relationship, consistent with current legal and custodial arrangements. Counselors are sensitive to the cultural diversity of families and respect the inherent rights and responsibilities of parents/guardians regarding the welfare of their children/charges according to law. Counselors work to establish, as appropriate, collaborative relationships with parents/guardians to best serve clients.

At times there are exceptions to gaining consent from a guardian of a minor. These exceptions include that of an emancipated minor client or court-ordered treatment (within a controlled setting such as a detention center, residential treatment center, or community agency). Additionally, some states allow for the treatment of minors without parent consent in circumstances that will serve public interests, such as substance abuse, sexually transmitted infections, or pregnancy (Koocher, 2003). Generally speaking, while consent is not a requirement for court-ordered counseling, it is generally wise to inform and update guardians when it is deemed appropriate, since guardians can play a major role in a helpful support system for the client during and after the required treatment. In addition, the counselor should also be mindful of where the child or adolescent will reside during and after treatment; if parents or guardians are involved in the treatment process, treatment can be enhanced and a smoother transition can occur.

Additionally, in emergency situations with minors, consent may not be a top priority on the list. For example, in life-or-death situations going through the informed consent process is most likely not appropriate prior to providing intervention. In these types of situations, consent must be sought as soon as possible but also at the appropriate time.

POINT TO PONDER

Informed consent is a critical part of the process of working effectively with clients. Create two lists. In List 1, identify your three main reasons for providing informed consent to the child/adolescent and then in List 2, the three main reasons for providing such information to their guardian/ parent. Then, consider how these two lists are similar or different. Finally, consider this—in what ways might the client or his or her parents/ guardians need further information, clarity, or guidance related to this critical document?

REPORTING ABUSE

Lawrence and Robinson Kurpius (2000) utilized the metaphor of Cinderella to describe the ethics of working with children and adolescents. They described this metaphor by assigning the following roles: Cinderella as the abused and neglected child; the stepmother, stepsisters, and absent father as the abusive caretakers; the prince as the state or the authoritative body; and the Fairy Godmother, who was charged with changing the environment to benefit Cinderella, was considered the counselor. Lawrence and Robinson Kurpius were correct in this metaphorical use in that these roles are ever present in counseling relationships with minors.

Working with children often presents complications and difficulties in choosing to report abuse. Because counselors have the *legal and professional* responsibility to identify and report child abuse, it is important for counselors to be aware of the legal and ethical issues as well as potential liability concerns (Lawrence & Robinson Kurpius, 2000). Beneficence and non-maleficence are important moral principles, especially when it comes to the counseling relationship and safety of our clients and future clients. While laws for reporting abuse vary from state to state, generally speaking professionals are required to report abuse or suspected abuse within a 48- to 72-hour time frame. In choosing to make reports, counselors should follow the rule of thumb that when in doubt consult with other licensed professionals. Because a report could potentially damage the counseling relationship (e.g., loss of trust in the counselor) or potentially put the child in harm's way (e.g., reporting abuse on a parent who is taking the child home after school), a counselor must always consider and put safeguards in place to protect minor clients prior to reporting.

In efforts to protect the relationship, counselors should set the stage at the first meeting or point of contact with the minor and his or her guardian. Mindful of the limits of confidentiality and informed consent, the counselor must ensure that child/adolescent clients and their parents understand the legal and ethical obligations of the counseling process (remember the limits of confidentiality and informed consent!). Limits of confidentiality and possible breaches should be included within the document and this conversation.

The developmental level in which a child or adolescent functions must also be factored into the equation. For example, according to Piaget's cognitive development theory, kids between the ages of 2 and 8 have difficulty distinguishing between fantasy and reality. In some cases the fantasy world becomes far more important to the child than actual reality. In play therapy it is not uncommon for children to have sword fights, fight and defeat dragons, discipline others in a "classroom," and openly explore play materials (toys) in the playroom. An inexperienced counselor (or a counselor not familiar with the high degree of fantasy during this stage) could easily misinterpret some of these play activities as being direct representations of the child's reality and begin to suspect abuse. Whether to discuss the meaning and symbolism of the play or to assess and recognize the developmental stage of the child as it relates to his or her play, supervision plays a key role in the development of a new counselor. And this is precisely why supervision is seen as essential for counselors new to counseling children.

In working with children and adolescents, counselors must also remember that following the session, the child does return home. Remember, the counselor cannot go home with the child, and the child cannot go home with the counselor. What would occur if the child is being abused in the home, and the counselor discusses the allegations with the abusing guardian prior to reporting? This can be quite complicated; what is the counselor to do?

I (Teri) was a supervisor for the following case involving a young child. If you were in this situation consider what you would you do.

A Licensed Professional Counselor–Intern was providing counseling services at an elementary school through a community agency. The counseling intern was providing play therapy services for a child who was approximately eight years of age but was slightly developmentally delayed. For the purpose of this example, the child will be called Mike. Mike functioned at a level similar to that of a 6-year-old. His referral for counseling was related to behavior difficulties in the classroom. Prior to the counseling process, little information was revealed by the single parent. After receiving the proper signed consent and release forms, the intern was able to communicate with school personnel. The information provided by teachers regarding classroom behaviors, socioeconomic status, interactions with others, and completion of school work was vital in providing adequate treatment and understanding of Mike's home life.

As part of the supervision process, which will be discussed in the next section of the chapter, the counselor intern was required to videotape sessions with clients. In reviewing the sessions, themes began to develop.

Mike adjusted to the makeshift playroom and play materials very quickly (within three to four sessions). This makeshift playroom consisted of a classroom that was converted to storage. The play area was separated by long tables and four-drawer filing cabinets. A wide variety of acceptable and appropriate play material was strategically placed on the tables for the child's play activities.

Sessions with Mike started out much like they would with well-adjusted children, partially because of the exploratory process in play therapy. When he became more comfortable in play and with the therapist, the themes of caretaking (cooking and feeding), nurturing (rocking a baby), and discipline ("whipping the kids") became commonalities. These behaviors did not occur all at once. There was a progression over approximately four consecutive sessions. Imagine a child "cooking" and then offering food then taking it away and saying, "Sorry you do not get to eat because you are not fast enough." This behavior soon led to nurturing a baby by rocking and feeding, and later using the rope ("whip") to hit the filing cabinets while rocking and yelling at a baby.

Children often play out scenes they may have seen on television or video games. Therefore, in reporting this case it was essential for the therapist to not misinterpret behaviors early on. Due to the progression of the behaviors and the assessment of information presented both in and out of the session, this case was reported. However, caution was taken because in most cases, children within this developmental level do not verbally say "I am being abused;" they say it nonverbally through play, a child's natural language (Landreth, 2012).

Because the child was seen for counseling as part of a contract with the school district, the school counselor was notified (permission was granted prior) and a report was made. To ensure the safety of the child, the department of family and protective services intervened while the child was at school. Because the field of counseling operates, at times, in very murky and gray areas, the decision to report or not report can take quite a toll on the counselor. This is a great case to highlight the need to seek professional consultation(s) at times in order to arrive at the best decision possible. Reporting and working with adolescents may bring about a different set of concerns. Because adolescents are more likely to verbalize abuse, it can, at times, be more easily detected. While there are many of the same concerns, such as whom the adolescent lives with, additional plans and approaches may also be necessary.

POINT TO PONDER

Here we ask you to stop and reflect on your own values, beliefs, and assertions. How will you detect abuse and neglect with the clients you see? We have, at times, worked with counselors-in-training who had the erroneous and problematic belief that all or many of their clients who happened to be youth, had at one time or other experienced abuse and/or neglect. This belief, thought pattern—dare we say, irrational view of counseling—of course, most likely stemmed from the counselor's own experiences in youth. Important to note though is that *not* all kids have been traumatized. In fact, many have not. Overdiagnosing is not the key to working effectively with this group. Rather, understanding the true warning signs and listening closely to the client's verbal and nonverbal stories likely yields more accurate assessment of such concerns.

The counseling relationship is one of trust, especially with the adolescent. At times adolescents may be hesitant to discuss incidences of abuse because of feeling or appearing "different" from their peers, limited coping skills, the risk of getting in trouble with their parents, feelings of inadequacy, or even fear. At such times it may prove helpful for the counselor to help the client understand how such disclosure may be helpful. Of course, if such reports are necessary, the adolescent client should be included to the greatest degree possible within the process. Oftentimes, the thought of reporting abuse may be terrifying for the adolescent; recognize, however, that if the guardian is a nonoffending party, his or her additional support could be beneficial for the client. Regardless, counselors must remember that reporting child abuse is the first step in ensuring children in need are protected (Lawrence & Robinson Kurpius, 2000).

Despite the counselor's need to take all reports of abuse seriously, occasionally adolescents make false claims. In situations such as these, it is not the counselor's role to play detective. Here again we reiterate the value of and need for professional consultation and/or supervision when instances necessitate. Making reporting decisions early in a counselor's career oftentimes should be a team decision as opposed to feeling as though the decision must be made alone. We cannot emphasize that enough. Counselors do not have to make these types of decisions in a vacuum, but rather they should be made within a collaborative and consultative approach that in most cases benefits the client. More often than not, we have found counselors who make reports of abuse solo (especially early in their careers) have jumped the gun and/or in actuality hurt the client by reporting a claim that turned out to be false. This, of course, is not to stop or halt reports but to remind counselors there is a greater value in consulting than in trying to make these life-changing/altering decisions alone.

Following the report of abuse or neglect, some counselors experience frustration that nothing is or was done. This seems to be true for many counselors and even more so with school counselors. Counselors should remember that due to large numbers of reports, budget reductions in state government, social or regional beliefs about abuse, and other factors, certain reports may have more immediacy than others (Koocher, 2003). Consequently, the fact that the department of family and protective services (or in some cases child protective services) does not quickly follow up or ask for additional details about potential abuse does not mean the child or adolescent is not important. What is important is the counselor did fulfill his or her professional role in an effort to assist in protecting the child.

ETHICAL DECISION MAKING

Making an ethical decision may seem like a simple task; however, a counselor must always remember simple rules for cause and effect. Every decision a counselor makes during a counseling session or in counseling-related activities can have repercussions. For this reason, counselors should utilize ethical decision making models, supervisors, peer counselors, and the legal hotlines of their state and national counseling associations to assist them in making ethical decisions. We have found that counselors who started using these resources early in their training and careers were far more apt to continue the process throughout their professional careers. Asking for help and assistance in interpreting direction in ethical gray areas is truly a sign of professionalism.

In the beginning, following the steps of an ethical decision making model may seem tedious; however, with practice the process becomes automatic for many counselors. Prior to utilizing ethical decision making models, counselors must acknowledge the importance of principals and virtues, ethical codes, ethical theory, case law, and peer consultation. Freeman's (2000) ethical decision model entails all of these aspects and is detailed here:

1. *Review* the situation and define the true problem.
2. *Review* ethical codes and relevant law to the defined problem.
3. *Review* ethical principles relevant to the problem.
4. If more than one ethical principle exists, create a *hierarchical* rank.
5. *Determine* action required based on ethical codes and law.
6. *Determine* action required based on applicable ethical principles and ethical theory (justify your actions!).

7. *Weigh* the action dictated by ethical principles/theory.
8. *Determine* course of action and associated rationale.
9. *Implement* decision and action.

The aforementioned model and similar models seem to work fairly well with adults; however, as a result of the dependency factors relating to children and adolescents, a modified model must be utilized in working with children. Because ethical decision making is an extremely sensitive issue when working with children and adolescents, additional factors must be considered to determine the most appropriate steps to take in regard to reporting and caring for child and adolescent clients. Following is what we, the authors (Sartor & McHerny, 2015), propose:

1. *Determine* the ethical dilemma.
2. *Evaluate* how the dilemma can impact the child–parent relationship.
3. *Evaluate* how the dilemma can impact the child–therapist relationship.
4. *Consider* and *determine* how relevant ethical codes and theories (especially developmental) impact the possible directions.
5. *Review* similar court cases and rulings in your state and nationally.
6. *Consult* with other professional counselors.
7. *Create* a plan.
8. *Follow through* with the plan and *continuously reevaluate* potential relationship concerns.
9. *Revise* plan when needed, and repeat Step 8.

The first step in our model suggests that the counselor determine the actual ethical dilemma. This can be of great challenge and require consideration of multiple factors. For example, in determining the dilemma, a counselor should consider what ethical guideline(s) are of concern, what the parameters of the dilemma are, and who are all of the key players in the dilemma. One of the challenges during this step in the process is to remain objective. However, this is a key part of the process in determining the next steps. Consultation and supervision aid greatly in processing the facts rather than hypothesizing and assuming based on emotional reactiveness. In this part of the process, counselors should assess if it is them, the system, the agency, the rules, and so on, or some combination of the same that are part(s) of the cause of the dilemma.

Once the dilemma has been clearly articulated, the next step is to perform a review of the impact the dilemma may have on the relationship between the child and the parent/guardian as well as between the child and the counselor. In this part of the process, care must be taken to empathize and recognize the scenario from the child's point of view. For example, one type of ethical dilemma that school counselors in rural areas can face is that of dual relationships (friends with the parents of clients they see). If the school counselor's good friend's child came for counseling and disclosed that his father was constantly telling him how awful his mother is (which was leading to significant stress on the child), the counselor may become quite torn between intervening as a friend with the family and breaking confidentiality. In this particular dilemma, the counselor would be forced to immediately consider the impact on the key parties involved, primarily her client, but secondarily, the parents (one of whom is her good friend).

Of course, the case just mentioned has several possible directions for successful resolution. In working toward a solution, the counselor would next want to consider the ethical standard(s) that may be of concern in this case. Standards that may apply to this case and need consider include A.4.a. Avoiding Harm and B.1.c Respect for Confidentiality.

The next two steps in the process have the counselor seek information from multiple sources. Making decisions regarding the best direction in cases when ethical issues arise can be challenging in a vacuum. By seeking literature, including court cases and rulings, and consultation with other professionals, the counselor is much better equipped to make a more fully informed, rational, and professional decision.

Once the counselor has garnered as much information as possible, considered ethical standards involved in the case, and thought through the potential implications on the relationships, it is time to make a plan. Oftentimes, if the previous steps have been adequately considered, this stage of the process brings some degree of relief. The counselor is now able to become unstuck and begin to take positive action. However, in some cases, there may be some degree of difficulty and challenge involved at this stage.

Throughout the next step, the counselor's role is to continually reassess the plan (and focus on impacts on the multiple relationships involved). The step leads to the final part of the process, which is to remain flexible and, with feedback from the previous steps, make any necessary adjustments.

What follows are some situations in which counselors may be forced to utilize an ethical decision making model. What would you do in these situations? Utilize the preceding steps to come up with your decision on what would be the ethical dilemma and the course of action.

CASE TO CONSIDER

The Case of Jennifer

Jennifer, a 16-year-old female, is brought to you by her mother, Tonya, a single parent. Jennifer is of high intelligence and has taken the steps to graduate high school at the end of the current school year. Tonya and her

---

husband, Tom, separated when Jennifer was 6 years old, and they have joint custody over Jennifer. During the initial interview, Tonya filled out the appropriate information and indicated she would bring the custody orders before Jennifer is seen for her first counseling session. Jennifer was not active in the initial interview and was hesitant to say much and did not appear interested when asked about goals for counseling and concerns about the counseling process.

Tonya informed you she is worried about her daughter's future and her desire to enlist in the military after graduation. She emphasized numerous times she "hopes you can talk some sense into her because Jennifer is throwing away her future." Tonya hopes you can convince Jennifer to go to the local community college so she can assist in caring for her little brother while Tonya is at work. After the initial interview, Tonya continues to make comments about you "making Jennifer listen" and "telling her to do what I say."

During Jennifer's first couple of counseling sessions, she was guarded. Jennifer expressed she was concerned you would tell her mom "everything I am saying" because her mom always threatens to tell you everything so you can "fix me." During the third session Jennifer started to become more comfortable with you and indicated she was excited about a presentation occurring at school later in the week. Upon further discussion, Jennifer indicated soldiers were coming to speak at her school about the available opportunities. Over the next several sessions, Jennifer informed you she hopes to join the army after graduation to gain money for college because her mom cannot afford to pay for a good university in her area of interest. Jennifer indicated her mom refuses to discuss anything with her other than attending the local college.

Considerations for Ethical Dilemma

Children and adolescents are often brought to therapy by parents when difficulties arise. In this case, Jennifer and Tonya do not see eye to eye on Jennifer's future plan. It is not uncommon for adolescents and parents to experience conflict over future plans, dating concerns, education, and so on. In such cases the therapist must be willing to mediate these disputes with the best interests, rights, and needs of the adolescent client in mind (Koocher, 2003). An additional area of concern involves Jennifer's father, Tom. Depending on the divorce decree, Jennifer's father may have to consent to treatment prior to treatment taking place.

HELP! I GOT A SUBPOENA!

In many cases newly minted and even veteran counselors fail to follow proper guidelines when receiving a subpoena. Receiving a notice to appear in court or to hand over counseling records through fax, verbal notification, or mail is not a valid subpoena. In such cases, counselors should consider the subpoena to be a request, not a mandate. On occasion, of course, counselors will be required to make a court-ordered disclosure. In such instances, counselors should follow the guidelines set forth the *ACA Code of Ethics* (American Counseling Association [ACA], 2014). Section B.2.d suggests when ordered by a court of law, counselors should "obtain written, informed consent from the client or take steps to prohibit the disclosure or have it limited as narrowly as possible because of potential harm to the client or counseling relationship" (p. 7). Because revealing any information from a counseling session can affect the counseling relationship, counselors should safeguard a client's information as much as possible. When specific circumstances do require confidential information to be revealed, only essential information should be disclosed.

Counselors should keep in mind that not all community agencies/organizations, school systems, or even attorneys view a subpoena as a request. Only special subpoenas, such as those that come directly from a judge, are actually mandates. Many subpoenas are simply requests by attorneys for information from the counselor. It is highly advisable that upon starting work at an agency or school, counselors find out the standard operating procedure for subpoenas. If modifications or alterations are necessary, the time to make such changes in protocol is *not* the moment you receive a subpoena.

In efforts to provide a clearer picture, we refer to the *Abrams v. Jones* case (Texas Supreme Court, 1999). In this well-documented court case, Abrams, a mental health professional, refused to release the records of a child client. Abrams refused because he believed there was a malicious intent in the use of records. Despite Abrams's refusal, the parents claimed the Parental Notification Act allows parents the right to access the records. The *ACA Code of Ethics* stipulates that "counselors provide reasonable access to records and copies of records when requested by competent clients. Counselors document the request of clients and the rationale for withholding some or all of the records in the files of the clients" (ACA, 2014, p. 8). According to the court document, a divorce took place and the parents wanted records to get an edge on each other in the custody battle. The rationale behind Abrams' refusal was that the child would be harmed if the records were released. This decision was based on the fact that the child only opened up after Abrams agreed information would be kept confidential to make the child comfortable enough to receive the services. Additionally, prior to a court proceeding the child client sent Abrams a letter reaffirming the request for confidentiality. Abrams noted he was acting on behalf of the child and in this situation the parents did not have the child's best interests because of their motivations behind seeking counseling for the child and the release of the records.

Ultimately, the court supported Abrams' decision to not release the child's records. This ruling supports the ethical theory or deontology otherwise known as Kantian ethics. In this regard, the intent needs to be right or just. In applying the related ethical principles this case supports fidelity, beneficence, and non-maleficence.

The case of *Abrams v. Jones* illustrates the reason why counselors need to know about parental rights and parental boundaries when it comes to minor clients. Furthermore, as indicated, counselors need to acknowledge when information is too much and when it is too little (ACA, 2014).

CONCLUSION

The legal and ethical mandates under which counselors work are not put there to burden the process or cause problems for the counselor or client. Rather, most are time tested and seem to clearly denote the values and inherent good of the best of counseling. Our field is anchored and based upon the premise of trust. Often trust emerges not through simply using words and phrases that catch the client's attention, but more holistically from simply doing the right thing. In cases where there are challenges to the counselor regarding what is the *right* thing to do, there are resources available and pre-set mandates upon which to rely.

DISCUSSION QUESTIONS/PROMPTS

1.   Informed consent is a cornerstone of our field. What makes it so important for quality care of clients?
2.   What are some ways you can handle situations in which the parents/guardians provide informed consent and feel they have a right to any and all information and discussion details from the sessions?
3.   The odds are very good that you will receive a subpoena in your career. Discuss/reflect upon your emotional reactions to being asked to turn in your case notes and perhaps even testify in a case related to your client.
4.   List and describe all of the possible resources available to you if you follow an ethical decision making model.
5.   After reading this chapter and reflecting on the information provided, what three things emerge for you as being absolutely critical in the ethical and legal counseling of children and adolescents?

UNDERSTANDING HOW PERSONAL AND PROFESSIONAL STRUGGLES CONTRIBUTE TO PRACTICE

Teri Ann Sartor, Bill McHenry, and Jim McHenry

INTRODUCTION

In this chapter, we will address some of the basic and advanced considerations related to *your* skills and resources in handling ethical and legal decisions. These resources may be internal (such as self-care) or external (supervision/consultation). Regardless, it is imperative that counselors utilize multiple means to handle the stress and strain of working with the gray area constructs that ethical decisions can present. Further, this chapter serves not only as a reminder of these resources but also as a primer for the chapters that follow, which include discussion of how various counselors utilized internal and external resources to benefit both the client and the counselor throughout the process.

SUPERVISION/CONSULTATION WITH OTHER PROFESSIONALS

Counseling children and adolescent clients can take enhanced and unique skill sets that may be even more complicated than those necessary to work effectively with adults. This statement is not intended to minimize counseling with adults, but rather to honor the fact that youth often present more challenges. Furthermore, working with minor clients takes specific knowledge unique to minor populations. Therefore, a counselor's competence in working with adults does not ensure a counselor will be effective in working with children and adolescents (Lawrence & Robinson Kurpius, 2000). Failure to acknowledge limitations in knowledge or skill could lead to significant ethical violations. Because beginning counselors may not be exposed to the knowledge and experience of counseling children and adolescents as frequently, supervision from an experienced child and adolescent counselor is seen as a necessity (American Counseling Association [ACA], 2014). In this regard, we have found that standard C.2.a Boundaries of Competence can be of concern for beginning counselors with this population.

Counselors who choose to work with children and adolescents must have additional knowledge of various developmental models (including emotional and social development), which is not needed by those who work mainly with the adult populations (Koocher, 2003). In working with children within the preoperational stage of development (ages 2 to 8), it is recommended that counselors who are not familiar working with this population seek supervision from an experienced child counselor. Because of the necessary skills specifically related to play therapy skills (tracking, reflecting, encouragement, etc.), counselors-in-training and supervisors must understand questions may not be appropriate for this age group due to their lack of cognitive abilities (Landreth, 2012; Ray, 2011). The ACA describes this in standard C.2.b New Specialty Areas of Practice. This standard states, "Counselors practice in specialty areas new to them only after appropriate education, training, and supervised experience. While developing skills in new specialty areas, counselors take steps to ensure the competence of their work and protect others from harm." In this, we find that the ACA subscribes to the fact that when entering a new realm of counseling (e.g., moving from adult to child or adolescent), counselors should put in place safeguards such as supervision and formal course work.

Older children and adolescents may be more adept in answering questions; however, sometimes they may struggle to effectively and clearly articulate and discuss their emotions. Whereas adults may be more able to verbally express their emotions, older children and adolescents may find it difficult to put their emotions into words. This could occur for several reasons, such as the following:

- More than one feeling exists.
- They cannot find a word or feeling that matches.
- They do not know what they are feeling.
- Saying it makes it real.
- They have been told some feelings are "bad."

Because clients of all ages arrive with varying abilities and skills, it is strongly suggested that trainees who work with younger children videotape sessions, and those who work with older children or adolescents video- or audiotape. Then, through reviewing video- and audiotapes (post hoc) with supervisors, counselors-in-training may receive additional direction, identification of strengths, and input regarding areas of growth from said supervisors.

As counselor supervisors, we have found that students and beginning professionals may be hesitant to tape sessions or actively participate in the supervision process due to fears of being viewed as inadequate in comparison to their peers. These fears are often common, as being a counselor does take advanced skills, insights, and awareness! Ronnestad and Skovholt (2003) provide several stages of counselor development that outline what counselors-in-training and experienced professionals encounter throughout their career. These stages of development are seen as extremely important as they clearly delineate the continuous need for growth and evaluation (self, peer, and supervisor) throughout a counselor's career.

Following are the commonalties of counselor development in accordance with Ronnestad and Skovholt's (2003) stages. The stages actually begin prior to admission into a graduate counseling training program, when the decision is made to become a counselor, and they continue throughout a counselor's career.

The Lay Helper

The lay helper is the first stage of counselor development. The lay helper is classified as a counselor without formal training. Therefore, this stage begins prior to and extends briefly into a counselor's graduate training. Within the lay helper stage much of the counselor's work is based on the ability to give advice and solve the problems of others; this is partially due to the beliefs in one's ability to assist others and the belief that he or she is such a great helper. We have found many counseling students tell a similar story that their family and friends come to them for advice and counsel—and this role seems to fit well with their personal needs in work. While the confidence in one's ability to help others is important, the lay helper tends to utilize sympathy instead of empathy and often overidentifies with the client. The lay helper stage is marked with a counselor's high levels of motivation and authenticity in conjunction with low levels of anxiety.

The Beginning Student

The beginning student is starting his or her formal training in the field of counseling. In this phase the student begins to realize it takes actual knowledge and skill to be a counselor. This realization also comes with the idea that lay concepts are no longer appropriate (sometimes even strongly challenged by the student's professors and supervisors). This phase is often marked by high levels of motivation and high levels of anxiety. Because authenticity is low to moderate in this phase, the beginning student may feel vulnerable, which will often lead the student to his or her supervisor for support, encouragement, positive feedback, and practical skills.

The Advanced Student

The advanced student is nearing the end of his or her academic training and is in the internship and supervision process. This student functions at the basic professional level. Because of his or her internalized standards and desire for excellence, he or she has a great deal of focus but exhibits little sense of humor in the counseling process. This focus on the *attempted mastery* of techniques overshadows the student's ability to be present, genuine, and authentic.

Advanced students often have a desire for autonomy but may be reluctant. Because of this reluctance, authenticity in the counseling process is relatively low. As a result of advanced students' low levels of authenticity and reluctance regarding autonomy, supervisors need to provide them with structure, support, modeling, and affirmative feedback. At this phase of development, motivation is seen as moderate, and high levels of anxiety are present. The fear of being found as an "imposter" can emerge as the student realizes the deeper level of therapy along with his or her own limitations. Additionally, the advanced student generally prefers one theory over the others. Therefore, the supervisor should accommodate the student's chosen theory and focus on the best general practice and counseling skill.

The Novice Professional

The novice professional is a new graduate from a counseling or counseling-related program. He or she is transitioning from the academic setting into the professional practice of counseling. At this phase the novice is considered the postgraduate intern (professional counselor interns) and will often challenge or question whether the graduate program adequately prepared him or her for practicing counseling. Additionally, at times the novice professional will question him- or herself regarding fit in the counseling profession. Generally speaking, most will respond with a renewed sense of energy and a desire for additional knowledge and application of theory. At this phase motivation starts out low but ends moderately. Authenticity is generally seen as moderate and is accompanied by high levels of anxiety.

The Experienced Professional

After several years of practice with a full counseling license, a developing counselor becomes an experienced professional. At this time, the central counseling role centers on integration into the professional role and maintaining a sense of authenticity in the practice. Here, the central task for the counselor is to integrate him- or herself into the professional role and maintain a sense of authenticity in his or her practice. Because of the counselor's level of experience, the experienced professional tends to believe he or she has seen it all, turning then to his or her inner self for direction. In cases in which the experienced professional has difficulty, he or she may play the game of "what would my previous mentor do?" to gain additional perspective or direction.

The experienced professional has come to tolerate ambiguity and has confidence within therapeutic relationships. Furthermore, the ability to manage personal and emotional wounds and maintain appropriate boundaries within the counseling relationship has been learned. With the increase in knowledge, experience, and confidence levels, authenticity is high and levels of anxiety are low. The experienced professional phase is also marked with moderate to high levels of motivation.

The Senior Professional

A counseling professional who has 20 or more years of experience is considered a senior professional. This professional is either in transition to or has established the elder status. In both practice and supervision process, the senior professional is realistic in his or her thinking and often shifts from "the counselor is the hero" to "the client is the hero." Furthermore, the senior professional is honored the client has chosen to include him or her, the counselor, in the journey. The senior professional practices with integrity and has a high level of authenticity. While levels of motivation are moderate and anxiety is low, some become bored with the counseling field; however, most remain involved in the counseling profession through their various roles as educators, supervisors, and membership in counseling organizations.

In looking at these stages of development and their happenings, it is evident supervision and consultation occur throughout the span of the counselor's career. Consultation with knowledgeable peers allows a counselor to ensure he or she is keeping up-to-date with common practices and ethical obligations; furthermore, it provides an accountability check to ensure other counselors would do the same in similar situations.

Now that we have reviewed the stages of counselor development, take a moment and reread them in relation to the specific skills set of working with children and adolescents. As you will see throughout this book, skills and techniques used with adults are not always transferrable to this population. Students and professionals who want to counsel children and adolescents need to enhance their formal educational training with as many opportunities as possible to *translate* material from adult tiers, techniques, approaches, and so on, to children and adolescents.

SELF-CARE

The most important aspect of being a counselor is emotionally and psychologically caring for others. However, in order for this to occur, the counselor must first care for him- or herself. The literature covering self-care is often linked to burnout and preventative measures. While specific consequences of doing "people work" are to be expected, preventative measures can be put into place to decrease the likelihood of their development. This is especially true for counselors working with children and adolescents.

Parents often seek therapy for their child for a sense of healing and support. Most parents want their child to feel better about him- or herself, live a fuller life, and be free of nagging psychological distress. Interestingly, of course, therapists, human beings that they are, also need the same type of support. Having such support may greatly lessen the personal stress that can arise for counselors as they work to help others (Bell, Kulkarni, & Dalton, 2003). Conversely, counselors who lack such support in their work (administrative, workplace, or supervisory) can experience burnout or other difficulties as a result of feeling overwhelmed.

Self-care is an especially significant point to consider in regard to the counseling profession since so much of what the counselor does involves working with people. This ongoing focus on people may cause the counselor to begin to merge and confuse his or her professional work with personal life. The literature suggests that maintaining a balance between the therapist's work and personal life seems to be a key element in preventing emotional strains brought on by working with people (Bober & Regehr, 2005; Pearlman, 1995, 1999; Saakvitne, 2002; Stamm, 1995; Tehrani, 2007). In short, the key aspect of self-care is the counselor's ability to separate one's self from the clients with whom he or she works.

Especially when working with children and adolescents, it is easy for counselors to become overly involved in their work. At a biological and cultural level, adults are programmed to defend, protect, and "save" children—sometimes at their own cost. Counselors who fail to recognize this innate tendency are more likely to slip from an effective functioning counseling role to that of *parent, guardian, savior, friend*, and so on. Paradoxically, the behaviors that most likely helped a counseling student succeed in graduate studies (writing a paper on a Friday night, studying all day Saturday rather than hanging out with friends or family) can actually become problematic at the professional level.

In this regard, maintaining a personal life outside of work is critically important. A degree of detachment in therapy may be needed in order to protect oneself (Iliffe & Steed, 2000; Ronnestad & Skovholt, 2003). Such detachment can be effected by gaining real awareness of the fact that the client and counselor are *not* the same person. In addition, this sense of separation between the two may help prevent therapists from overidentifying with clients (Bell et al., 2003). Overidentification and the lack of detachment can eventually lead to boundary crossings due to the desire to help and may lead to additional ethical violations. Additional ethical violations include but are not limited to dual relationships, enabling or creating a sense of dependence, and even breach of confidentiality.

Hesse (2002) suggested stress reduction techniques are essential to maintaining a balanced work and personal life. These techniques include making adequate time for rest and relaxation, meditation, eating right and exercising, spending time with nature, and participating in creative and expressive activities such as drawing, writing, painting, and sculpting. In short, therapists must allot a specific time frame for work and time to enjoy their lives without the stress that is often placed on them by others. Though admittedly an unscientific, nonempirical observation, I (Jim) found that several counselor colleagues and I independently chose woodworking as one common diversion.

In taking time out for the self or self-care, for counselors, there never seems to be a good time. There may always be too many clients who "need to see me." While it may be hard to find such time, Wicks and Buck (2014) suggests using the alone time a counselor already has and making it more purposeful. A repurposed sense of quiet time for relaxation, breathing, meditation, self-awareness, exercise, or just for thought may assist in the process. According to the ACA (2014), counselors should be aware of the signs of physical, emotional, and mental impairment.

Counselors must remember impairment also includes symptoms of burnout such as tiredness, lack of energy, change in sleeping patterns, stress, depression, headaches, a sense of lacking personal accomplishment, depersonalization, and even cold or flu-like symptoms (Acker, 2010; Maslach, 2003). When impairment of the self is noted, counselors are professionally and ethically mandated to take the necessary means to ensure client welfare. Saakvitne (2002) suggests counselors do this by simply asking themselves "How am I doing?" (p. 447) as a means to assess their own psychological health and well-being. Counselors must be willing to do "me work" during times of emotional, psychological, intellectual, or spiritual distress. In fact, it is not uncommon for counselors to have their own counselors. If counselors cannot effectively treat clients without causing harm, counselors should refer current clients to other qualified professionals or suspend their practice until impairment is no longer an issue.

PERSONAL VIEWS ON MEDICATION OF KIDS AND PARENTING STYLE

Medication is not a cure-all for every difficulty children have. However, in some cases appropriate medications are necessary to assist with difficulties as a result of different neurological issues (brain chemistry, levels of serotonin, dopamine, norepinephrine) (McHenry, Sikorski, & McHenry, 2014). If a child or adolescent is on psychotropic medication, it is recommended they also take part in individual or group counseling.

Counseling provides certain aspects that cannot be adjusted or altered by administering medication. For example, psychoactive medication does not assist in the development of coping skills, whereas counseling does. Because the body has the natural ability to become immune to certain substances introduced into the body, specific medications or doses may not be effective in the long run; however, the development of coping skills may provide the necessary tools.

Furthermore, as a result of children's and sometimes adolescent's feelings and emotions being presented through behaviors, simply addressing the behavior may not solve or relieve the difficulty. Counseling can be utilized in conjunction with psychoactive medications to process the emotions underlying such behaviors.

Medication can change brain chemistry in children, therefore caution should be utilized prior to its administration. Because children are considered a vulnerable population (i.e., experiencing substantial developmental growth in short time periods), the long-term effects of medications may be unseen for years (Ingersoll, Bauer, & Burns, 2004). In many cases parents take their children and adolescents to their primary care physician and have them "tested" and placed on psychoactive medication. It should also be clearly recognized that no single test can provide a diagnosis. However, when used in conjunction with each other, tests *and* assessments can assist in supporting a diagnosis. Additionally, of course, medical practitioners may not be aware of the potential side effects, uses, dosages, and potential harmful interactions caused by some psychoactive medications (Glasser, 2008).

It is for this reason that counselors should educate parents on the need to seek the assistance of a psychiatrist to ensure the child or adolescent gets the appropriate medication and correct dosage. In speaking with the psychiatrist, the parents should ensure they are honest in their reports of current behaviors and emotional difficulties.

In treating a client who is on psychoactive medication, the counselor may be required to advocate for the client. To ensure the treatment process is consistent, counselors should obtain a release of information enabling communication with the prescribing physician or psychiatrist. Additionally, through communicating with the prescriber, counselors can assist parents in reporting atypical symptoms and educating them on the purpose of the medication. By providing good and accurate information on medications and their purposes, counselors can also assist guardians in making an informed decision regarding medicating their child (Ingersoll et al., 2004).

Of course, with all of this being said, yet another element in the medication process for children and adolescents emerges—specifically, the role of the counselor in the medication process. Because we are seen (rightly so) as being experts in psychological issues, oftentimes we have found that parents/guardians consult with us on the types of medications their children and teens are on—or have been suggested to take. Certainly, counselors must understand that they are not medically trained, nor are they able to prescribe pharmaceuticals. Having said that, however, and since counselors will be consulted by parents/guardians and the like, our professional response to medications must be augmented not only by our anecdotal evidence (personal views), but also from awareness of the current literature. By failing to understand current trends in both effective medication regimens and *overmedication* of certain hot-button diagnoses, counselors may sometimes play a role in causing harm to their clients. We strongly encourage students and practitioners to develop and maintain an engagement with trends in medications. The statement "I don't believe in medications" is a personal choice—not a professional stance. In fact, if a counselor espouses this view and works to get all of his or her clients to stop taking psychoactive medications, the following ethical standards are most likely being broken: A.4.b Personal Values and C.7.a Scientific Basis for Treatment. Some of the children we serve and adolescents we counsel *will* and *should* be on psychotropic medications. As professionals we must assume the role of best practices within the world we live in (counselors function within the team, including the prescribing doctor and allied professionals).

DIVERSITY ISSUES

Counseling child and adolescent populations includes several aspects related to diversity. Diversity concepts outside of counseling theory often include socioeconomic status, race/ethnicity, age, disability, cultural beliefs and values, and cultural parenting practices. The ACA has identified several standards related to the effective and professional practice of counseling diverse clients, including A.2.c Developmental and Cultural Sensitivity and E.8 Multicultural Issues/Diversity in Assessment. Beyond specific standards that call out diversity by name, at its core, the ACA standards and the practice of counseling is built upon one "primary responsibility": "The primary responsibility of the counselor is to respect the dignity and promote the welfare of clients." This statement, at the beginning of Section A of the ACA standards, both encapsulates and reinforces the very nature of counseling as individualized, personalized, and anchored in promoting optimal human development.

One consideration that must always be taken into account when counseling children and adolescents is that of Maslow's Hierarchy. Oftentimes, a child or teen who is starving or in great fear of his or her personal safety *cannot and probably should not* be focused on higher order issues such as self-esteem and social connections. Although counselors are not social workers or case managers, there are times when we must take on the role of coordinating additional services to remedy or address the most pressing *basic needs* of the client. Can you imagine asking an adolescent whose family has been displaced in the midst of the Hurricane Katrina disaster to work with you on career issues?

Another issue that surfaces when we consider counseling children and adolescents in regard to issues of diversity is that of cultural rules. One of the concerns that can emerge here is a mismatch between the counselor's "cultural rules" and those of the family system. For example, a counselor may believe that parents should never spank their child, while, in fact, in some of the family systems, this is a norm.

CASE TO CONSIDER

Suzie is a beautiful 14-year-old girl. She is coming to counseling because her parents and she agree that her self-esteem is very low. In the initial session, she jokes about not being allowed to date until she is 18. You sense that this is a real rule in her family. What do you do? How might this family cultural rule impact Suzie's life, her self-esteem, and the counseling process?

CONCLUSION

Inherent in the job duties and professional conduct of professional counselors is the necessity to recognize the varied and various resources available to them. Especially important for beginning counselors is the need to monitor their self-care and seek consultation/supervision regularly. Far too often we have seen good counselors leave the field because they could not effectively cope with the pressures and persistent weight of difficult cases on their mind.

DISCUSSION QUESTIONS/PROMPTS

1. Self-care is a critical part of a professional therapist working effectively for many years. In what ways do you practice self-care?
2. This chapter provided two different concepts related to developmental status. The first was the recognition that children are directly impacted by the developmental stage they are in (e.g., cognitive ability to understand and communicate complex thoughts). How do you or will you prepare to meet kids at their developmental level?
3. Take an honest assessment of your current level. Of those provided in this chapter, which are you and how will you continue to work toward the next level?
4. Good or bad, medications are prevalent in our society. How do you view medications and how will such a perspective inform your work with clients?
5. In response to your reflection and answer to Prompt 4, discuss your thoughts and beliefs on medications with at least three other current professionals in the field. How are your views similar and different?

THE ETHICAL AND LEGAL DIFFERENCES AND SIMILARITIES OF WORKING WITH CHILDREN AND ADOLESCENTS IN CLINICAL MENTAL HEALTH COUNSELING AND PROFESSIONAL SCHOOL COUNSELING

Trigg A. Even

INTRODUCTION

So far in this text, you've learned to recognize some of the unique ethical challenges faced by counselors who work with children, adolescents, and their families. In addition, you've reviewed both ethical and legal aspects of counseling with minors. Up to this point, the discussion in this book has emphasized general ethical principles and legal precedent as it relates, universally, to minors entering a professional relationship with any counselor. However, as this and the following chapters will address, many specialty areas exist within counseling. These specialized professional organizations publish a code of ethics for all members of the organization to address ethical and legal challenges unique to the specialty area.

This chapter considers the similarities and differences in ethical and legal issues faced by clinical mental health counselors (CMHCs) who work with minors and professional school counselors (PSCs). Specific topics discussed in this chapter include the systemic factors contributing to these similarities and differences, the similarities and differences with respect to documentation and record keeping, confidentiality, and a special consideration for CMHCs who practice in the school setting. You are encouraged to review the American Counseling

Association (ACA, 2014) *Code of Ethics*, the American Mental Health Counselors Association (AMHCA, 2010) *Code of Ethics*, and the American School Counselor Association (ASCA, 2010) *Ethical Standards for School Counselors*.

AUTHOR'S PERSONAL PREFACE

Soon after I finished my master's degree in community counseling, I was thrilled to join my LPC-S and a small team of clinical mental health and family therapy professionals doing something really innovative: therapy in schools! Prior to this, I was on staff with a residential treatment center and had spent a few years doing crisis intervention with at-risk youth in a nonprofit agency. I quickly learned that I knew very little about the school environment and how counseling fit into the larger mission of primary and secondary education.

At the time, counseling in schools was primarily thought of as a career guidance and academic support service. It was not well understood outside of the profession that school counselors also performed many other functions, including crisis counseling, mental health assessment and intervention, behavior management, consulting, and special education support. As the ASCA National Model (2005a) came into view, school districts were beginning to appreciate the enormous need for comprehensive developmental guidance and counseling programs to meet the needs of all students. I observed that the school environment and its fundamental mission and purpose were—and still are—reacting to the paradigm shift brought on by the ASCA National Model that was itself a response to meeting the ever-increasing demand placed on schools and school professionals. The philosophical debate is ongoing regarding the appropriateness and validity of certain counselor duties as they relate to the school environment and its mission. My experience as a CMHC working in a school setting enlightened me to these issues and strengthened my identity as a professional counselor. The ideas and opinions expressed in this chapter come from my own experiences with navigating this territory and balancing the parameters of my license with the expectations of a work setting that often presented new and different experiences and challenges for which I had little prior knowledge, training, or experience.

SYSTEMIC FACTORS CONTRIBUTING TO ETHICAL AND LEGAL DIFFERENCES

In my experience, differences between the ethical and legal challenges that CMHCs and PSCs face are most influenced by two primary systemic factors: (1) external and internal stakeholder influences that impact the autonomy of the counselor to perform specific duties and (2) the degree of shared professional identity among professional colleagues in the work setting. In the former, whether an ethical or legal dilemma emerges at all may have something to do with how congruent the system's values are to those of the counselor. For example, in a community agency setting whose mission is primarily to serve a transient and homeless population with basic needs for shelter, food, and clothing, the clinical mental health counselor may be met with opposition when attempting to secure informed consent prior to providing counseling to a minor. In this example, the system within which the counselor works may exert pressure on the counselor to provide a service under the agency's mission without consideration for the counselor's unique ethical and best practice standards.

CMHCs and PSCs generally work within different systems. In educational environments, the system is primarily oriented toward student academic achievement. While PSCs are responsible (through the ASCA National Model) for addressing personal/social development, career development, and behavioral intervention and support, the system within which the PSC works is typically most interested in those programs and service activities that can be shown to directly influence academic achievement gains (Studer, 2015). Ethical and legal dilemmas emerge when the PSC owes a *fiduciary duty* to a minor client that the system itself may not consider to be relevant to its mission or purpose.

In community mental health centers, private practices, and other counseling agencies where CMHCs typically work, the system is primarily oriented toward mental and behavioral health assessment and treatment, mental health wellness, psychiatric stabilization, and family therapy. In these settings, the external and internal stakeholder influence on ethical and legal challenges include, but are not limited to, the source of funding (i.e., grants, contracts, other third-party payers), program policy and procedures, variability among the qualifications of direct service and administrative staff, and as illustrated earlier, agency mission or purpose.

The second systemic factor that contributes to differences between the ethical and legal challenges that PSCs and CMHCs experience has to do with who the counselors work with and for. These counselors—relevant to work setting—experience ethical and legal challenges that, in some cases, are owned only by the counselor and no other professional with whom the counselor interacts. For example, on a certain school campus, the professional school counselor may be the only professional on staff with counselor training and certification. By default, the professional school counselor is the only person obligated to act within the parameters of a counselor's code of ethics or standards or practice. Similarly, a CMHC may be employed by an agency or practice staffed by social workers, advanced nurse practitioners, and a supervising psychiatrist. In this example, the CMHC (i.e., LPC) may experience a legal or ethical duty that the other mental health–serving professionals do not. All counselors—regardless of certification, licensure, or work setting—are advised to regularly review both ethical and legal standards relevant to the specialty area and work setting and utilize consultation and supervision with similarly credentialed colleagues.

Common Ethical and Legal Challenges

If PSCs and CMHCs (and the settings within which they practice) were the same, we would not be having this conversation. The reality is—despite both professionals having earned an advanced degree with a common set of core content standards—the specialty area, credentials, and work settings of PSCs and CMHCs vary considerably. As such, the ethical and legal issues faced by counselors with different credentials and work settings also differ. This section examines more closely some of the common ethical and legal challenges faced by PSCs and CMHCs and explores their unique similarities and differences. Specifically, the ethical and legal issues related to documentation and record keeping, confidentiality, evidence of potentially harmful behaviors, and the primary role of the counselor will be reviewed.

DOCUMENTATION AND RECORD KEEPING

Documentation and record keeping is often understood by counselors as a legal and ethical duty necessary for protecting oneself and one's legal right to practice, proving that the work performed as a counselor is consistent with professional standards, and justifying decisions or actions made within the scope of practice. In other words, counselors often think of record keeping as a necessary mandate for them; not doing so places the counselor's license or certification in jeopardy. While these reasons for maintaining accurate and sufficient records are valid, a closer examination of ACA (2014) and both AMHCA (2010) and ASCA (2010) reveals that documentation and record keeping are more accurately understood to be an ethical and legal commitment to clients that serves to promote the client's autonomy and well-being. In all three documents, the ethical practice of documentation and record keeping is categorized under the headings Client Welfare (ACA, 2014), Responsibilities to Students (ASCA, 2010), and Commitment to Clients (AMHCA, 2010). This section reviews the ethical and legal issues relative to informed consent, authorization to release and receive, and case notes.

Informed Consent

At the outset of the counseling relationship, one of the more important ethical and legal issues that counselors who work with children and adolescents must be prepared for pertains to who the counselor can provide counseling with and whether the counselor needs permission to do so (Hess, Magnuson, & Beeler, 2012). This is true for PSCs as much as it is true for CMHCs. While there are some exceptions allowed under the law that vary state by state (See Table 5.1 in Erford, 2011, p. 83), the practice of obtaining informed consent is both a legal matter and an ethical best practice that promotes client and student well-being and autonomy. This is achieved by engaging the minor client and her or his parent or legal guardian in deciding from whom they want to receive counseling services and under what circumstances (Geldard, Geldard, & Yin Foo, 2013), ensuring that they understand in a developmentally appropriate way what the counseling relationship entails (Kanyal, 2014; Ledyard, 1998), and signaling the beginning of the counselor's legal and ethical duty to act in the best interest of the minor client (Lawrence & Robinson Kurpius, 2000; Wilcoxon, 1990).

In community counseling and clinical mental health settings, CMHCs are advised to obtain written consent from all parents or legal guardians before initiating the counseling relationship with a minor client. In many locations, this is a legal requirement established by licensure board regulations. According to AMHCA (2010), "Mental health counselors provide information that allows clients to make an informed choice when selecting a provider. Such information includes but is not limited to: counselor credentials, issues of confidentiality, the use of tests and inventories, diagnosis, reports, billing, and therapeutic process" (p. 4). Furthermore, AMHCA (2010) advised:

> When a client is a minor or is unable to give informed consent mental health counselors act in the client's best interest. Parents and legal guardians are informed about the confidential nature of the counseling relationship. Mental health counselors embrace the diversity of the family system and the inherent rights and responsibilities parents/guardians have for the welfare of their children. Mental health counselors therefore strive to establish collaborative relationships with parents/guardians to best serve their minor clients.
>
> (p. 5)

Professional school counselors also exercise due diligence in securing written informed consent from the parents or legal guardians of school clients and attempt to engage and collaborate with all parents or guardians (ASCA, 2010). However, because PSCs are legally permitted and obligated to act in loco parentis, school counselors are generally and legally permitted to provide counseling services without a parent or guardian's written informed consent (Glosoff & Pate, 2002; Ledyard, 1998). One exception to this pertains to group counseling in schools in which PSCs are advised that "best practice is to notify the parents/guardians of children participating in small groups" (ASCA, 2010, A.6.b; Studer, 2015).

Regardless of setting or credential, counselors who work with minors and their families are advised to consider this general process relative to state licensure laws, relevant codes of ethics, institutional policies, and developmental needs of the minor client:

1. With consideration of developmental, language, cultural, and other contextual factors, clearly communicate both verbally and in writing the nature, purposes, goals, potential risks and benefits, limits to confidentiality, alternatives

to counseling, and counselor qualifications for any authorized counseling practice or related service available to a minor client or student.

2. Exercise due diligence in securing the signatures of all parents or legal guardians on the informed consent document(s). This includes making attempts to engage all parents or guardians when divorce and custody orders are in place (ASCA, 2015; Sealander, 1999; Souders, Strom-Gottfried, & DeVito, 2009). Retain and update records of your efforts to secure informed consent.

3. Approach informed consent as an ongoing responsibility that serves to protect the welfare of the minor client or student.

4. Consult with other colleagues and established laws, policies, and relevant codes of ethics for guidance when issues pertaining to informed consent require clarification.

Authorization to Release and Receive Confidential Information

An essential part of securing informed consent has to do with clearly communicating for understanding the nature and limits of confidentiality. Subsequently, an essential part of documentation and record-keeping practices for counselors who work with minors has to do with obtaining permission prior to disclosing confidential information to a third party. Confidentiality will be discussed in the following section. This section addresses the counselor's use of an Authorization to Release and Receive Confidential Information document. First, let's take a look at this composite case example from real-life practice.

CASE TO CONSIDER

An elementary school counselor received an e-mail request for records from a community counseling agency. Because the school counselor knew that the community counseling agency specialized in home and social studies for family court proceedings, he presumed that the request for records was made as part of this process. The e-mail request appeared to be signed by the legal guardian of the student, but the school counselor noted that the request was received after the return-by date listed on the request. The request for records also indicated that a hearing was scheduled, but this date was also previous to the date that the school counselor received the request. On the one side of the counselor's dilemma was whether he had a legal and/or ethical obligation to release confidential information. On the other side was the issue of the community counselor's adherence to sound ethical and legal principles and best practices when requesting the authorization and records.

As this scenario illustrates, counselors are often faced with an ethical dilemma related to exchanging confidential information about a minor client and her or his family. As discussed previously, the reason these dilemmas emerge has as much to do with work setting and variability in credentials among the professionals involved as it does with the client-specific scenarios themselves. Counselors often wonder about the circumstances under which confidential information can and should be shared, the proper procedure for doing so, and the necessary documentation and record-keeping practices that protect the client as well as the counselor.

In short, however, regardless of setting or credential, counselors should never disclose confidential information to an unauthorized third party. Although there are exceptions to this permitted under the law, discussed later, this standard practice will serve counselors well by protecting client/student information from unnecessary and potentially harmful release while protecting counselors from liability issues that are likely to arise. As such, counselors in any set-ting are advised to secure a signed authorization form with specific requests and limitations clearly cited on the document, for each proposed disclosure. Without the signed form, counselors should not disclose or attempt to receive confidential information. Oftentimes, counselors can secure standardized forms in the public domain; from licensure boards, agency or school policy and procedure manuals, and staff handbooks; and through consultation with legal representation (law offices and attorneys).

At a minimum, an Authorization to Release and Receive Confidential Information form should include

1.   Name and affiliation of the requestor, including contact information.
2.   Name of the client/student and parent/legal guardian.
3.   Date of the request for information and the expiration date of the request/ authorization.
4.   Name and affiliation, including contact information, of the party to whom confidential information will be released.
5.   A specific indicator of the type of information requested and/or released (i.e., intake assessment, treatment plan, case notes, termination summary, medical history, dates of appointments, etc.).
6.   A specific indicator of the parameters/limitations of the information requested or received (i.e., during a specified time period, relating only to a specific diagnosis or treatment, etc.). All counselors are advised to request and/ or release only the minimum amount of information necessary to satisfy the need for the information.
7.   A specific statement about the intended use of the confidential infor-mation (i.e., for treatment collaboration, consideration of placement in a counseling-related program, continuity of care, diagnostic support, etc.).
8.   An acknowledgment of understanding and agreement, and a signature, by the minor client and her or his parent or legal guardian(s).

Case Notes and Memory Aids

As stated previously, the issue of documentation and record keeping is one that pertains most importantly to client/student welfare and the counselor's responsibility to that minor client/student (ACA, 2014; AMHCA, 2010; ASCA, 2010). That being said, any response to the counselor's question (mine and yours) about "What do I *have* to document?" and "How much should I actually write?" should be considered within this ethical duty to promote client welfare (Wehrman, Williams, Field, & Schroeder, 2010). The simple summary, in my opinion, is that counselors who work with children and adolescents should write case notes and progress notes with enough substance or content to ensure that the client/student's welfare is not jeopardized—now or in the future—yet without so much substance or content that disclosure of the record could be reasonably foreseen as potentially harmful to the client/student. For example, the volume of information may leave too many things open for subjective interpretation should the documents be released or subpoenaed at a later time. Ideally, case notes (i.e., progress and process notes) should be a chronological accounting of the counseling services rendered relative to specific goals and objectives, the client/student's response/progress, and any counselor decisions, justifications, and actions relative to these goals and progress.

However, when it comes to documentation and record keeping, there appear to be more differences than there are similarities between the legal and ethical standards for CMHCs and PSCs. For example, the AMHCA (2010) advised CMHCs to "create and maintain accurate and adequate clinical and financial records" (E.1, p. 13). Considered by itself, there appears to be a lack of guidance relative to *what* and *how much* a CMHC should be expected to document. However, AMHCA also advised counselors to use and continuously review and revise "integrated, individual counseling plans that offer reasonable promise of success and are consistent with the abilities, ethnic, social, cultural, and values backgrounds, and circumstances of the clients" (B.1, p. 4). In addition, AMHCA (2010) specified that clients have the right "to a clear working contract in which business items, such as time of sessions, payment plans/fees, absences, access, emergency procedures, third party reimbursement procedures, termination and referral procedures, and advanced notice of the use of collection agencies, are discussed" (B.7.c, p. 7). Counselors will find that state licensure boards also specify clearly the expected frequency and content of case notes and related documentation relative to providing clinical mental health counseling services.

By contrast, ASCA (2010) advised PSCs to "maintain and secure records necessary for rendering professional services to the student . . . keep sole possession records or individual student case notes separate from students' educational records" (A.8, p. 3). Furthermore, ASCA (2015) advised PSCs to "only keep minimal notes, containing student name, time, and a few details as a memory aid" while implying that detailed case notes were reserved for more critical incident encounters, such as child abuse cases. Relative to counseling plans, ASCA (2010) appeared to prefer prescribing an ethical duty to PSCs for "provid[ing] students with a comprehensive school counseling program that parallels the ASCA National Model" (A.3.a, p. 2) rather than prescribing an ethical duty to establish individualized counseling plans with single students.

To be sure, the enormity of work responsibilities, the pace of the counseling work environment, and the probable high volume of clients/students seeking services with counselors makes case notes and progress reporting a necessary, but challenging, task (Wehrman et al., 2010). Regardless of setting or credential, counselors are advised to do the following:

1. Consult relevant legal standards for your practice setting and credential as well as your agency or institution's policies, procedures, and administration for specific guidelines relative to case notes, progress notes, and related record-keeping requirements.
2. Develop and regularly review/update an individualized counseling or treatment plan for each client/student with whom you are providing counseling services. Include specific, observable, and measurable goals and objectives.
3. Maintain an adequate record for each counseling interaction that includes the client/student name or initials, the date of session, the type of session, the primary focus of the session, client self-other-report of progress on relevant goals and objectives, and the counselor's specific intervention to address goals and objectives. In situations where small-group counseling is the recommended counseling intervention, keep a separate record of both the general focus of each group session with no identifying information and an individual record, as applicable, documenting the individual client/student's participation in the group.
4. Write progress and process notes as objectively as possible. For example, "Student reported . . ." or "Counselor observed. . . ." If you must include your subjective interpretation or opinion, specify it as such. When you document having applied a particular intervention or strategy—particularly if it is not standard or general best practice—provide a citation to the author or scholarly source to establish empirical support of its use.
5. Retain the records as long as the regulatory body specifies (state board, agency, occupational code, etc.). These differ for CMHCs and PSCs, and these differ by location. In general, records made by a CMHC are retained for a minimum of 5 years (AMHCA, 2010). Records created by a PSC are retained until the student transfers to another campus level (ASCA, 2015).

CONFIDENTIALITY

Defined as a "professional's promise or contract to respect clients' privacy by not disclosing anything revealed during counseling except under agreed upon conditions" (Glosoff & Pate, 2002, p. 22), confidentiality is for counselors who work with children one of the more problematic legal and ethical issues (Lawrence & Robinson Kurpius, 2000). These legal and ethical issues are complicated further by ambiguity within and between the laws and codes for CMHCs and PSCs. This section will briefly review the similarities in law and ethics for both CMHCs and PSCs, review key differences within and between relevant codes, and examine best practices for navigating the ethical and legal challenges associated with confidentiality and minors in counseling.

To begin, let's review what we already know about confidentiality. First, confidentiality is an ethical concept that exists as a standard rule of practice by our profession (Remley, 1985, as cited by Ledyard, 1998). What this means for all of us is that—by membership in the profession—we agree to be bound by this general ethical duty. It is fundamental to our profession and the trust of the public who seeks the service of our members that confidentiality is honored. As Mitchell, Disque, and Robertson (2002) illustrated, "confidentiality is the cornerstone of counseling and should be guarded at extreme costs, lest the profession redefine itself" (p. 158).

Second, confidentiality is an ethical right that belongs to minor clients in counseling, not a legal right (Glosoff & Pate, 2002; Lawrence & Robinson Kurpius, 2000; Ledyard, 1998; Sealander, 1999). The parent(s) or legal guardian(s) of a minor client retain(s) the legal authority and responsibility to make decisions on the child's behalf, including those related to professional services (Ledyard), and to request, review, restrict, and/or otherwise influence access to private and protected information about the child (Sealander) without restricting the minor child's access to other basic, human, and welfare rights (Such, 2014).

Third, there are exceptions to confidentiality permitted under law, codes of ethics, and professional best practices. Particularly with respect to counseling children and adolescents, it is generally permitted and at times, required, for counselors to breach confidentiality when (1) the counselor suspects or receives information about abuse or neglect; (2) the minor client reports or implies intent to harm self or others, especially if the risk is clear and imminent, and including, but not limited to, potential harm resulting from contagious, life-threatening disease; (3) a court order mandates disclosure or release of confidential information; and (4) disclosure of limited protected and confidential information is necessary for supervision, consultation, billing, practice management, and data management (ACA, 2014; AMHCA, 2010; ASCA, 2010; Erford, 2011; Glosoff & Pate, 2002; Lawrence & Robinson Kurpius, 2000; Ledyard, 1998). All counselors are advised to consistently review ethical codes, case law, and legal precedents for their specialty area, practice setting, and jurisdiction.

While there are similarities inherent to the laws and ethical codes relevant to confidential CMHC and PSC practice, several key differences can also be found, specifically in regard to the permissibility of sharing noncritical (i.e., unrelated to a psychiatric crisis) confidential information without authorization or consent. Counselors might find it useful to categorize these ethical and legal differences according to the descriptors given in the literature. These dilemmas about breaching confidentiality without consent can be categorized as pertaining to a right-to-know, a need-to-know, and qualified privilege.

A right-to-know scenario is one in which the counselor is permitted to share confidential information without consent of the minor client or the parent/legal guardian because the non-parent person receiving the information has a right-to-know. That a person is determined to have a right-to-know does not guarantee that that same person has a legitimate need-to-know (see later discussion).

The ACA (2014) articulated support for a strict adherence to confidentiality. For example, "Counselors disclose information only with appropriate consent or with sound legal or ethical justification" (B.1.c, p. 7). Similarly, "When counseling minor clients . . . counselors seek permission from an appropriate third party to disclose information. In such instances, counselors inform clients consistent with their level of understanding and take appropriate measures to safeguard client confidentiality" (B.5.c, p. 7). Furthermore, ACA (2014) cautioned counselors who are consulting with colleagues to "not disclose confidential information that reasonably could lead to the identification of a client . . . unless they have obtained the prior consent of the person" (B.7.b, p. 8).

The charge of the AMHCA (2010) regarding confidentiality is comparably persuasive. For example, CMHCs are said to "have a primary obligation to safeguard information . . . communicated to others only with the person's consent" (I.A.2, p. 1) and released only "under the most extreme circumstances" (I.A.2.b., p. 2). Finally, it is apparent that CMHCs are not authorized in principle to release confidential and identifying client information "unless accompanied by a specific release of information or a valid court order" (I.A.2.d., p. 2).

While the ACA (2014) and AMHCA (2010) appear to be necessarily restrictive when it comes to breaching confidentiality, the ASCA (2010) recognized that the environment in which PSCs work permits some appropriate and careful exchange of confidential information without student or parent consent or release. For example, PSCs

Recognize their primary obligation for confidentiality is to the students but balance that obligation with an understanding of parents'/guardians' legal and inherent rights to be the guiding voice in their children's lives. . . . Understand the need to balance students' ethical rights to make choices, their capacity to give consent or assent and parental or familial legal rights and responsibilities to protect these students and make decisions on their behalf.

(A.2.d, p. 2)

In addition, ASCA (2010) described a responsibility that PSCs have to the school and school environment to "inform appropriate officials, in accordance with school policy, of conditions that may be potentially disruptive or damaging to the school's mission, personnel and property while honoring the confidentiality between the student and the school counselor" (D.1.b, p. 5). While this is not to be interpreted as clear freedom to breach confidentiality (Glosoff & Pate, 2002; Mitchell et al., 2002; Moyer, Sullivan, & Growcock, 2012), it does seem to serve as a reminder of PSCs' ethical duty to facilitate school safety and positive learning environments as a member of the professional staff. Should information or conditions present during the course of a confidential exchange between a student and PSC, the PSC may have an ethical duty to inform, but must do so in a manner that honors and protects confidentiality as much as possible.

Who, then, is a person having a right-to-know? For the CMHC, a person with the right-to-know might be, for example, an administrator of a residential treatment center or outpatient community mental health agency, an interdisciplinary co-facilitator of a psycho-educational group, or the social worker/case manager at a juvenile detention center. However, it must be noted that there is no clear indication in either ACA (2014) or AMHCA (2010) that a breach of this sort is permissible with one of these individuals. The responsibility for determining right-to-know and, subsequently, upholding the confidentiality of the client rests with the counselor.

For the PSC, a person having the right-to-know may include but is not limited to the campus administrator, the local education agency police or security department, or the central administrative coordinator of the guidance and counseling department. Sealander (1999) also indicated that under the Family Educational Rights and Privacy Act (FERPA, 1974), the term *parent* is loosely defined to include "a natural parent, a guardian, or an individual acting as a parent in the absence of a parent or guardian" (p. 124). Under this definition, a person with the right-to-know might include a "noncustodial or nonresidential parent . . . unless the agency has been provided with evidence that there is a court order, state statute, or legally binding document relating to such matters as divorce, separation, or custody that specifically revokes these rights" (p. 124). School staff, such as teachers, administrators, and other support staff, because they operate in loco parentis (ASCA, 2015), might also be considered as qualifying as having a right-to-know. Again, the responsibility for determining who has a right-to-know falls on the counselor and also very significant here is the fact that the right-to-know does not necessarily mean a person has a need to know.

In the literature describing confidentiality issues for the PSC, a need-to-know scenario is one in which the counselor is permitted to share confidential information about the child or adolescent client/student because the person receiving the information has a legitimate need-to-know. The

ASCA (2015) clarified that determining the validity of a need-to-know scenario or person also requires that the person receiving the information has the authority or autonomy to benefit the student as a result of acting on the information received. Furthermore, the need-to-know in educational environments requires a determination that the probable benefit to the student is related in some way to the school's mission of "optimiz[ing] a student's learning" (para. 8).

Clinical mental health counselors are challenged to consider scenarios in which the CMHC is bound ethically, and in some cases legally, for providing continuity of care in the counselor's absence. For example, AMHCA (2010) specified that "assistance is given in making appropriate arrangements for the continuation of treatment, when necessary, during interruptions such as vacations and following termination" (B.5.a, p. 6). Consider the possibility in which a CMHC provides a brief overview of a client to the agency's intake, assessment, or crisis coordinator "just in case a client calls for an appointment while I'm gone." Similarly, it is common practice for CMHCs to have a specific plan in place for transfer of clients in the event that the CMHC becomes unexpectedly incapacitated or is deceased. In these examples, the receiving provider or other professional can be said to retain a legitimate need-to-know that serves to benefit the CMHC's client.

Closely related to the need-to-know and right-to-know rules is the concept of *qualified privilege*. Usually cited in cases when an accusation of defamation or slander has been levied, qualified privilege protects a person from sharing or receiving confidential information that would otherwise be considered inappropriate for disclosure because the receiving party has a valid interest in the information, the sharing of which is purposeful and necessary to accomplish a specific goal (Wheeler & Bertram, 2012):

> So long as such communications are made in good faith, with appropriate permissions or releases from the clients where needed' express only facts as known to the counselor; and are made only to persons having a proper interest in receiving the information, they will usually be protected.
>
> (p. 69)

For both PSCs and CMHCs, qualified privilege protects the client in that the counselor exercises due diligence to establish reasonable assurance of benefit to the client as a result of the disclosure and limits the confidential information shared to only that which is essential and factual. This due diligence also protects the counselor by ensuring that the counselor has fully evaluated alternatives to a proposed breach, has carefully weighed the risks and benefits of such a disclosure, and has made considerable effort to restrict unnecessary and nonfactual information from the disclosure or report.

Regardless of work setting or credential, counselors who work with children or adolescents are advised to do the following:

1.   With consideration of developmental, language, cultural, and other contextual factors, clearly communicate both verbally and in writing the nature of confidentiality and the limits to confidentiality at the beginning of the counseling relationship and at regular intervals, as necessary (Huss, Bryant, & Mulet, 2008).

2.   Discuss with the child or adolescent client and family specific scenarios in which the counselor is likely to breach confidentiality (i.e., to protect safety and well-being) (Lawrence & Robinson Kurpius, 2000).

3.   Clarify with parents and others (i.e., principals, administrators) the significance of confidentiality to the counseling relationship and seek a collaborative resolution to any concerns about sharing or withholding information (ASCA, 2015).

4.   Consider asking for the name and contact information of at least two other adults with whom the parent(s) or legal guardian(s) authorize you to have contact in the event of an emergency or the unavailability of the parent(s) to receive confidential information (i.e., emergency contacts). Include this in your initial informed consent process and update or revise as necessary.

5.   Prepare a professional, friendly, and diplomatic response for situations in which you may be asked to share confidential information. Practice your response (ASCA, 2015).

6.   Approach confidentiality as an ongoing ethical and legal duty with very few valid exceptions. Do everything you can to protect yourself and your minor clients from disclosure of confidential information. Never share confidential information unless it has been authorized and/or the situation qualifies as a legitimate need-to-know and right-to-know.

7.   Make it your practice to ask for signed authorization to release and receive confidential information. Even in situations where you may be permitted to breach confidentiality, this practice will help ensure that your clients and their parent(s) or legal guardian(s) are protected from unnecessary disclosure.

8.   Consult regularly with colleagues about ethical and legal responsibilities pertaining to confidentiality in order to stay up-to-date about changes or challenges to codes and laws. Always consult your colleagues and relevant codes of ethics, laws, and policies and procedures prior to and during the course of a request or need to breach confidentiality (Lawrence & Robinson Kurpius, 2000).

CASE TO CONSIDER

Upon returning to the office from a home visit, a CMHC working for a community agency was surprised to learn that during the CMHC's absence one of his coworkers—a nonlicensed case manager—had received a phone call from an attorney's office and proceeded to answer the attorney's direct questions about a client's presenting problem, treatment plan, and participation in services. The CMHC later discovered that the attorney who called (and who ultimately subpoenaed his testimony) represented the estranged spouse of the client in a suit for child custody. What potential legal and/or ethical issues may arise from this event?

EVIDENCE OF POTENTIALLY HARMFUL BEHAVIORS

Bodenhorn (2006) reported on an exploratory study in which approximately 100 school counselors were surveyed about their most frequently occurring ethical challenges. Although the participants were PSCs, CMHCs might relate to these common ethical dilemmas. In addition to issues related to confidentiality, parental rights, and dual relationships, these counselors indicated that they experienced frequent ethical challenges related to their responsibility to act (or not) on information of danger to self or others. Counselors who work with children and adolescents understand that some of their minor clients (but not all) will disclose or be observed engaging in behaviors that are considered risky, unhealthy, or potentially harmful. These behaviors include, but are not limited to, substance use, sexual activity, self-injurious behaviors, suicidal ideation or gestures, and various forms of violence and aggression.

As if decisions to breach confidentiality while promoting our client's autonomy and well-being weren't challenging enough, the presence of a risky or potentially harmful behavior history or report complicates the issues even more. As illustrated by Moyer et al. (2012), the criteria for deciding to breach confidentiality when faced with evidence of potentially harmful behaviors are not clearly or consistently detailed in the literature. Furthermore, there is a lack of agreement on how to operationally define risky, harmful behaviors that signal clear and imminent danger to the safety and well-being of self or others (Isaacs, 1997; Moyer & Sullivan, 2008). For example, ACA (2014) advised counselors that the ethical requirement to keep disclosures confidential "does not apply when disclosure is required to protect clients or identified others from serious and foreseeable harm or when legal requirements demand that confidential information must be revealed" (B.2.a, p. 7). Furthermore, AMHCA (2010) reiterated that CMHCs "have a primary obligation to safeguard information . . . communicated to others only with the person's consent" (I.A.2, p. 1) and released only "under the most extreme circumstances" (I.A.2.b., p. 2). While these ethical mandates or permissions are necessarily prescriptive, the lack of clarity with respect to establishing the threshold of "serious and foreseeable harm" and "extreme circumstances" makes it difficult for counselors when the evidence of risky or potentially harmful behavior does not *precisely* fit these definitions.

For the PSC who encounters an ethical dilemma about reporting risky or potentially harmful behaviors, the ASCA (2010) offered a similar admonition to report and "prevent serious and foreseeable harm to the student" (A.2.c, p. 2), but further clarified that "serious and foreseeable harm is different for each minor in schools and is defined by students' developmental and chronological age, the setting, parental rights and the nature of the harm" (A.2.c, p. 2).

For any counselor who works with children or adolescents, promoting the health, safety, and well-being of the minor client or student is both common best practice and an ethical mandate; in some cases, a legal duty as well. Yet, as illustrated by Bodenhorn (2006) and others (Isaacs, 1997; Issacs & Stone, 2001; Moyer & Sullivan, 2008; Moyer et al., 2012), the lack of clear guidelines for establishing harm intersects with variability between counselors in how harm is identified and determined. Glosoff and Pate (2002) reminded counselors that parents have a legal right to be informed of risky behaviors occurring with their minor child, and this does not negate the counselor's ethical duty to uphold confidentiality if at all possible (see also Ledyard, 1998).

A review of relevant literature offers some assistance when counselors attempt to establish and define what constitutes serious and foreseeable harm; that is, when to breach confidentiality and report to parents, administrators, or others having a right-to-know and/or a need-to-know. First, counselors are advised to practice prevention and informed consent (Glosoff & Pate, 2002). By establishing at the beginning of a counseling relationship—with the help of local policies, laws, and codes of ethics, and through consultation—the conditions under which a counselor will report evidence of potentially harmful behavior, the counselor is more prepared to navigate the ethical dilemma without rupturing the trust that has been established. Second, counselors are advised to consult with other counselors of similar credential and work setting in order to review and establish what is considered usual, customary, and reasonable best practices (ASCA, 2015; Lawrence & Robinson Kurpius, 2000). In addition to establishing consistency across providers, when counselors engage in the process of aligning their practices with other professionals' policies and procedures, counselors are more likely to identify gaps in their knowledge and understanding of ethical and legal issues and to subsequently resolve and prevent issues arising from this oversight or omission.

Regardless of work setting or credential, counselors are also encouraged to consider the frequency, intensity/severity, and duration or history of the risky behavior (Moyer & Sullivan, 2008). This practice requires counselors to engage in both informal and formal assessment, including assessment of lethality, and to place the evidence of risky behavior in context. Moyer and Sullivan discovered that counselors were more likely to breach confidentiality and engage a parent or other third party when the risky behavior occurred with some combination of greater frequency and intensity (See also Isaacs & Stone, 2001).

Fourth, according to Moyer et al. (2012), counselors were more likely to report on evidence of risky or potentially harmful behaviors when the behavior occurred with a younger child. Mitchell et al. (2002) advised counselors to also consider developmental level alongside chronological age and degree of dependence on the parents or guardians when considering whether a report is legally or ethically justified. The fifth factor worthy of consideration to determine permissibility of reporting has to do with the visibility of the risky or potentially harmful behavior. Moyer et al. (2012) discovered that school counselors, in particular, were more likely to report evidence of risky behavior when that behavior was observed rather than simply reported. In addition, if the behavior was observed by the counselor on the school campus, the counselor appeared to be more likely to report. For all counselors, considering the context within which the risky or potentially harmful behavior is reported or observed may impact the decision to report its occurrence to a parent or other third party.

Regardless of work setting or credential, all counselors who work with children, adolescents, and their families are encouraged to practice the following:

1. Carefully consider your own values, beliefs, and experiences with behaviors that are often considered risky or potentially harmful to a minor's well-being or safety. Consult with your colleagues about ethical and legal best practices and willingly reflect on any biases you may have regarding these behaviors and your ethical and legal duties (Glosoff & Pate, 2002; Moyer & Sullivan, 2008).

2. With consideration of developmental, language, cultural, and other contextual factors, clearly communicate both verbally and in writing to your clients, parents, and other relevant third parties your policies about confidentiality and the limits to confidentiality with respect to risky or potentially harmful behaviors. Give specific examples and clearly communicate what you intend to do (or not) if/when these behaviors are reported or observed (Mitchell et al., 2002).

3. Decide now if and when you will—either by mandate or professional best practice—immediately report without hesitation a risky or potentially harmful behavior. Determine the conditions under which you will automatically report. Define what factors will qualify the report or observation of a risky behavior as worthy of an immediate breach.

4. When confronted with an ethical dilemma involving risky or potentially harmful behaviors, review relevant codes of ethics, laws, and best practices; consult with colleagues; apply an ethical decision-making model, and document the process.

5. Recognize that as a counselor who works with minors, the public, parents, and other third parties, you must make a reasonable effort to keep a minor client or student safe (ASCA, 2015). Recognize also that their beliefs and values about these behaviors may differ from yours.

6. Recognize that each counselor is individually responsible for providing continuity of care and support to see a situation through (ASCA, 2015).

In most instances, this ethical mandate is satisfied when the parent or legal guardian assumes responsibility for providing for the child's safety and any necessary medical, psychiatric, or other professional services to eliminate or minimize the potential for harm.

CASE TO CONSIDER

Imagine that it's the afternoon of the last workday before a holiday break. You're a counselor working full time in a salaried position. The workday is almost over. You've already worked 40+ hours, all your paperwork is completed, and your bags are packed to leave town for much-needed time with family and friends. As you and your colleagues tidy up and start heading for the doors, your adolescent client shows up in a crisis. Do you have a *legal* obligation to stay after hours? Do you have an *ethical* obligation to stay after hours? Does it make a difference if you are a professional school counselor/at school versus a clinical mental health counselor/at an agency? Does it matter that your client is a minor versus an adult?

SPECIAL CONSIDERATION FOR CMHCs IN SCHOOL-BASED SERVICES

With increasing frequency, school districts are employing clinical mental health counselors to complement the comprehensive developmental guidance program, particularly in the area of responsive services (Erford, 2011). Within the ASCA (2005b) National Model, *responsive services* refers to individual, small group, crisis, and referral counseling necessary for addressing the immediate behavioral and emotional health needs of students, and in some cases, their family members. Clinical mental health counselors might be employed full or part time by the school district, provide services under a subcontractor agreement with the school district, or work within the school setting as assigned by an outside entity (such as a nonprofit agency, professional practice group, or grant-funded program). Another opportunity for CMHCs to work within the school setting is as a counselor who provides *counseling as a related service* with students served by the district's special education department. Regardless of the specific employment arrangement, CMHCs who work for and within schools encounter similar ethical and legal challenges to those already discussed, but often discover that the intersection of setting and licensure/credential magnifies the issues by blurring the lines between primary role, ethical responsibility, and legal liability.

CASE TO CONSIDER

Consider the case of a CMHC who was hired by a school district to work with the general education student population as an intervention counselor. This counselor kept an office in the counseling center near the principal's office and accepted referrals for responsive services counseling from all schools within the feeder pattern (PK–12) from the school counselor, teaching staff, parents, and even students (self-referrals). While this intervention counselor was considered to be a part of the counseling staff on the assigned campuses, this counselor was actually supervised and evaluated directly by the school district's administrator of guidance and counseling.

One afternoon, a district-level administrator approached the intervention counselor with a request for counseling records. The administrator explained that the parent of a student had filed a grievance against the school district for failing to provide necessary and reasonable academic and behavioral accommodations and support for her child as was required by her child's special education designation. The district-level administrator stated that a copy of the record must be made immediately available in order for the district to prepare an informed response to this pending legal matter. The CMHC explained to the administrator that, to her knowledge, a determination had been made previously that the student was not eligible for special education services. The CMHC identified that an *educational need-to-know* threshold was not met by this request, and she refused to release a copy of the record to the administrator.

How then, should a CMHC working in the school setting confront and manage ethical and legal dilemmas? One the one hand, the CMHC may be obliged to follow school district policy and procedure; on the other, the CMHC may be held responsible to adhere to a more or less restrictive legal or ethical mandate by the licensure board. In schools with dedicated CMHCs available to address crisis and mental health needs of students, are PSCs released from a duty prescribed by the ASCA National Model (2005b) and supported in principle by PSC ethics (ASCA, 2010)? To be sure, both CMHCs and PSCs will benefit from collaborations that maximize student accessibility to necessary mental health services (Erford, 2011). Even so, these professionals "face the challenge of establishing their role and professional identity within a shifting framework of services" (Hess et al., 2012, p. 14).

A lot more can be said about CMHCs who work in school settings, but this last quote is, for me, the one that holds the key. We're different.

Our training—while similar in so many ways—is different. Our credentials, scope of practice, and primary mission are also different. Within school-based services, the coming together of professionals with unique identities that are embedded within the larger, shared professional identity of counseling results not in impassable obstacles but in opportunities to navigate ethical and legal challenges together, and learn to support and understand the other through this collaborative process. Studer (2015) recommended that counselors pursue collaborations with the following characteristics: flexibility, collaborative commitment to goals, and process reflection. According to Studer, "richer solutions will emerge when professionals meet to brainstorm solutions to dilemmas. As each professional contributes suggestions, a repertoire of answers that are fundamentally different and more innovative than what would be provided by an individual professional member emerges" (p. 410).

Clinical mental health counselors and their PSC colleagues are advised to do the following, relative to preventing and managing ethical and legal challenges in the school setting:

1. Form and maintain collaborative and collegial partnerships with other professionals in the school environment—in particular, other counseling professionals and administrators (ASCA, 2015).
2. Clinical mental health counselors are advised to learn as much as they can about the school, its mission, and the general school environment. Ask questions, attend district-level meetings, take a graduate course in school counseling, and so on. Because you may not have "insider information" about schools and how they operate that comes from years in the classroom, you will benefit from accelerating your on-the-job training.
3. With the help of campus administrators, lead counselors, and district-level coordinators/directors, establish clear roles and responsibilities for all counseling professionals, including the policies and procedures for managing student or campus crises (Studer, 2015) and operating within an organizational chart ("chain of command").
4. Be an advocate for the profession of counseling and for your unique professional identity. Inform others about your credentials, scope of practice, role and responsibility in the school environment, and any ethical and legal mandates that may be in conflict with the school environment or standard operating procedure. Invite conversation ahead of time about how these conflicts can be resolved in a way that promotes students' well-being without undermining the integrity of the school environment or mission.
5. Review and update policies and procedures relative to ethics codes and current licensure laws for all counselors. Share specific details of your ethics code and licensure law with your colleagues and learn from theirs. Take time periodically to process real or hypothetical case scenarios, paying particular attention to arriving at an acceptable ethical decision-making outcome.

6.   When faced with ethical and legal dilemmas, consult. In addition to the standard use of colleagues for consultation, know that school districts and most professional associations provide no-cost legal advice for all employees or members.

7.   When in doubt as to the most ethical way to resolve a challenge or conflict, counselors are encouraged to align their actions with the most conservative option necessary for promoting student/client welfare. For CMHCs working in the school setting, the most conservative option will likely be the one pre-scribed by your licensure board. Similarly, the licensure laws in your state may specifically require or prohibit certain actions that are mandated or prohibited in the school setting. Again, your licensure board and legal counsel will advise in a way that ultimately seeks protection of student client welfare and your license.

CONCLUSION

This chapter discussed some of the similarities and differences in ethical and legal issues faced by clinical mental health counselors who work with minors and professional school counselors. The ACA (2014) *Code of Ethics*, the AMHCA (2010) *Code of Ethics*, and the ASCA (2010) *Ethical Standards for School Counselors* were consulted for guidance on common ethical challenges, including those related to documentation and record keeping, confidentiality, and disclosure of risky and potentially harmful behaviors. The limitation to these topics certainly falls short of discussing the numerous other ethical and legal challenges counselors will face. While recommendations were given, the reader understands that these were limited to interpretation of current code, best practices, and my own experiences. By approaching ethical practice as a process more than an event, and engaging in dialogue, consultation, reflection, and review of codes and laws, counselors will find empowerment to navigate even the most treacherous of ethical and legal dilemmas.

DISCUSSION QUESTIONS/PROMPTS

1.   Imagine that you receive a referral to counseling for a 15-year-old who is not living at home. The adult who brings the teenager to your office reports that she is providing a place for the teen to stay and that she has no legal guard-ianship. The teenager's parents are not available or willing to assign any type of guardianship to the adult caretaker. Discuss the circumstances under which a counselor is permitted to provide counseling to a minor without parental or legal guardian's consent. Are these different for CMHCs and PSCs? Would you see the teenager even though you cannot obtain informed consent from a parent or legal guardian? Discuss the ethical principles and legal standards related to this scenario.

2.   Various codes of ethics prescribe record keeping and documentation practices as a means of ensuring client welfare and promoting client well-being. Discuss and illustrate how obtaining informed consent, revising a counseling treatment plan, or charting the results of a pre- and post-counseling assessment promotes client or student well-being. Under what circumstances might it be harmful to a client's or student's well-being to make and keep records?

3.   Define *responsive services*. List and describe the differences and similarities in applying ethical codes and legal standards between CMHCs and PSCs who provide responsive services in the school setting.

4.   Imagine that you are approached by an agency or school administrator who demands to know specific details of your counseling interactions with a child or adolescent client. Think about how you would respond to this request. Under what circumstances would the request for confidential information be warranted and appropriate, and how would you proceed? Under what circumstances would the request for confidential information be inappropriate, even for a school or agency administrator, and how would you proceed?

5.   Counselors are advised (in as much is possible) to clarify policies and procedures before ethical and legal challenges arise. Make a list of those policy and procedures you want to ask about and clarify before you begin employment in a counseling position. Make a list of those policies and procedures you want to explain to your child and adolescent clients (and their family members) before you start counseling with them. Share specific strategies and language with your peers/colleagues.

ETHICAL AND LEGAL ISSUES IN ADOLESCENT RESIDENTIAL TREATMENT, ADOLESCENT GROUPS, AND WORKING WITH SEVERE EMOTIONAL AND BEHAVIORAL DISORDER (SEBD) POPULATIONS

Don Redmond

INTRODUCTION

Providing counseling services to adolescents in a residential treatment setting can be highly rewarding but also exceptionally challenging. From an ethical perspective, like other environments and according to the foundation of "do no harm," you are responsible for ensuring the safety of clients who are often vulnerable and in some cases have suffered abuse. The narratives of these are wide-ranging; often the only commonality one resident shares with another is a pattern of dangerous behaviors. Treatment outcomes also vary greatly, and there is rarely a consensus on factors that contribute to success; family involvement in treatment and discharge planning seems to clearly improve outcomes (Landsman, Groza, Tyler, & Malone, 2001; Wilmshurst, 2002). Mood disorders may have greater likelihood of improvement versus behavior disorders (Peterson & Scanlon, 2002), and the trajectory of benefits from treatment may level out within the first 6 months, regardless of how much additional residential treatment an adolescent receives (Noftle et al., 2011). Otherwise, however, on a day-to-day basis a residential treatment setting, particularly one serving SEBD adolescents, can seem an intimidating and complex mixture of behavioral interventions.

With so many variables, how can a counselor effect the most positive change while practicing within preferred and necessary personal and ethical boundaries? Before discussing specific characteristics of residential treatment, it can be helpful to consider an underlying philosophy of child and adolescent develop: parenting styles. As any parent or teacher can likely attest, finding the right balance between warmth and control can be difficult. Too much warmth, or unconditional positive regard, without structure and expectations can leave a child unmotivated or entitled. However, if a child is not shown consistent love and support, but is rather inundated with messages that they are flawed and incapable, she may respond with chronic acting out or belligerence. Parenting scholars suggest that finding a balance between warmth and control—termed *authoritative parenting*—results in children and adolescents who are more likely to reach their social and academic potential. Conversely, indulgent-permissive parenting (too much warmth with too little control) and authoritarian parenting (too much control with little consistent warmth) results in children who show lower academic achievement and more impulsivity, among other less preferable behaviors such as substance abuse (Baumerind, 1991). Further, for children and adolescents to thrive, both the school and home environment have complimentary authoritative characteristics: Expectations and rules are clear, as are consequences for misbehavior; however, successes are recognized and rewarded.

Many children arrive in a residential treatment setting because their home environment was chaotic and unsafe in a way that the structure and safety of a school couldn't compensate. When residential treatment works, the success often can be attributed to a child or adolescent belatedly finding the combination of consistent structure and warmth previously missing from his or her life.

Two counselor roles in residential treatment settings, directly related to finding a balance of warmth and control while also often presenting ethical challenges, are administrative supervision and group counseling.

ADMINISTRATIVE SUPERVISION

By virtue of holding a master's degree, a counselor in a residential treatment setting may be put in the role of administrative supervisor. This role can be very different from the one a CACREP-master's curriculum prepares you for. When supervising staff, you must create an environment that is supportive enough that a worker can deal with behaviors that would test the patience of a saint: Why would a direct-care staff subject themselves to daily verbal aggression—if not the physical type requiring a multiple person therapeutic restraint—if they did not feel supported by their supervisor? Gray et al. (2001) conducted a study of counselor trainees' experiences with counterproductive supervision events and found that the following constitutes a negative experience: a supervisor asking a question with suspicion; a supervisor being judgmental regarding a trainee's thought and feelings; a supervisor who inappropriately self-discloses; a supervisor who only emphasizes mistakes, has overly harsh reactions to a trainee's seemingly normal concerns, and engages in repetitive negative interactions with the trainee. Perhaps one of the greatest challenges of administrative supervision of direct-care staff working with SEBD populations is this: Children who have the most severe behaviors are also the ones who are most likely to provoke a reaction by a direct-care staff member that may require termination of employment.

So how does an administrative supervisor find balance between ensuring the safety of residents and adequately supervising and supporting direct-care staff?

First, before accepting a role or promotion to administrative supervisor, a counselor should be well versed in the following portions of the *ACA Code of Ethics* (American Counseling Association [ACA], 2014):

D.1.g. Employer Policies

The acceptance of employment in an agency or institution implies that counselors are in agreement with its general policies and principles. Counselors strive to reach agreement with employers regarding acceptable standards of client care and professional conduct that allow for changes in institutional policy conducive to the growth and development of clients.

D.1.h. Negative Conditions

Counselors alert their employers of inappropriate policies and practices. They attempt to effect changes in such policies or procedures through constructive action within the organization. When such policies are potentially disruptive or damaging to clients or may limit the effectiveness of services provided and change cannot be affected, counselors take appropriate further action. Such action may include referral to appropriate certification, accreditation, or state licensure organizations, or voluntary termination of employment.

F.1.a. Client Welfare

A primary obligation of counseling supervisors is to monitor the services provided by supervisees. Counseling supervisors monitor client welfare and supervisee performance and professional development. To fulfill these obligations, supervisors meet regularly with supervisees to review the supervisees' work and help them become prepared to serve a range of diverse clients. Supervisees have a responsibility to understand and follow the *ACA Code of Ethics*.

(Reprinted from *ACA Code of Ethics* [ACA, ©2014].
American Counseling Association. Reprinted with permission.
No further reproduction authorized without written
permission from the American Counseling Association.)

Within an administrative supervision and organizational context, staff orientation, level systems, and regular staff meetings/trainings are an important way to maximize the likelihood that adolescents will be treated in an ethical manner.

Orientation

Many residential treatment settings have a formal system for the prevention and management of aggressive behaviors such as the Nonviolent Crisis Intervention training provided by the Crisis Prevention Institute. Programs such as these teach de-escalation strategies but also safe restraint and seclusion techniques in the event that less restrictive interventions fail to mitigate aggression. As might be expected, seclusion and restraints should be used as a last resort, and need to be closely monitored to avoid excessive use or undue force. Other types of training include educating direct-care staff on developmental theories such as Erik Erikson's theory of psychosocial development. In my experience, this helps a direct-care staff avoid being drawn into provocations by residents. If a professional helper is able to recognize that a 13-year-old SEDB resident is actually much younger from an emotional standpoint, then she will be less likely to be surprised, and frustrated, by a behavioral outburst by the same 13-year-old bearing a strong resemblance to a "temper tantrum."

Level Systems

Behavioral level systems are a hallmark of successful behavior modification systems in residential treatment settings. To an outsider, and often many new residents of residential treatment centers and psychiatric hospitals, level systems might seem to be the definition of authoritarian leadership or "micro-management." However, given the lack of impulse control of residents, it's usually necessary from a therapeutic standpoint to provide consequences for everyday behaviors that wouldn't be tolerated in nonresidential settings. Examples of these include physically fleeing an environment when you are uncomfortable, deviating from a schedule because you don't feel like following it, physically invading other people's space, making derogatory and sarcastic remarks to authority figures, and failing to take responsibility for misbehavior. Level systems not only help residents learn to refrain from these types of negative behaviors, they also provide a measure of how long a resident can maintain positive behavior. If these systems can seem unduly restrictive to some (including, for example, person-centered individual counselors whose goal is to create an in-session environment that's as *least* restrictive as possible), they also can provide transcendent accomplishments: When an adolescent does attain a behavioral milestone such as reaching a new level or earning discharge home or to a step-down program, a sense of liberation can be seen in the resident over accomplishing something she didn't think was possible.

Staff Meetings

Regular staff meetings and trainings are an important way to allow staff to express concerns as well as a means where a counselor administrative supervisor can instill the message that the environment will never be completely stress free. Also, based on my experience, this is a way to cover necessary nonserious remedial topics without the need to single out individuals who, again, might already be bombarded with negative statements from residents. An example is being sure to rotate on certain chart auditing duties. As a supplement to regular staff meetings, communication logs can also help to maximize communication between administrative supervisors and direct-care staff as a way to ensure a high level of consistency. For example, a common phenomenon in residential treatment, similar to that of many two-parent and/or intergenerational households, is what can be termed *splitting staff*. This takes place when a child/resident does not want to accept "no" from one person, and thus tries to find another authority figure to give them a "yes" without disclosing their initial request. In residential treatment, this tactic can have a higher success rate in that there are typically multiple shift changes during a typical week. A communication log helps with ensuring not only that staff are following the same rules and procedures, but also that they are interpreting any gray areas consistently and thus presenting a unified front, which is important to a child's development.

POINTS TO PONDER

When growing up, what type of parenting characterized your home environment? Did you have a parent who erred on the side of praise? A father who was either authoritarian or absent for long time periods? A verbally abusive stepparent? When working with an SEBD adolescent with a documented history of abuse, how will your environment during your formative years influence the way you process a resident's negative emotions and behaviors? If you're an individual counselor, will you support the behavior management level system even when this system keeps your client from reaching an important long-term goal?

GROUP COUNSELING

Group counseling provides therapeutic benefits that can be absent from individual counseling. In an inpatient setting, in addition to benefits, there are several challenges that are atypical of nonresidential settings. First, a counselor should be familiar with the following ACA codes (2014):

A.9.a. Screening

Counselors screen prospective group counseling/therapy participants. To the extent possible, counselors select members whose needs and goals are compatible with the goals of the group, who will not impede the group process, and whose well-being will not be jeopardized by the group experience.

A.9.b. Protecting Clients

In a group setting, counselors take reasonable precautions to protect clients from physical, emotional, psychological trauma.

(Reprinted from *ACA Code of Ethics* [ACA, ©2014].
American Counseling Association. Reprinted with permission.
No further reproduction authorized without written
permission from the American Counseling Association.)

One tenant of group therapy is that not only is informed consent used, but group members are free to leave the group without penalty. Given that the group members live with each other in residential settings, there is perhaps a greater possibility that group members would have to work through a "storming" phase (Tuckman, 1965) away from the group setting in that they would need to coexist with each other outside the group milieu as well. Related to this concern, maintaining confidentiality can be even more difficult when a conflict in a group may carry over to, for example, the dining hall. And even if social media can be controlled for by restricting access to cell phones and the internet for noneducational purposes, it's also impossible, even within a locked treatment setting, to prevent one resident from using another member's group topic as a way to antagonize. A second inherent ethical risk within a residential treatment setting is that the groups must often be open; that is, new members are admitted at any time, and thus the groups sometimes struggle to get to a "norming and performing" stage (Tuckman, 1965).

A way to counter this risk is for direct-care staff to be diligent about monitoring the behaviors of residents during non-group treatment hours. This can even often be an opportunity to get a better idea of dynamics of residents (in a military setting, this might be termed *intelligence gathering*).

POINTS TO PONDER

You are sitting in a common area of a locked residential treatment unit when two residents begin arguing. You're the closest staff member to the commotion and one of the residents is your individual counseling client. As you approach, the conflict escalates first to shoving, then to a punch being thrown. The punch misses the intended target and instead catches you in your left eye. What do you do? What if other staff members encourage you to press charges? What if you get the impression the clinical director prefers you do not press charges? What additional details would help you decide for and against pressing charges?

CASE EXAMPLE

In a residential treatment setting, one ethical dilemma that is common with clients in residential treatment involves legal guardianship and treatment. Most social workers/caseworkers would attest to the importance, whenever possible, of having biological relatives, if not a biological parent, involved in treatment. The motivation of the child or adolescent, in addition to the likelihood of a successful long-term placement, as previously mentioned, increases when biological/custodial family take part in treatment and treatment planning. However, a common dilemma often arises when legal custody resides with a caseworker but a biological parent is permitted to have supervised contact with the resident. In these instances, the desire to have regular communication between the parent and child can be offset by issues that led to the parent initially losing custody; for example, perhaps the parent had a drug or alcohol problem, engaged in illegal behavior, or suffered from a serious mental illness. Family courts typically are careful to provide clear directives to professionals in residential treatment with a list of family members with permission to have contact with residents.

At a hospital serving children with severe emotional behaviors, an adolescent female struggled with depressive symptoms. [For the purposes of this example, the resident will be called Allison.] Allison had a love–hate relationship with her mother. She realized that her mother sometimes was a negative influence in her life, but she also clearly loved her mother and was motivated by the goal of returning home to live with her. However, based on the mother's own significant mental health issues, she had lost custody of Allison. The mother's ability to talk with Allison was dependent upon the authorization of Allison's caseworker, and phone calls were to be monitored by a staff member. One day, a staff member observed Allison becoming tearful when talking to her mother, and requested that the phone call be cut short. When the staff member processed the call with Allison, she was alarmed to hear that Allison's mother shared with her daughter that she, Allison's mother, had made an unsuccessful suicide attempt the previous night.

While this example is disturbing, it may be important to remember the foster care radio ads that state "you don't have to be perfect to be a perfect parent." It's tempting in a situation like this to advocate, immediately, for termination of contact between biological parent and child and even a change in the discharge plan to exclude the possibility that Allison can return to live with her mother. How can Allison possibly overcome her own depression when she gets such updates from her mother? Certainly, the caseworker should be notified, and contact should be suspended. But what are other options that would still leave open the possibility of renewed regular contact between Allison and her mother, if not a goal of reinstatement of parental rights? One short-term solution could be psycho-educational interventions with the mother. Another, perhaps obvious in hindsight, would be phone calls taking place on speaker phone, or in-person visits only with supervision. These options would provide the safety Allison requires and deserves, while still providing motivation for reunification between Allison and her mother.

The following ACA code is relevant in this example:

B.5.b. Responsibility to Parents and Legal Guardians

Counselors inform parents and legal guardians about the role of counselors and the confidential nature of the counseling relationship, consistent with current legal and custodial arrangements. Counselors are sensitive to the cultural diversity of families and respect the inherent rights and responsibilities of parents/guardians regarding the welfare of their children/charges according to law. Counselors work to establish, as appropriate, collaborative relationships with parents/guardians to best serve clients.

(Reprinted from *ACA Code of Ethics* [ACA, ©2014].
American Counseling Association. Reprinted with permission.
No further reproduction authorized without written
permission from the American Counseling Association.)

CONCLUSION

Many counselors, counselors-in-training and/or practicum and internship students, and recent master's graduates who are pre-license will have the opportunity to work in a residential treatment setting. This experience can be exceptionally meaningful, but also challenging: Working with adolescents in a residential treatment setting is a stark example of the difference between theory and practice. To succeed, you must be able to display a range of qualities, including, but not limited to, patience, compassion, morality, and resolve. Perhaps most importantly, considering the stories of the residents you'll be working with and your attempt to ultimately help them, perhaps your first task should be this: convincing yourself, and your clients, that despite sometimes overwhelming messages to the contrary, every day is an opportunity to display strengths.

DISCUSSION QUESTIONS/PROMPTS

1. In this chapter, the idea that a new counselor may be asked to assume the role of supervisor is presented. How well prepared are you to assume such a role and in what ways can you develop such a skill set?

2. Regardless of whether you will ever serve as a therapist in an inpatient setting, working with children and teens *may* result in the need for you to intervene physically. How comfortable are you with such an intervention? What steps have you taken or can you take to ensure that you follow acceptable practices for safe physical management?

3. Group homes often use what is called a *points system* based on good or inappropriate behavior. Discuss the pros and cons to using such a behavioral model.

4. This chapter posits a rather challenging question regarding how the home environment for some clients may play a huge role in the development of ineffective thoughts and behaviors (which resulted in the client being placed in the group home setting). Discuss the concept of returning kids to homes that have not changed.

5. When you consider children and teens who have been adjudicated to a group home setting, what is your impression/belief of how they came to be that way?

LEGAL AND ETHICAL ISSUES IN COUNSELING LGBTQ CHILDREN AND ADOLESCENTS

Cyndi Matthews

INTRODUCTION

Counseling with lesbian, gay, bisexual, transgender, and questioning/queer (LGBTQ) children and adolescents can lead to a number of ethical dilemmas for counselors, ranging from competence, to confidentiality, to conflicting values on the part of the counselor with the client. On the other hand, LGBTQ children and adolescents may find the coming-out process extremely difficult in a heterosexist society and could seek out allies, such as counselors, to help them through this difficult process. It is imperative that counselors support and advocate for their LGBTQ clients and not become part of the overall damage their clients may experience through the process of coming out in a heteronormative society.

This chapter will focus on the American Counseling Association (ACA, 2014) ethical principles that counselors must adhere to when counseling with LGBTQ clients, including

1.   when counselors experience personal value discrepancies between themselves and their client;
2.   how counselors need to increase their counseling competence by enhancing their personal awareness, knowledge, and skills regarding LGBTQ children and adolescents;
3.   when and why counselors need to take a social justice perspective and orientation in advocating for LGBTQ clients both outside and inside the counseling relationship;
4.   how and when counselors will find it necessary to maintain confidentiality in the counseling relationship with LGBTQ youth even when parents are pressing for information from the sessions.

BOUNDARIES OF COMPETENCE AND PERSONAL VALUES VERSUS PREJUDICE AND DISCRIMINATION

The 2014 American Counseling Association (ACA) *Code of Ethics* recommends in standard C.2.a, "Counselors practice within the boundaries of their competence, based on their education, training, supervised experience, state and national professional credentials, and appropriate professional experience." Many mental health professionals in the past have read this to mean that if they are uncomfortable in working with LGBTQ individuals, they can refer their clients to other counselors. Ford and Hendrick (2003) found that when counselors were presented with a values conflict, 40% referred the client to another professional, and 25% of mental health professionals discussed the value conflict with their clients. Clients who have been referred to other counselors or treated unfairly by their counselor because of their sexual orientation have reported feeling discriminated against and as suffering psychological harm because of the referral (Francis & Dugger, 2014). *Counselors need to understand that referring clients because of personal values is not a competence issue—it is a discrimination issue.* Regardless of a counselor's personal values, ethical mandates of the counseling profession maintain that counselors seek additional training and supervision in order to counsel with LGBTQ clients rather than refer (Granello & Young, 2012).

Counselor values can be communicated subtly through nonverbal communication, by what the counselor chooses to ignore or discuss, and by the interventions the counselor chooses to use in the counseling session. The preamble to the *ACA Code of Ethics* (ACA, 2014) states that counselors should empower their clients to achieve their goals, and standard A.4.a states "Counselors act to avoid harming their clients." As counselors work to empower their clients, they need to set aside their personal values in order to help clients achieve their goals. Standard A.11.b of the ACA (2014) *Code of Ethics* states,

> Counselors refrain from referring prospective and current clients based solely on the counselor's personally held values, attitudes, beliefs, and behaviors. Counselors respect the diversity of clients and seek training in areas in which they are at risk of imposing their values onto clients, especially when the counselor's values are inconsistent with the client's goals or are discriminatory in nature.

This means that as a counselor, it is not acceptable to refuse to treat or work with a client based solely on one's personal values. Counselors need to seek out training when their values are inconsistent with the client or if there is a risk of being discriminatory, and learn to "bracket" their own values in order to work with their client in a nonjudgmental, empathic counseling environment (Herlihy & Corey, 2015). They need to learn to work with their clients within their client's value system and help their clients find their own way (Remley & Herlihy, 2014).

In regard to working with LGBTQ individuals, several legal cases have come to light within the counseling community. In *Bruff v. North Mississippi Health Services, Inc.* (2001) and *Walden v. Centers for Disease Control and Prevention* (2010), counselors Bruff and Walden referred their LGBTQ clients to another counselor because it went against their religious values to counsel someone who was LGBTQ. Both counselors filed lawsuits against their employers when their employers placed them on administrative leave or fired them. Both Bruff and Walden claimed that their employers had violated their religious rights under Title VII of the Civil Rights Act of 1964. The courts ruled against Bruff and Walden, claiming that referring LGBTQ clients to other counselors put undue hardship on their fellow colleagues and that counseling with LGBTQ clients did not violate their civil rights.

Two similar legal cases have also played out prominently in the academic world with respect to the training of counselors. In *Ward v. Wilbanks* (2010) and in *Keeton v. Anderson-Wiley et al.* (2011a), two different graduate counseling students refused to counsel with or complete personal remediation plans for working with LGBTQ clients because of the counseling students' religious values. Both students were dismissed from their respective programs by their universities. In one case, the courts found in favor of the university, stating that the student's actions went against the *ACA Code of Ethics* and that the student was trying to impose their personal values and religious views on the client. In the other case, the student and university settled outside of court. In neither case were the students allowed to continue their training at their respective universities.

The *ACA Code of Ethics* standard C.5 (ACA, 2014) states:

> Counselors do not condone or engage in discrimination against prospective or current clients, students, employees, supervisees, or research participants based on age, culture, disability, ethnicity, race, religion/spirituality, gender identity, sexual orientation, marital/partnership status, language preference, socioeconomic status, immigration status, or any basis proscribed by law.

Counselors and mental health workers are required to become aware of their personal values, work toward not forcing these values upon their clients, and gain competence through supervision, education, and further training.

Shiles (2009) suggested that clinicians choose to refer their LGBTQ clients to other mental health professionals because (a) referring clients is seen as a normal activity in the mental health community (however, it could be a case of invisible heterosexism or microaggressions against the LGBTQ community); (b) clinicians maintain their self-efficacy by rationalizing that referring is in the best interest of the client; (c) referring clients is easier than engaging in self-reflection, gaining additional training, and seeking supervision and consultation. However, discriminatory referrals occur when mental health professionals do not seek supervision or further training to increase their capacity to provide counseling services, but instead refer when the client's presenting concern is against their values or religious beliefs (Shiles, 2009).

Some counselors and counselors-in-training, such as those mentioned in the preceding legal cases, believe their rights to their beliefs and values are being violated when asked to counsel with LGBTQ individuals. However, clinicians are not asked to change their beliefs or values. Counselors are required to bracket their personal values so as to create a therapeutic environment for their client (Remley & Herlihy, 2014). *ACA Code of Ethics* standard A.4.b states, "Clients are aware of their own values, attitudes, beliefs, and behaviors and avoid imposing values that are inconsistent with counseling goals. Counselors respect the diversity of clients, trainees, and research participants" (ACA, 2014). It is crucial that counselors and counselors-in-training learn to, when necessary, separate their own values from the counseling relationship in order to help their clients work through their issues in a safe, nonjudgmental counseling space. If students struggle in this area, they can seek supervision, consultation, and training to help clients work within the client's value system.

CASE TO CONSIDER

Cassandra is a graduate counseling student in the internship phase of her courses. She has been working with Jessie, a female adolescent client age 16, about issues of self-esteem, assertiveness, and healing from emotional abuse from her father. Cassandra has reported to her supervisor/instructor that she feels the sessions are going well and that a level of trust has been established between counselor and client. During the fourth session together, Jessie starts to discuss how she is struggling with being open and honest with her partner, Cathy. Cassandra maintains an impassive composure, but internally starts going through all of the reasons she can no longer be Jessie's counselor. Cassandra was raised to believe that being lesbian or gay is a sin. Cassandra starts to think of all of the reasons why she should refer Jessie to another counselor. During the session, Cassandra says nothing to Jessie about her thoughts. During her next supervision session, Cassandra brings up referring Jessie to another counselor with her supervisor.

Questions to Consider and Discuss

* How should the supervisor respond?
* Should Cassandra refer Jessie to another counselor? Why or why not?
* How might it hurt Jessie if Cassandra did refer her to another counselor?

* How might it hurt Jessie if Cassandra continues to counsel Jessie with Cassandra's current beliefs?
* What does Jessie need to do in order to become a more ethically competent counselor?

ADOLESCENCE AND LGBTQ

KEY TERMS FOR COUNSELORS TO UNDERSTAND

Heteronormative: Heteronormative views are views that promote heterosexuality as the preferred or normal sexual orientation.

Heterosexism: Heterosexism is discrimination against the LGBTQ population with the assumption that heterosexuality is the norm. A heterosexist society tends to reject and malign non-heterosexual behavior (Herek, Cogan, Gillis, & Glunt, 1997).

Heterosexual Privilege: Heterosexual privilege is defined as the unearned benefits one receives as a result of being heterosexual. Some examples include social acceptance of heterosexual relationships and being able to express affection to a partner in public.

Homophobia: Homophobia is defined as negative beliefs and attitudes held toward LGBTQ individuals (Chutter, 2007).

Internalized Homophobia: Internalized homophobia is when individuals take outward societal negative messages about sexual orientation and gender identity and turn those messages onto themselves (Bernal & Coolhart, 2005).

Microaggressions: Microaggressions are those words or actions that degrade socially marginalized individuals (Sue et al., 2007).

Transphobia: Transphobia is the negative attitudes, beliefs, and stereotypes held toward transgender individuals (Chutter, 2007).

Ethical considerations are paramount when working with LGBTQ youth, particularly in terms of counselor self-awareness, counselor competence, and counselor advocacy. However, there are also other developmental considerations that need to be taken into account when working with LGBTQ adolescents. Adolescence is a time of transition and is traditionally a time of role identity versus role confusion (Erikson, 1959), when adolescents start to move from concrete to abstract reasoning (Piaget, 1972), when teens start to question and define their spiritual and religious beliefs (Fowler, 1981), and when beliefs and norms are internalized regarding gender identity and sexual orientation (Gilligan, Ward, & Taylor, 1988).

Researchers have noted that during adolescence, teens and preteens become aware of their own sexuality, including their gender identity and sexual orientation (Kinsey, Pomeroy, & Martin, 1948; Sorenson, 1973). The average age that LGBTQ adolescents and preteens become aware of their same-sex attraction and gender identity is usually between 10 and 15 (Grossman & D'Augelli, 2006; Grov, Bimbi, Nanin, & Parsons, 2006), although children may be aware of feeling different from the others as early as ages 4 and 5 (Cass, 1979, 1984). In the United States, various studies have indicated that at least 5% to 12% of the population identify as LGBTQ, indicating that at least one in five families may include someone who is LGBTQ, and similarly, in an average school size of 1,000 students, 50 to 120 students may be LGBTQ (Gates, Ost, & Birch, 2004; Kinsey et al., 1948; Zinmesiter, 2006). Because adolescence is a time of transition, counselors with heteronormative prejudices may not believe or take seriously the feelings and thoughts of teens coming to terms with their gender identity and sexual orientation. Throughout this chapter, the author will mostly be referring to adolescence as the time when most youth start to explore their gender identity and sexual orientation and seek counseling.

Coming-out in a heteronormative society can be extremely challenging for LGBTQ youth (Chutter, 2007; Wright & Perry, 2006). Coming-out is a process that includes acknowledging one's sexual orientation or gender identity, disclosing one's sexual orientation or gender identity to others, and associating with other LGBTQ individuals (Grov et al., 2006; Mosher, 2001). Lack of family support, negative and sometimes hostile societal attitudes, and lack of peer support represent some of the challenges adolescents face as they come to terms with and express their sexual orientation and gender identity (Hollander, 2000; Morrison & L'Heureux, 2001; Rosario, Schrimshaw, & Hunter, 2004).

In the Minority Stress Model, Meyer (2003) described how minority status individuals, such as LGBTQ individuals, experience daily stressors and microaggressions that are above and beyond everyday stressors. These daily negative and hostile messages or microaggressions, whether intentional or not, can range from derogatory name-calling, to being ignored, to death threats. The stigma of being LGBTQ in a heteronormative, homophobic, hostile environment can lead to prejudice and discrimination that in turn can lead to a higher occurrence of mental disorders (D'Augelli, 2002; Meyer, 2003).

The Gay, Lesbian & Straight Education Network (GLSEN) (Kosciw, Greytak, Bartkiewicz, Boesen, & Palmer, 2012) reported that LGBTQ adolescents are five times more likely to commit suicide than their heterosexual peers because of minority stress, and seven times more likely to be victims of a hate crime. In the 2012 GLSEN report, 82% of LGB teens reported being verbally harassed while 64% of teens reported being verbally harassed because of their gender expression; 64% of teens felt unsafe at school because of their sexual orientation and 44% felt unsafe because of their gender expression; 40%

of teens reported being physically harassed because of their sexual orientation and 27% reported harassment because of their gender expression; 55% of LGBTQ youth reported having experienced cyberbullying or bullying via text messages, Facebook, or other electronic media; and LGBTQ teens reported they are likely to hear antigay slurs 26 times during an average school day and that 82% of faculty and staff never intervened when slurs were made against them (Kosciw et al., 2012).

In addition to daily microaggressions that LGBTQ individuals face, researchers have found that many counselors do not want to work with LGBTQ clients (Green, 2003). Thus, not only are these youth marginalized and discriminated against by society in general, they are also ignored and discriminated against by the professional counseling community (Espelage & Swearer, 2008; Twist, Murphy, Green, & Palmanteer, 2006).

There has been increased recognition within the counseling profession that counselors need to be more cognizant and informed regarding the coming-out process, gender identity, and sexual orientation for sexual minority youth (Singh, 2008; Stone, 2003). Sue and Sue (2013) recommended that in order for counselors to become multiculturally competent, they need to

1. become self-aware by assessing and taking stock of their own attitudes and personal biases/prejudices against LGBTQ individuals;
2. increase their knowledge regarding the LGBTQ community, including terms and healthy developmental models; and
3. learn appropriate intervention strategies in working with LGBTQ adolescents and children.

Self-Awareness

Counselors need to have a willingness to self-examine and to address their own personal homo-prejudice and heterosexism. In a heteronormative society, it can be difficult for members of the dominant heterosexual culture to become aware of their own biases and prejudices. McIntosh (1988) discussed how privilege, such as white or male privilege, encouraged lack of self-awareness on the part of a majority member. Heterosexual privilege works in the same way—counselors may be unaware of the invisible, unearned advantages that they may have that LGBTQ minorities do not. These advantages may include being able to talk about a relationship with others, not worrying about being fired from a job because of being LGBTQ, being able to date a person of their choice, and receiving social support from family and peers for their relationship. Self-awareness on the part of the counselor can be increased through reading articles such as the ALGBTIC (Association for Lesbian, Gay, Bisexual, and Transgender Issues in Counseling) Competencies, education at counseling training events, supervision, and consultation with knowledgeable colleagues.

For school counselors, the American School Counselor Association (ASCA) clearly states that school counselors

> are aware of their own beliefs about sexual orientation and gender identity, are knowledgeable of the negative effects that result from stereotyping individuals into rigid gender roles, and are committed to the affirmation of youth of all sexual orientations and identities.
>
> (ASCA, 2007, p. 28)

This mandate requires that school counselors put aside potentially contradictory personal values and go beyond just ensuring a safe environment for lesbian, gay, and bisexual youth. ASCA also requires that school counselors work toward establishing a school environment free from judgment, bullying, and ridicule for their students. When school counselors' or any counselors' bias and prejudice go unchecked, it may result in the unethical and harmful treatment of LGBTQ children and adolescents (Field & Baker, 2004).

Knowledge

In order to be an effective counselor working with LGBTQ youth, it is essential that counselors become knowledgeable of both helpful and offensive terms, such as those listed below, and learn healthy sexual and gender identity developmental models (Remley & Herlihy, 2014; Singh, 2008).

KEY TERMS TO KNOW AS A COUNSELOR

Ally: Allies are typically non-LGBTQ individuals who support the rights of LGBTQ, although LGBTQ individuals can also be allies among themselves.

Bisexual: Bisexuals are those individuals attracted to both males and females. They are more attracted to another individual's personality than they are concerned about the individual's biological sex.

Coming-Out: Coming-out is an ongoing lifelong process of coming to terms with one's sexual orientation in a heterosexual normative society and sharing that information with themselves and others around them. Individuals who have not shared their sexual orientation with others are referred to as "in the closet."

Gay: Gays are males who are emotionally, romantically, and or sexually attracted to individuals of the same sex. The term *gay* can also be used as an umbrella term used to refer to both lesbians and gays, although *lesbian* is the preferred term to refer to women being attracted to women.

Gender Identity: Gender identity is the inner sense of being male or female, or somewhere in between, and does not necessarily conform to biological sex.

Gender Expression: Gender expression is how one manifests masculinity or femininity. This may include hair style, clothing, speech, movement, behavior, and other nonverbal expressions as to how we wish to be understood in terms of being masculine/feminine or male/female.

Lesbian: Lesbians are females who are emotionally, romantically, and/or sexually attracted to other women.

Pansexual: Someone who self-identifies as pansexual generally pursues romantic relationships without regard to biological sex, gender, or gender identity.

Questioning: Questioning individuals are those who are exploring their sexual orientation, gender identity, and gender expression. They may be either internally asking questions about their sexual orientation and/or exploring their sexual orientation through experimentation with males and females.

Queer: The term *queer* is used by younger generations as an umbrella term to describe the LGBTQ population. Older generations may find the term offensive.

Sexual Orientation: Sexual orientation refers to the emotional, romantic, and/or sexual attraction to men, women, or both genders, such as identifying as lesbian, gay, bisexual, asexual, or pansexual.

Transgender: Transgender is an umbrella term for individuals who do not conform to traditional notions of male or female gender or the gender assigned at birth.

OFFENSIVE/INAPPROPRIATE TERMS/MODELS NOT TO USE AS A COUNSELOR

Gay Agenda: The term *gay agenda* reflects a fear that the LGBTQ community has a negative or sinister plan for society. In contrast, those who are LGBTQ have the same desire for equality as every other individual within the general community.

Gay/Homosexual Lifestyle: Being gay is not a lifestyle; it is a sexual orientation. Just as those who are heterosexual have many different facets that make up their life, so do those who are LGBTQ. The term *lifestyle* also suggests that being LGBTQ is a choice, which it is not.

Homosexual: The term *homosexual* is usually seen as an offensive term by the LGBTQ community. In 1973, the American Psychiatric Association took homosexuality out of the third edition of the *Diagnostic and Statistical Manual* as a psychological disorder. Those who use the term are usually associated with those who suggest that being LGBTQ is being clinically, psychologically, or emotionally disordered.

Reparative Therapy/Conversion Therapy: Conversion or so-called reparative therapy attempts to change someone who is lesbian, gay, or bisexual into someone who is heterosexual. The American Counseling Association, the American Medical Association, the American Psychological Association, and the American Pediatric Association, along with the White House and several states, consider the methods and underlying premise of conversion therapy unethical and harmful toward those who are LGBTQ.

Sexual Preference: The term *sexual preference* denotes that one's sexual orientation is a choice, which researchers and the LGBTQ community report is not the case.

Several developmental models have been developed to describe a healthy sexual identity process (Carrion & Lock, 1997; Cass, 1979, 1984; Troiden, 1988). Criticism does exist for these models as they present sexual identity formation as a linear instead of a fluid, individual process (Eliason, 1996). However, these models help counselors and clients alike understand that sexual identity formation is not easy in a heterosexual society. Cass's Sexual Identity Model describes how an LGBTQ individual moves from identity confusion, to identity comparison, to identity tolerance, to identity acceptance, to identity pride, and finally to identity synthesis. The LGBTQ individual can successfully navigate from shame, guilt, denial, and bewilderment to a level of healthy functioning (Bernal & Coolhart, 2005; Carrion & Lock, 1997; Mosher, 2001; Singh, 2008). When counselors and clients understand that moving through these stages is a normal part of growth and development, counselors can help clients navigate the sexual identity formation process in an affirmative way.

There are many resources for counselors to become more knowledgeable about working with adolescents in the LGBTQ community. Textbooks such as *Transgender Subjectivities: A Clinician's Guide* (Drescher & Leli, 2004) and *Casebook for Counseling Lesbian, Gay, Bisexual, and Transgender Persons and Their Families* (Dworkin & Pope, 2012) can be helpful to counselors in understanding how to conceptualize and counsel with their clients. Books such as *Is It a Choice? Answers to the Most Frequently Asked Questions About*

Gay & Lesbian People (Marcus, 2005), *What the Bible Really Says About Homosexuality* (Helminiak, 2000), and *Coming Out of Shame* (Kaufman & Raphael, 1996) can be utilized to educate both counselors and clients regarding common myths about LGBTQ individuals and the effects religious messages have on feelings of worth and self-efficacy. Websites and organizations such as GLAD (Gay and Lesbian Advocates and Defenders), PFLAG (Parents, Families and Friends of Lesbians and Gays), and GLSEN, along with other resources listed at the end of the chapter, can be extremely helpful in providing necessary knowledge in working with LGBTQ adolescents and children.

Experiential learning when working with LGBTQ individuals in counseling can also be effective and provide powerful learning opportunities (Remley & Herlihy, 2014). When experiences in practicum and internship are paired with knowledgeable supervision, counselors-in-training can become competent in their knowledge of working with LGBTQ individuals.

Skills

Counselors need to develop culturally appropriate skills in working with LGBTQ adolescents and children. Many traditional approaches may not work with culturally different individuals whose problems originate in societal oppression (Meyer, 2003; Remley & Herlihy, 2014). Limiting counseling interventions to intra-psychic methods may only increase feelings of internalized homophobia and cause adolescent clients to blame themselves for feelings of depression, shame, guilt, and anxiety.

Counselors need to understand that conversion, or reparative therapy, has been deemed unethical and even harmful by the American Counseling Association (2013), the American Psychological Association (2009), the American Psychiatric Association (2000), and the American Academy of Pediatrics (2013). So-called reparative therapists view those who are LGBTQ as psychologically disordered and try to "repair" clients by changing them into heterosexuals. Researchers across the spectrum have found that conversion therapy does not lead to changing sexual orientation, but instead leads to greater depression, anxiety, and suicidal ideation (AAP, 2013; ACA, 2013; APA, 2000, 2009). The *ACA Code of Ethics* (ACA, 2014) standard C.7.a states, "When providing services, counselors use techniques/procedures/modalities that are grounded in theory and/or have an empirical or scientific foundation." Counselors would need to inform clients who seek reparative therapy that this type of therapy could potentially harm their client and that they will not offer conversion therapy. On the ACA website (www.counseling.org) there are scenarios discussed regarding working with clients who seek out reparative/conversion therapy. The ACA specifically urges counselors to discourage their clients from seeking this type of therapy as it is potentially harmful to clients.

Counselors need to develop skills that take into account larger social systems. For example, Crisp and McCave (2007) recommended that counselors work with LGBTQ individuals from an affirmative, strengths-based approach. They suggested that counselors consider the person in his or her many environments, such as school, family, and social settings, and how much the youth discloses about him or herself within these different environments. Crisp and McCave (2007) also suggested that counselors support young clients in how they self-identify and to whom they disclose their sexual orientation, focusing on their strengths and not pathology, and by countering homophobic/internalized homophobic/heterosexist messages.

The Integrative-Empower Model (Matthews & Salazar, 2012) depicted in Figure 6.1 focuses on a holistic, systemic process that assesses both the internal processes for the individual and also their external environment. The counselor then determines the strategies and interventions by focusing on both the internal and external factors for the client. Recognizing that external factors can affect internal processes of the client, the counselor considers the sexual-identity stage of the client, the amount of internalized feelings of homophobia, the internalized self-esteem of the client, and the mental health coping behaviors of the client, such as cutting, alcohol or drug use, journaling, meditation, and so on. The counselor then assesses the external environment of the client, such as family support or lack of support, the school/peer environment, supportive organizations such as Gay–Straight Alliances (GSAs), racial/cultural factors, religious background and beliefs, and previous counseling experience of the client. Hays' ADDRESSING Model (2001) focused on how individuals are an integration of many potential cultural identities and are not a result of one identity or category. Effective counselors understand that LGBTQ individuals do not come only for counseling to address gender identity or sexual orientation issues and that such areas are addressed only when they are necessarily indicated. A transgender, Baptist, African American male may present different counseling issues than a transgender, nonreligious, Caucasian male. Just because two individuals are transgender males does not mean their counseling issues will be the same. Understanding the intersectionality of identity is essential in realizing the backgrounds that our clients come from (Greene, 1994).

Once an overall assessment of the client is completed, including their intersectionality of identities and their external environment, the counselor can determine how to work with the client. Interventions may include educating the client about LGBTQ developmental models, addressing internal homophobia and heterosexism through cognitive behavioral therapy, and possibly working with parents and family members. Counselors can help adolescent LGBTQ clients work through their shame, guilt, and bewilderment by addressing the specific needs of their clients based on a thorough, holistic assessment of the client's many environments.

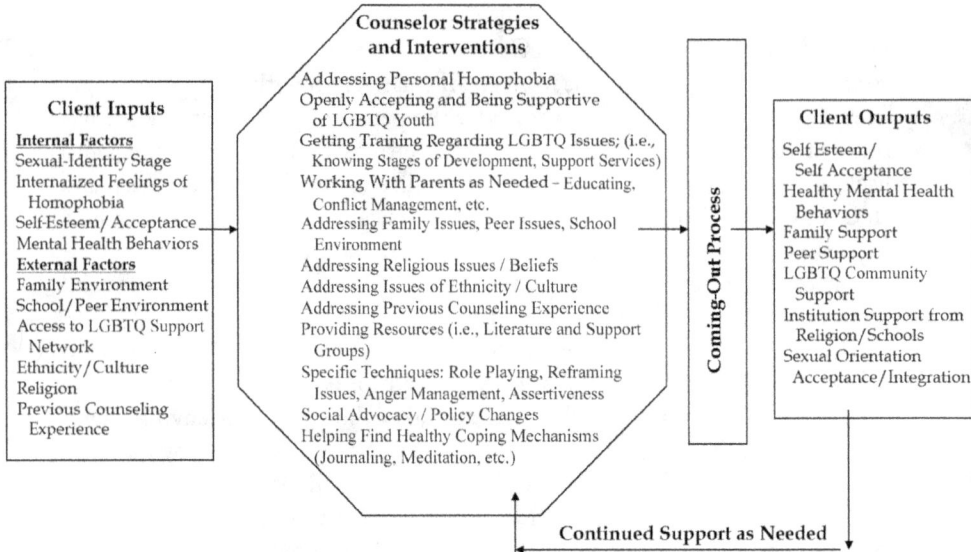

Figure 6.1 An Integrative-Empower Model for Counselors Helping LGBTQ Youth Through the Coming-Out Process

---

CASE STUDY TO CONSIDER AND DISCUSS: JUAN

Juan considers himself to be a multiculturally competent counselor. He has been working with adolescents for a number of years and prides himself on understanding the intersectionality of identities that most individuals possess. As a Hispanic, bisexual male, he feels he has a "handle" on understanding how sexual orientation and ethnicity have played a role in shaping his own identity. Juan agrees to see a new adolescent client, Sean. His client, 15-year-old Sean, admits to having feelings of attraction to other males. Sean discusses how he even masturbates to thoughts and pictures of one male individual in his class and how horribly guilty he feels after each time he thinks about or acts on these feelings. Sean tells Juan that he has heard of reparative and conversion therapy. Sean begs Juan to utilize conversion therapy to turn him straight, as Sean knows his parents, family, and friends will not approve of him being gay. Sean admits that he has being utilizing self-injury/cutting to deal with his internal struggle and has spent numerous days fasting and praying for his God to heal him from his "gayness."

Questions to Consider

* How should Juan proceed with this client?
* What role do clients play in determining the direction of counseling?

> * What issues are going on for this client, Sean?
> * What factors does Juan need to consider as he puts together a treatment plan for Sean?

AWARENESS OF LGBTQ MODELS/SOCIAL JUSTICE PERSPECTIVE

HELPFUL TERMS FOR COUNSELORS

Advocacy: Advocacy denotes not only an intellectual support for a marginalized group but also commitment through action. Advocates try to influence decisions within institutions, organizations, and social systems.

Social Justice Counseling: Social justice counseling embraces the notion that counselors advocate on behalf of their clients for change and growth (Lewis, Ratts, Paladino, & Toporek, 2011).

The Association for Multicultural Counseling and Development (AMCD) and the Association for Counselor Education and Supervision (ACES) developed a list of competencies known as the Multicultural Counseling Competencies and Standards (Arredondo et al., 1996). They are available at http://www.counseling.org/knowledge-center/competencies. These standards were operationalized to help counselors competently meet the needs of marginalized populations. They include counselors becoming aware of their own cultural values and biases, becoming aware of the client's worldview, and developing culturally appropriate intervention strategies. A set of Advocacy Competencies was also adopted in 2003 by ACA that encouraged counselors to help empower marginalized clients and students not only within counseling sessions, but also advocate for and behalf of clients on levels ranging from an individual level or microlevel all the way to a sociopolitical level or a macrolevel (Lewis, Arnold, House, & Toporek, 2003). These competencies are also available at http://www.counseling.org/knowledge-center/competencies.

Advocacy requires counselors to step out of their traditional role of staying in the counseling office to working within institutions and the political arena to help change policies, procedures, and decisions to assist in equitable and fair treatment of minority populations. The ACA Advocacy Competences can be found on the ACA website under "Competencies" at www.counseling.org. The Association for Lesbian, Gay, Bisexual, and Transgender Issues in Counseling (ALGBTIC) also created and operationalized competencies for working with lesbian, gay, bisexual, queer, questioning, intersex, and ally individuals (2012). Another document was created for working with transgender individuals (ALGBTIC, 2009). Both of these can also be found under "Competencies" at www.counseling.org. Both documents are essential reads for counselors trying to educate themselves and understand the competencies required in working with LGBTQ individuals.

A counselor's professional obligations extend beyond meeting the needs of his or her LGBTQ adolescent clients in the office during counseling sessions. The obligation also includes providing and promoting a psychologically and physically safe environment that supports the healthy development of LGBTQ adolescents and children (ALGBTIC, 2012; American School Counselor Association, 2007; King, 2008). The GLSEN report of 2012 estimated that 28% of LGBTQ students drop out of school because they feel unsupported by school faculty and staff (Kosciw et al., 2012). According to this same report, the average grade point average (GPA) for LGBTQ students who could identify supportive staff and faculty at their school was 3.1, while the GPA for those who could not identify supportive staff and faculty was 2.9. Higher rates of victimization also correlated with lower GPA for students—3.2 for non-victims versus 2.9 for victims. Absentee rates were higher for those LGBTQ students who felt victimized or harassed at school. It is essential that counselors, including school counselors, help provide healthy, safe environments for their clients and students.

CASE TO CONSIDER

Saymora is a school counselor at Bellview High School. She has noticed that it is commonplace in the staff room for teachers to make negative or derogatory comments about the LGBTQ students at the school. Saymora has seen other students making derogatory comments about the LGBTQ students and watched as staff and teachers either laugh or do nothing about the situation. Several of Saymora's student clients have come to counseling complaining about how they are treated by both faculty and students. They discuss how they are pushed against lockers, are called names, are made fun of, have their books thrown to the ground, and are ostracized because of their sexual orientation.

Questions to Consider

*   How should Saymora work with the student clients dealing with bullying?
*   What should Saymora do about nonsupportive faculty and staff at Bellview High School?
*   What can Saymora do about the students who are doing the bullying of the LGBTQ students?

THE NEED FOR CONFIDENTIALITY FOR LGBTQ ADOLESCENT CLIENTS

When working with children and adolescents in general, confidentiality can become a major issue, but it can be especially important when working with LGBTQ youth because of the sensitive nature of the material they may discuss. Many minors would not seek out counseling if parental permission was required or if session information was shared by counselors with parents. Laws vary from state to state regarding confidentiality of sessions with minors. The *ACA Code of Ethics* (ACA, 2014) recommends that counselors work in the best interest of their clients. However, it is difficult to determine whose best interest is being served when it comes to sharing counseling session information with parents and/or keeping the information confidential with the adolescent client. The ACA ethics standard B.5.b requires counselors to discuss with parents and legal guardians the role of counselors, to respect the role and rights of parents/legal guardians, and to work to achieve collaborative relationships with parents (ACA, 2014). Forms can be signed and agreements can be worked out between parents and counselor on limits of confidentiality, ensuring that when a child/adolescent is a danger to self or others, parents will be informed. Standard B.1.c states that "counselors disclose information only with appropriate consent or with sound legal or ethical justification."

Dugger and Carlson (2012) suggested when working with adolescents and children that counselors initially have a separate parent consult before meeting with the adolescent. During this consultation, the counselor can determine what the parents view as the dominant issues for the adolescent or child, as well as discuss the limits of confidentiality between counselor and child. During the second session, the counselor then meets with the parents and child together at the beginning of the session to discuss confidentiality and the importance of trust in the client/counselor relationship. The counselor discusses that confidentiality will be maintained unless the child is at risk of harming self or others. In this way, the child/adolescent understands that his privacy is valued and parents understand the value of creating a trusting environment.

When working with LGBTQ adolescents, confidentiality can be an issue because teens and preteens may disclose information that parents and guardians may potentially find distasteful or against parental values. In order to maintain an environment of trust necessary in the therapeutic environment, counselors will need to work carefully with their clients in maintaining confidentiality. If parents/guardians press for information, the counselor can work with the client to determine what information will be shared, who will share the information, who it will be shared with, where it will be shared, and when it will be shared. Counselors can discuss, role-play, and work through coming-out scenarios with their clients as well as potentially work with parents to help create a supportive environment for the teen (Matthews & Salazar, 2012).

Counselors need to respect and balance the adolescent client's need for privacy, adolescent's need to control sharing of non-life-threatening information, and the parents' need/wish for information.

CASE STUDY TO CONSIDER

Gregory is in private practice specializing in working with adolescents dealing with depression. Gregory has been seeing Julia, a 14-year-old female, for the past 2 months in a counseling relationship. Julia has confided in Gregory that she has been attracted to several females in her grade and has even had dreams about them. Julia has been feeling very guilty about her feelings of same-sex attraction. Julia has described her parents as antigay and feels herself drifting further apart in her relationship with her parents as she starts to question her own sexual orientation. One night Gregory receives a call from Julia's father. The father yells at Gregory that he needs to stop talking about "homosexuality" in the session and "putting homosexual thoughts" into his daughter's head. The father insists that he be privy to everything Gregory and Julia talk about in session from now on and threatens a lawsuit if discussions ensue regarding "homosexuality."

Questions to Consider

*   How should Gregory respond to Julia's father?
*   What conversation should have occurred before any therapy began between Gregory and Julia?
*   How can Gregory address this issue with Julia?
*   If you were Gregory, what would you do?

CONCLUSION

Counseling with adolescents and children regarding issues related to gender identity and sexual orientation can be both challenging and rewarding. The *ACA Code of Ethics* (ACA, 2014) specifically warns that counselors cannot discriminate against individuals regarding sexual orientation and gender identity. It also states that counselors cannot refer their clients to other counselors because of personal values conflicts, nor can counselors impose their personal values on their clients. Counselors need to learn through supervision, consultation, and training to bracket their own values in order to work with clients whose values may be different from their own.

In order to be successful in counseling with LGBTQ adolescents, counselors need to constantly assess their personal biases and prejudices; gain knowledge of current LGBTQ terms and models of human development, interventions, and research; and become aware of their own areas of privilege. The ACA Social Justice Competencies, ALGBTIC Competencies, and AMCD Multicultural Competencies are excellent places for counselors-in-training to begin understanding the perspectives and lives of LGBTQ individuals and what counselors need to know. Counselors need to work with LGBTQ clients from a societal, environmental perspective, understanding that many mental health issues LGBTQ adolescents present with in counseling are related to "minority stress" experienced in a predominantly heterosexual/heterosexist society.

In terms of advocacy, counselors also need to learn to step out of their role as counselors in their office to working outside of the office within institutional and political arenas for the sake of their clients. Social justice advocacy requires counselors to create safe environments for their clients not only in their offices but in the outside world.

Confidentiality can be a difficult facet of counseling when working with LGBTQ teens. Most adolescent clients need privacy and confidentiality in order to feel they have an environment of trust and nonjudgment. However, counselors are required to work with parents to establish collaborative relationships and balance providing necessary information with the teen's need for privacy. Initial discussions and agreements with parents before counseling begins can help when counselors work in private practice. School counselors, however, may need to discuss issues of privacy after counseling begins, depending on state school rules. All information from a session that relates to a client potentially harming self (suicide) or others (homicide) needs to be discussed with parents.

The *ACA Code of Ethics* (ACA, 2014) provides an excellent resource and guide for working with LGBTQ adolescents and children. However, it is essential that counselors become aware of their own biases, obtain necessary knowledge, and be able to apply appropriate interventions that meet the needs of their clients. Working with supervisors, consulting with colleagues, and gaining training through workshops and reading are all continually necessary in continuing to learn to be an effective counselor.

DISCUSSION QUESTIONS/PROMPTS

1. What will you do to increase your competency (i.e., personal awareness, knowledge, and skills) to prepare for and when working with LGBTQ individuals?
2. How will you ensure that your own biases/values/beliefs do not interfere with or harm your LGBTQ clients?
3. How will you work with a client who is homophobic and may be bullying or mistreating individuals who may be LGBTQ or perceived to be LGBTQ?

4. As a counselor, how will you work within a less than supportive environment for LGBTQ individuals?

5. What will you do to ensure you assess the whole LGBTQ client instead of looking at issues/problems related to sexual orientation or gender identity?

HELPFUL ONLINE RESOURCES FOR COUNSELING LGBTQ YOUTH AND FOR LGBTQ CLIENTS

GLAD: Gay and Lesbian Advocates and Defenders—an online resource for understanding legal rights for LGBTQ adults and adolescents: www.glad.org and www.glad.org/youth

GLSEN: Gay, Lesbian & Straight Education Network—a great online resource for school counselors regarding antibullying of LGBTQ: http://www.glsen.org/

GSA: Gay–Straight Alliance Network—teaches adolescents to empower themselves in schools and colleges: https://www.gsanetwork.org/

It Gets Better Project—an online community that communicates to LGBTQ youth that the world gets better and to try to inspire change to create that better world: http://www.itgetsbetter.org/

Lesbian, Gay, Bisexual, and Transgender Health: Centers for Disease Control and Prevention—Resources for LGBTQ youth and their families: http://www.cdc.gov/lgbthealth/youth-resources.htm

PFLAG: Parents, Family, and Friends of Lesbians and Gays—both a face-to-face group and an Internet website that offers various resources: https://community.pflag.org/

Safe Schools Coalition—an online resource providing resources for school faculty and staff to provide support for gay, lesbian, bisexual, transgender, queer, and questioning youth: www.safeschoolscoalition.org

StopBullying.gov—website with the goal of creating a safe environment for LGBTQ youth and those perceived to be LGBTQ: http://www.stopbullying.gov/at-risk/groups/lgbt/index.html

The Trevor Project—provides crisis intervention and suicide prevention for LGBTQ youth: http://www.thetrevorproject.org/

PROFESSIONAL AND ETHICAL USE OF EXPRESSIVE ARTS

Andrea Davis

INTRODUCTION

While the use of expressive arts in therapy is relatively new, humans have always used the arts as a form of expression. As an artist and art therapist, I firmly believe that all humans have a birthright to express creativity. While anyone can make art, dance, play music, sing, or write poetry, a special kind of therapy has emerged from the expressive arts. In 1970, Expressive Arts began at Leslie College Graduate School in Cambridge, Massachusetts. That same year the International Expressive Arts Therapy Association (IEATA) was formed. In 1984, the Person Centered Institute was formed by Natalie Rogers. The expressive therapies, through practice and research, are becoming more popular and recognized as legitimate therapies. Today one can earn degrees, certifications, and licenses in Art Therapy, Music Therapy, Dance Therapy, Play Therapy, and Drama Therapy. This chapter seeks to provide an overview of the field, defining the modes of expression, as well as explore some of the unique legal and ethical dilemmas found in the expressive therapies.

Recently a counseling student made an appointment to come to my office for advice. She had been seeing a client during her internship and having the client draw about emotions resulting from sexual abuse. The images were intense, graphic, and raw. The client was quite a good artist, able to express herself in imagery with relative ease, and had expressed a preference for art making over talking. As a board certified art therapist, I was concerned that this student was in over her head with this client. After all she had no training in art therapy. She was attending a counseling program that did not offer any course work in the expressive arts, yet here she was using art with this client. Would she be able to process the art in a manner that was not harmful to the client? Would she be able to appropriately provide a sense of the art being "contained"? Were the intern and her supervisor at legal risk providing this therapy without proper education?

According to the American Counseling Association (ACA) *Code of Ethics*,

C.2.a. Boundaries of Competence

Counselors practice only within the boundaries of their competence, based on their education, training, supervised experience, state and national professional credentials, and appropriate professional experience. Whereas multicultural counseling competency is required across all counseling specialties, counselors gain knowledge, personal awareness, sensitivity, dispositions, and skills pertinent to being a culturally competent counselor in working with a diverse client population.

C.2.b. New Specialty Areas of Practice

Counselors practice in specialty areas new to them only after appropriate education, training, and supervised experience. While developing skills in new specialty areas, counselors take steps to ensure the competence of their work and protect others from possible harm.

(Reprinted from *ACA Code of Ethics* [ACA, ©2014].
American Counseling Association. Reprinted with permission.
No further reproduction authorized without written
permission from the American Counseling Association.)

The intern and her supervisor were definitely exhibiting unethical behavior by not referring this client to a credentialed art therapist. Should the client have been harmed, she would have had grounds for litigation. The best approach for any counselor, of course, is to enroll in an educational program and legitimately earn a degree in the expressive art of choice and have a supervisor who can adequately guide one as an intern. If you have the inclination to use expressive arts in therapy with clients, the ethical obligation on the part of any licensed professional is to be competent and trained to use interventions.

Expressive arts therapy utilizes the spectrum of art, music, dance, play, and drama. Within each of these modes of expression a therapy has developed. There is a difference between making art and art therapy, making music and music therapy, and so on. It is very important to take a closer look at each expressive mode and the definition of that therapy.

In the 1950s, art therapy became formalized as psychotherapy by the mother of art therapy, Margaret Naumberg. At this time, art was also used by Carl Jung and Sigmund Freud in work with patients. Today, art therapists must have a master's degree in art therapy and can be found working with many diverse populations. Schools, hospitals, psychiatric wards, and homeless shelters are just a few of the places one may find art therapy being utilized.

Art therapy is a mental health profession in which clients, facilitated by the art therapist, use art media, the creative process, and the resulting artwork to explore their feelings, reconcile emotional conflicts, foster self-awareness, manage behavior and addictions, develop social skills, improve reality orientation, reduce anxiety, and increase self-esteem. A goal in art therapy is to improve or restore a client's functioning and his or her sense of personal well-being. Art therapy practice requires knowledge of visual art (drawing, painting, sculpture, and other art forms) and the creative process, as well as of human development, psychological, and counseling theories and techniques.
(American Art Therapy Association, 2015)

Because of the therapeutic nature of the experience and the goals associated with art therapy, it certainly differs in many ways from what we consider basic art "activities." For example, art activity is basically teaching art skills while art therapy contains no lessons or teaching but rather provides a nondirective approach to therapy through the use of expression in art. Beyond that basic major difference, there are other ways to understand the inherent differences between the two. In art therapy, themes emerge from the participant, while in art activities themes are typically provided to the students; in art activity, the art teacher demonstrates how to produce art, while in art therapy, the client makes the art through the artistic means he or she chooses; in art activity, the participant needs to be able to follow verbal and/or written instructions and complete tasks, while art therapy does not necessarily require a high level of verbal understanding; art activity is a leisure activity, while art therapy is used to process an individual's emotional life; and finally, art activity is typically open to the public and created to display or share, while art therapy is a personal and private experience that is to remain confidential.

Music therapy is defined as "the clinical and evidence-based use of music interventions to accomplish individualized goals within a therapeutic relationship by a credentialed professional who has completed an approved music therapy program" (http://www.musictherapy.org/about/quotes, para. 1). The American Music Therapy Association clarifies how music therapy is defined apart from casual use of music. Like art media, music has the potential to be therapeutic, but not all use is therapy.

Music therapy is an established health profession in which music is used within a therapeutic relationship to address physical, emotional, cognitive, and social needs of individuals. After assessing the strengths and needs of each client, the qualified music therapist provides the indicated treatment, including creating, singing, moving to, and/or listening to music. Through musical involvement in the therapeutic context, clients' abilities are strengthened and transferred to other areas of their lives. Music therapy also provides avenues for communication that can be helpful to those who find it difficult to express themselves in words. Research in music therapy supports its effectiveness in many areas such as overall physical rehabilitation and facilitating movement, increasing people's motivation to become engaged in their treatment, providing emotional support for clients and their families, and providing an outlet for expression of feelings (American Music Therapy Association, 2015).

More information about music therapy is available on the website for the American Music Therapy Association. Music therapists abide by a code of ethics as outlined by the American Music Therapy Association (http://www.musictherapy.org/about/ethics/).

Drama therapy is defined differently:

> Drama therapy is the intentional use of drama and/or theater processes to achieve therapeutic goals. Drama therapy is active and experiential. This approach can provide the context for participants to tell their stories, set goals and solve problems, express feelings, or achieve catharsis. Through drama, the depth and breadth of inner experience can be actively explored and interpersonal relationship skills can be enhanced. Participants can expand their repertoire of dramatic roles to find that their own life roles have been strengthened.
>
> (North American Drama Therapy Association, 2016.
> Reprinted with permission from the North American
> Drama Therapy Association.)

And, play therapy has yet a different definition:

> Play therapy is defined as "the systematic use of a theoretical model to establish an interpersonal process wherein trained play therapists use the therapeutic powers of play to help clients prevent or resolve psychosocial difficulties and achieve optimal growth and development."
>
> (Association of Play Therapy, n.d.)

Special legal and ethical questions need to be examined across the spectrum of the expressive arts. What are the responsibilities of the expressive therapist regarding the materials used in a session? Once a creation is made in a session, what happens to the artifact and to whom does it belong? What are the risks of compromising confidentiality when the artifact is left in the therapy office? Under what circumstances, if any, can the artifact be displayed or shared? What are some special ethical considerations for using expressive arts in group settings? I will address each of these questions, but not all ethical dilemmas have a clear-cut answer.

The materials used in expressive arts vary from paint, clay, sand, and costumes to hammers, fabric, masks, and musical instruments. Whichever the expressive tool, the therapist must be aware of the potential dangers that can put a client at risk. The therapist must provide a safe space for the therapy, which includes having knowledge about materials. Knowing which paint contains cadmium (which is poisonous) is as important as knowing how to ensure proper ventilation when using clay or printmaking. Learning more about keeping clients safe around materials includes knowing which materials to avoid in order to prevent emotional flooding and how to provide containment and comfort (Jennings, 1997). The therapist also has a duty to use materials that will best meet the needs of a client. The Expressive Therapies Continuum is a helpful tool for determining where a client will best be served on the spectrum of expressive materials. One example of a client that can be harmed with certain materials is a client who is experiencing psychosis. Giving this client unstructured experiences and loose materials such as watercolors or wet clay can promote a less grounded state. Helpful choices would be those materials that offer a sense of control and grounding such as pencil, collage, and very structured experiential.

The "material" of music therapy is the musical composition or melody. Sound is difficult to contain. Music therapists must also work to ensure confidentiality of sound. Keeping the therapy room soundproofed is a challenging but essential achievement. When parents can hear what is happening in the therapy room, it is tempting to question their child about what they heard. Music therapists work to contain confidentiality of musical sounds in a way that is equal to the confidentiality of words in a talk therapy session (Davis, Geller, and Thaut, 2008).

Teenaged clients are typically very interested in music and have identified with a particular music genre that speaks to their personal belief system. Tania Cordones, music therapist, explains that using music to build rapport with clients is appropriate even if not trained in music therapy. A client may bring in a playlist to share with the therapist. When developing a therapeutic bond, this can be helpful. After that the therapist must examine whether or not the playlist is enhancing the therapy.

Expressive arts therapists are trained to provide a safe space for therapy in the same ways as traditional therapists. With the addition of art materials, instruments, sound, or physical movement, there are more concerns for liability. In addition to maintaining malpractice insurance specific to their certification or license, these therapists educate themselves with the intent of protecting clients from potential harm. According to the American Art Therapy Association Ethics (AATA, 2013),

> 1.8 Art therapists strive to provide a safe, functional environment in which to offer art therapy services. This includes: a. proper ventilation; b. adequate lighting; c. access to water; d. knowledge of hazards or toxicity of art materials, and the effort needed to safeguard the health of clients; e. storage space for artwork and secured areas for any hazardous materials; f. allowance for privacy and confidentiality; g. compliance with any other health and safety requirements according to state and federal agencies that regulate comparable businesses.
>
> (Reprinted with permission from the American
> Art Therapy Association.)

Having a good working knowledge or art materials safety is absolutely essential. Knowing that using clay or sand can be dusty and can cause problems for those with asthma helps the therapist best meet the client's needs for safety. When working in a hospital setting, I yearned to have space for an art therapy room. I secretly dreamed of having a kiln and being able to fire clay pieces. But the hospital could not install a kiln without causing air pollution for patients. In that situation, I used a kind of clay that came in individual, single-use packages. This clay was not optimal and did not allow for detail work, but it was adequate for some expressive work. Protecting client's emotional needs is always more important than the expressive product (Hinz, 2013).

Some modes of expression such as music and art result in some kind of artifact, whether it is a musical composition or an art piece. The general rule in art therapy is that what is created in a session by a client belongs to that client (Junge & Asawa, 1994; Knowles, 1996). The American Art Therapy Association (AATA, 2013) outlines the use of art here:

4.0 Client Artwork

Art therapists regard client artwork as a form of protected information and the property of the client. In some practice settings client artwork, or representations of artworks, may be considered a part of the clinical record retained by the therapist and/or agency for a reasonable amount of time consistent with state regulations and sound clinical practice. 4.1 Client artwork may be released to the client during the course of therapy and upon its termination, in accordance with therapeutic objectives and therapeutic benefit. 4.1.a The client is notified in instances when the art therapist and/or the clinical agency retain copies, photographic reproductions or digital images of the artwork in the client file as part of the clinical record. 4.1.b If termination occurs as a result of the death of the client, the original artwork is released to relatives if (a) the client signed a consent specifying to whom and under what circumstances the artwork should be released; (b) the client is a minor or under guardianship and the art therapist determines that the child's artwork does not violate the confidentiality the child entrusted to the art therapist; (c) the art therapist received and documented clear verbal indications from the client that the client wanted part or all of the artwork released to family members; or (d) mandated by a court of law. 4.2 Art therapists obtain written informed consent from clients or, when applicable, legal guardians, in order to keep client artwork, copies, slides, or photographs of artwork, for educational, research, or assessment purposes. 4.3 Art therapists do not make or permit any public use or reproduction of client art therapy sessions, including dialogue and artwork, without written consent of the clients. 4.4 Art therapists obtain written informed consent from clients or legal guardians (if applicable) before photographing clients' artwork or video-taping, audio recording, otherwise duplicating, or permitting third party observation of art therapy sessions. 4.5 Art therapists obtain written, informed consent from clients or legal guardians (if applicable) before using clinical materials and client artwork in any teaching, writing, and public presentations. Reasonable steps are taken to protect client identity and to disguise any part of the artwork or videotape that reveals client identity. 4.6 Art therapists disclose client artwork to third parties, members of inter-disciplinary teams and supervisors with the consent of the client or legal guardians (if applicable). 4.7 Art therapists explain how client artwork will be stored while the client is receiving art therapy services and the duration of retention for the actual artwork, photographs or digital images.

(Reprinted with permission from the American
Art Therapy Association.)

However, in music therapy it is not always the case that what is created in a session can be taken from a session. The music therapist is trained to determine whether the composition made by the client will be recorded. As a rule, many music therapists do not record music expressions that repeat traumatic memories. The reason for this is rooted in neuropsychology. The therapist prefers the client to leave the therapy session with recorded music as a tool for maintaining therapeutic goals. Tania Cordonia, licensed music therapist, explains,

The therapist protects the client from the exposure to repetitive negative, hopeless messages. A music therapist will help a client to rewrite, and find a melody and harmony to build a new neurological pathway to healing. Music therapists work to use the power of music to train the brain for hope and healing.

(personal communication, 2016)

WHAT WOULD YOU DO?

An adolescent client brings a guitar into the session and sings an original composition about suicidal despair.

Many times in work with children in art therapy, a client will gift their artwork to the therapist. It is okay to accept the art. If fact, it is essential as the artwork is an extension of the self. To accept the art is to accept the client. An example of an opportunity to show how you have unconditional positive regard happens when a client wants to throw their art in the trash can. When this happens, I ask the client what it is they do not like about the art. Following that discussion, I ask if I may have permission to keep the art. In this way, I am communicating my acceptance of the art and the value I see in the client, while creating a holding space for acceptance in the client–therapist relationship.

In my practice I ask clients to sign a form acknowledging that they consent to my taking a digital image of the art for their file. I also provide a separate consent for specific art images that I would like permission to use in presentations, publications, or with student interns.

Often art is left in the office to be completed in several sessions. This artwork is positioned so that names are not showing. During the intake, I explain that their artwork, when it is left in the office, is similar to their file being open in the room. I have not had a client yet who has expressed unwillingness to leave art in the room. It is important that they understand that their art will be cared for in their absence (Gussak and Orr, 2005). I have a rule that other people's artwork may not be touched by anyone entering the office. "We must be vigilant toward the rights of our clients, the rights of their images and our own rights and responsibilities" (Moon, 2006). Sometimes, it may happen that an art piece will crack or fall apart. This can be used as part of the therapy process. Working through having one's art turn out other than how one intended is a great metaphor for life's hard times.

When I was an intern, working with Latino female immigrants with low-birth-weight babies, I decided it would be a great therapeutic benefit to have an art exhibit of the women's art. The women all spoke Spanish as a first language and could not speak fluent English. However, with art making they could communicate their dilemmas. (At times, a translator was available to aid in discussion.) At the clinic, they would arrive in the morning and the babies would be cared for and have access to the mother as needed during the day. The mothers attended classes to learn English, job skills such as computer training, and other skills designed to increase possibility for successful integration into self-sufficiency. These women came from poverty, some experienced domestic violence, and while some had great support systems, others did not (Vick, 2011). An art exhibit would give the opportunity for them to be seen as artists extending their identities. I discussed the idea of having an exhibit, and the women agreed that the art would be saved for the exhibit.

The Icehouse Cultural Center, a local community art center that specialized in Latino art, agreed to let us do a "pop up" exhibit and reception. The women invited their families and friends. Watching the women share their art with their children, I saw them transformed from immigrant mothers to artists. A new identity emerged. The ladies gathered together and took a group portrait. It was soon announced that the art would be hung permanently in the new Low Birth Weight Clinic. This type of process is highly recommended and consistent with the American Art Therapy Association's thorough guidelines for exhibiting client artwork.

The American Art Therapy Association (AATA, 2013) has thorough guidelines for exhibiting client artwork:

5.0 Exhibition of Client Artwork

Exhibiting artwork created in art therapy provides an opportunity for clients to show their artwork to the general public or those in their agencies who would not normally see their artwork. Art therapists affirm that the artwork belongs to the clients, and an exhibition of client artwork has the potential to inform the public and empower the clients, while decreasing stigma and preconceptions. In preparation for an exhibition of client artwork, art therapists and clients or legal guardians (if applicable) weigh the benefits of exhibiting against the potential unintended consequences for the clients. 5.1 Art therapists engage clients who wish to exhibit their artwork in a thoughtful and intentional conversation regarding the rationales, benefits, and consequences of exhibiting artwork created in art therapy. 5.2 Art therapists ensure proper safeguards in exhibition to ensure that clients and their imagery are not exploited, misrepresented, or otherwise used in ways that are not approved by the clients. 5.3 In selecting artwork for exhibition, art therapists help clients make decisions based on several factors, including reason(s) for the display of the artwork, the therapeutic value of the artwork to the clients, the degree of self-disclosure, and the ability to tolerate audience reactions. 5.4 Art therapists discuss the merits and detriments of including artwork created outside of the art therapy session in the exhibition with clients or legal guardians (if applicable). 5.5 Art therapists discuss with clients or legal guardians (if applicable) the importance of confidentiality (e.g., personal history, diagnosis, and other clinical information) and anonymity (e.g., name, gender, age, culture) with regard to the display of clients' artwork. Art therapists respect the rights of clients who wish to be named in exhibits. 5.6 Art therapists obtain written informed consent from clients or, when applicable, parents or legal guardians, in order to exhibit client artwork. Art therapists discuss with clients, parents or legal guardians how the exhibition will be described and advertised to the public and viewing audience to ensure their consent in being associated with the exhibition. 5.7 In the event that exhibited artwork is for sale, the art therapist and client discuss the potential therapeutic impact before a sale of artwork is initiated. Art therapists ensure that clients and responsible parties (if applicable) are aware of and agreeable to how profits are used and who will specifically benefit from them (e.g., clients, agency[ies], social cause[s]). 5.8 Art therapists clearly state where and when exhibitions will take place to ensure that clients understand the range of possible audience members and degree of public exposure. 5.9 With regard to on-line exhibitions, art therapists make clients aware of the widespread availability of images, and therefore the enlarged viewing audience, as well as the potential for their images to be downloaded, forwarded or copied by on-line viewers.

(Reprinted with permission from the American Art Therapy Association.)

All such situations must be handled carefully and individually. Consider the implications of arranging an exhibition of client artwork to educate the public about depression. Assessing whether a client is a good candidate for inclusion in the exhibit means the difference between harming a client and providing an experience that can help the client move beyond identity with the diagnosis. Utilizing the guidelines set forth by the American Art Therapy Association, think about an approach to this endeavor.

Suppose you are employed by an advocacy center that specializes in counseling services for children who have experienced sexual abuse, and the center's development team would like to fund-raise using client artwork. Your boss asks you to start gathering art made by clients that will be auctioned to the public. What dangers could this pose to the clients? How would you navigate fulfilling your job duties versus following the ethical duty to protect? What can therapists do to educate nonprofits about fund-raising while simultaneously respecting client confidentiality and maintaining client dignity? *What would you do?*

Special problems can occur when using music with clients. For example, if a client brings lyrics, without music and harmony, into a session and shares them with a trained talk therapist, that professional should be able to use language as the foundation for the therapy. It will not be music therapy, but it will be a therapeutic exploration of words or poetry. The power of words is safer without melody. The therapist can ask the following to determine if a music therapist is needed: Did the client write a song or is it actually a poem? Does it have musical content, melody, harmony, rhythm? If is a poem, it can be processed using language. If it is a melody, harmony, or rhythm, is it memorable? Does it have a hook or a melody that is catchy and can replay in the mind? Repetition develops neurological pathways in the brain. (Neurologic Music Therapists like Michael Thaut are actively researching music and the brain.) Consider what the client is gaining by singing or hearing this song over and over. In this situation, a therapist who is not trained as a music therapist will be ethically obligated to consult with a trained music therapist.

Drama therapy is another of the expressive arts therapies. Through drama, clients can explore their inner experiences and social interaction, "trying on" new ways of solving problems. Whether problem solving, expressing feelings, setting goals, telling one's story, or working to achieve catharsis, drama can tap into the playful creative action of acting. Ethical issues that are especially important in drama therapy encompass good boundaries and ethical principles of touch.

7. Principles of Physical Contact, Role-Play, and Other Drama Therapy Activities

Drama therapists are responsible to practice in a manner that maintains professional boundaries, based on the individual's therapeutic goals, safety, and best interests. a. A drama therapist uses physical contact, movement, and/or role-play: 1) when they are consistent with the client's therapeutic goals, 2) with the client's informed consent, and 3) in a safe, respectful, and culturally sensitive manner. A drama therapist never engages in any behavior that is intended for sexual stimulation nor makes intentional contact with any private area of the client's body, and communicates that objective at the beginning of the professional relationship. b. A drama therapist never imposes or requires that an individual make physical contact, and informs the client that they may refrain from or refuse physical contact at any time. c. A drama therapist makes continuous assessments regarding the usefulness of physical touch with each client, and periodically renews the consent from the client. They also document the use of physical touch and its therapeutic effects. d. A drama therapist appreciates that physical contact may evoke strong feelings from the client and seeks consultation on a regular basis regarding their use of physical contact.

(North American Drama Therapy Association, 2016.
Reprinted with permission from the North American
Drama Therapy Association.)

For those who are trained to do it, using drama in a therapy session has very strong therapeutic potential. Drama therapists use physical contact and movement which carry some risk. Working with clients who have had trauma requires sensitivity. The client may feel uncomfortable with physical interactions. Informed consent is essential when working with personal boundaries. It builds trust and maintains awareness and a feeling of safety for the client.

What would you do if a client came to therapy to seek help after sexual assault? How would you set limits about touch? How would you prepare your client(s) for expressive therapy?

Using expressive arts interventions is very complimentary to group work. However, using art and expressive therapies in groups with adolescents requires attention to the teenagers' search for identity and need for acceptance. If a teen draws a picture and it is considered "bad" by anyone in the group, that teen can shut down and quit drawing. One approach would be to minimize any types of art making that could easily elicit judgment and, instead, stick to using stencils, clay, magazine collage, and torn tissue collage, for example.

I have experienced working in a juvenile detention center with female teenagers. Stencils were used to draw inside mandala circles, a circular image that is used in many cultures. The circle acts as a container for the images. The stencils offered to the girls gave them an option besides free drawing. Asking girls who are in a juvenile detention center to be vulnerable where it is absolutely not safe to trust peers can be a recipe for disaster. Although not a great way to be exclusively expressive, the use of stencils gave the girls a way to be expressive while remaining safe from being teased, insulted, or humiliated. Of course, any group work utilizing expressive means may elicit some degree of vulnerability. Being mindful of this and preparing accordingly will ensure that clients feel safe even when other group members may not necessarily be bonded.

We have explored some ways that expressive arts can evoke powerful responses from clients. A trained professional cannot be prepared for every ethical dilemma that will present itself. It is always important to be active in a peer supervision group or your local professional association, or have a peer you can consult with on a regular basis. A few years ago, I was at a training taught by a founding art therapist, Don Jones. He told us that as therapists we must "sink or swim." We dive into the waters not knowing if dangers lurk below the surface. Being prepared to swim through the rough spots with our clients comes with practice. That is why they call it a therapy *practice*, right?

With each expressive art that is integrated into therapy, a number of ethical problems can arise. Shining a light on some of these ethical situations instills a deeper respect for the ability for expressive arts to heal and also harm. Exploring the subtleties that come with the various expressive modalities does not end here. As we move forward into the new terrain of virtual therapy using Internet connections, therapists are developing more methods for navigating ethical limits. Therapists must continue the ethical conversation as they navigate the path.

DISCUSSION QUESTIONS/PROMPTS

1.   Does receiving a master's degree in counseling prepare you and, further, cover you legally to use expressive arts therapies as you see fit? Discuss this question in regard to practicing within your scope of competence.
2.   This chapter provided guidance from multiple professional organizations. If you are not an active member of these organizations, are you mandated to follow their standards when using a particular type of expressive art?
3.   Consider a client with severe emotional issues who has never experienced drama therapy. How would you explain and prepare the client for the powerful impact such an approach may make?
4.   Is it ethical and professionally competent to avoid the use of all expressive art approaches?
5.   What resources will you incorporate if you use expressive arts as a part of your practice?

LEGAL AND ETHICAL ISSUES IN ADMINISTERING AND INTERPRETING TESTS AND ASSESSMENTS WITH CHILDREN AND ADOLESCENTS

Darren E. Dobrinski and Joseph R. Engler

INTRODUCTION

Counseling children and adolescents is multifaceted. Counselors serve various roles when working with minors. To be an effective agent of change, counselors rely on gathering as much information as possible to ensure effective treatment. In addition to interviews, informal and formal observations, and counseling techniques, counselors also rely on psychological and educational assessments to assist in gathering information for effective outcomes for children and adolescents. According to the American Counseling Association (ACA, 2014) counselors administer, score, and interpret tests for the purpose of educational, mental health, psychological, and career assessment. Information obtained from these various types of assessments provides invaluable data to the counselor and his or her client in making effective decisions. Sattler (2014) states that sound practice in the arena of assessment includes knowledge in psychometrics, child development, personality theory, ethical guidelines, and clinical experience. The understanding of these areas collectively is used to arrive at appropriate decision-making for the client.

In considering the area of measurements, you, the reader should clearly recognize that in some way, shape, or form your life has already been impacted because of assessment. For example, you were required to take either the SAT or ACT to get into college. After graduating college, you may have been required to take the GRE to get into graduate school. Upon successfully completing your graduate program, you were (or will be) required to pass state licensing exams. The purpose of those assessments was (or will be) to gather information and make a prediction about the likelihood of your success at each level. By reading this book, I am assuming that the scores you obtained were predictive of your success, and you are enjoying the career field that you have chosen.

What, however, would have happened if the assessments that were given to you did not end in favorable results? Would you be angry? Sad? Disappointed? It is quite possible that all the aforementioned emotions would be interwoven. To further exacerbate the situation, what would happen if the person administering and scoring each of the tests was not competent? What if, for example, the tests being used were not predictive in their ability to discriminate between successes and failures? Would this change your emotional disposition? Unfortunately, many individuals have in fact been placed in this position, and their lives have been negatively impacted by assessment. Therefore, the purpose of this chapter is to identify common ethical situations that practitioners may encounter in their professional practice and also discuss the ethical guidelines that assist in the decision-making process.

As we navigate through this chapter, it is imperative that you have a framework for understanding the history of assessment since it provides clarity into the current challenges you may experience as an assessor. Moreover, there are many examples throughout the past 100 years that have influenced both professional and public opinion regarding assessment.

ROLE OF COGNITIVE TESTS IN ASSESSMENT

Assessment, particularly cognitive assessment, is relatively new within the historical context of measurement. Although measurement can be traced back hundreds of years, it was not until the early 20th century that Alfred Binet designed the first cognitive test to measure intellectual abilities. The genesis of the Binet-Simon Scale was in response to the French government mandating public education for all children. Consequently, the French government was particularly interested in the assessment of children to determine which students were likely to succeed within the traditional school setting and which would need to receive additional educational resources with services in an alternative setting. Although it was not Binet's intention, herein lies what will soon spark a number of controversies associated with outcomes related to those with inferior scores.

Decades later, as the Binet-Simon Scale (newly revised as the Stanford-Binet) was gaining popularity, the United States sought the use of cognitive tests to assist in strengthening their military. Moreover, the Army Alpha and Army Beta were developed to ascertain current intellectual abilities on thousands of military personnel. The scores obtained were then used to determine military ranking, with higher ranks available only for those individuals with higher cognitive scores. Again, cognitive tests were used to predict the success of an individual while relying relatively little on additional sources of data. As with the Binet-Simon Scale, criticism continued to build as certain individuals' futures were decided primarily based on their intellectual abilities.

During the latter third of the 20th century, cognitive tests remained in the forefront of professional and public dissention as ethnic differences in IQ scores began to surface. In the 1970s and 1980s, a number of legal cases resulted from the use of cognitive tests with ethnic minorities. Three landmark cases regarding this issue were *Larry P. v. Riles, Diana v. Board of Education*, and *Guadalupe v. Tempe Elementary School District*. The underlying contentions of the aforementioned cases centered on potential test biases and educational placement disparities between ethnic majorities and ethnic minorities. As a result, there was a call to change practices surrounding the use and misuse of IQ and academic tests for ethnic minorities. To exacerbate the situation, one of the most controversial and publicly scrutinized books was published regarding cognitive assessment in the early 1990s. Hernstein and Murray (1994) published *Bell Curve: Intelligence and Class Structure in American Life*, which reported varying levels of intellectual and academic ability levels across different ethnic groups favoring the majority. In reacting to this result, governing bodies such as the American Counseling Association, American Psychological Association, and National Association of School Psychologists have continually increased the importance of cultural competence and sensitivity in assessment with each passing revision of their ethical codes.

It is certainly not our intention to present cognitive tests in an overly negative light, as cognitive tests did not make these decisions, people did. Further, many of the most popular and widely used cognitive tests do, in fact, exhibit excellent psychometric properties and provide valuable information. Rather, our intention is that when a cognitive test, or any test for that matter, is used inappropriately, negative outcomes are likely to occur for the clients we serve. Of course, in cases where the information is misinterpreted or misused by the professional, legal and ethical citations may result. For example, despite intellectual and academic achievement tests having stronger psychometric properties than social-emotional measures, practitioners are more likely to end up in a legal situation over the use of the former (Whitcomb & Merrell, 2013). Fortunately, as mental health professionals, we have governing bodies and codes of ethic such as the American Counseling Association (ACA, 2014), American Psychological Association (APA, 2010), National Association of School Psychologists (NASP, 2010), and the American Educational Research Association, American Psychological Association, and National Council on Measurement in Education (AERA, APA, & NCME, 2014) to provide guidelines for appropriate uses of tests.

Although legal and ethical decision-making may initially appear to be black and white, the more you work with children and adolescents, the more shades of gray you see. That is, sometimes the results of testing and assessment can be in conflict with the counselor's objectives to provide services to the client.

Let us consider a real-world case study in which the counselor found herself in an ethical bind. It is not a coincidence that the first case study involves the use of cognitive test within the assessment process as this underscores the care needed when administering such instruments.

CASE TO CONSIDER

Susie, a recent graduate, just received her first job offer to work as a school counselor in a rural school district in the Midwest. The school she worked at was a K–12 school with a total of 153 students. Her first year practicing as a school counselor was going extremely well as she was implementing a number of programs at the school, classroom, and individual level that were showing efficacy in regards to social-emotional learning. As the school year continued, Susie had a growing concern that one of her fourth grade students, Jayden, was undergoing some emotional turmoil. Susie had noticed that Jayden had suddenly become much more emotional than he had been previously, as he was crying in class and began refusing to complete his homework. Susie and the school administrator requested a meeting with Jayden's parents to discuss this issue further. Jayden's parents were at a loss and requested that he be evaluated for special education under the classification of emotional disability, which would then entitle him to receive extra services and supports within the school. All parties at the meeting agreed. Consent was signed and the evaluation began. Susie was trained in emotional assessment and administered a number of tests that clearly showed elevated levels of depression. The last piece of the evaluation was an intelligence test, as schools are required to document that the emotional difficulties were not due to cognitive deficits. Susie had called the school psychologist to complete the intelligence test a number of times to no avail. Meanwhile, Jayden's behaviors escalated resulting in a physical altercation with another student. The principal, fed up with how long it was taking the school psychologist, asked Susie to administer the Wechsler Intelligence Scale for Children—Fifth Edition (WISC-V) because it was only a "formality" for qualification in special education. Further, the principal told Susie that she had some familiarity with standardized tests, and it would be easy for her to learn in a day or two. The principal told Susie that the client was her number one priority and the longer they waited, the worse things were going to be for Jayden. Susie agreed and administered the WISC-V. Jayden ended up with a Full Scale IQ of 75, and the team determined the behaviors were not due to a cognitive deficit so Jayden qualified for special education under the educational classification of Emotional Disability.

This case presents an interesting ethical dilemma that needs to be discussed further. When solving ethical dilemmas, we rely on a condensed five-step problem-solving model that was adapted from Armistead, Williams, and Jacob (2011).

The first step in the problem-solving model is to *identify the problem*. It is our experience that beginning practitioners do not spend an adequate amount of time during this problem identification step. Rather, they tend to haphazardly bypass this step to brainstorm potential solutions. Unfortunately, however, if the problem is not initially correctly identified, each subsequent step will likely lead to erroneous conclusions. This case involves one problem with contributing factors. The problem relates to whether the counselor should have administered the WISC-V to the student rather than waiting for the school psychologist. The contributing factors were pressure from the administration and lack of follow through from the school psychologist.

The second step is to *identify all relevant parties* within the ethical situation. In Case Study 1, the relevant parties are Jayden, the school psychologist, Susie, and the administrator. The school psychologist, Susie, and the administrator are the professionals involved in this case.

The third step is to *describe the ethical principles* most relevant to the case. The most relevant ethical principles from ACA (2014) are outlined next:

E.1.b Client Welfare (p. 11)

Counselors do not misuse assessment results and interpretations, and they take reasonable steps to prevent others from misusing the information provided. They respect the client's right to know the results, the interpretations made, and the bases for counselors' conclusions and recommendations.

E.2.a. Limits of Competence (p. 11)

Counselors use only those testing and assessment services for which they have been trained and are competent. Counselors using technology-assisted test interpretations are trained in the construct being measured and the specific instrument being used prior to using its technology-based application. Counselors take reasonable measures to ensure the proper use of assessment techniques by persons under their supervision.

E.2.b. Appropriate Use (p. 11)

Counselors are responsible for the appropriate application, scoring, interpretation, and use of assessment instruments relevant to the needs of the client, whether they score and interpret such assessments themselves or use technology or other services.

E.2.c. Decisions Based on Results (p. 11)

Counselors responsible for decisions involving individuals or policies that are based on assessment results have a thorough understanding of psychometrics.

The fourth step is to *seek supervision and consultation* with colleagues. When problem-solving an ethical situation, it is imperative to seek both supervision and consultation. This is especially necessary for beginning practitioners. The purpose during this step is to make sure that you are thoroughly analyzing the situations and not overlooking any pertinent information. It is important to know that during this step, you should still be maintaining confidentiality of your client's personal information and only providing need-to-know information. From our experiences, it is best to look at Step 4 as a linear progression from the previous steps.

During your supervision and consultation, the team will likely determine that the ethical dilemma centers on standard E.2. Competence to Use and Interpret Assessment Instruments from the *ACA Code of Ethics*. As a consultative team, it is recommended that all members of the team process each of the identified ethical principles involved in this case. In regards to E.2.a. Susie had not been formally trained in either cognitive theories or tests (which are often a prerequisite from major testing companies for the purchase of cognitive tests). The lack of any formal training is directly related to E.2.b. because if Susie was not trained in the WISC-V, it is entirely possible that her administration, scoring, and interpretation were invalid. Our experience is that learning a new test takes extensive reading of the test manual, practice, and seeking supervision after the practice administrations to decipher any scoring discrepancies that may exist. It is highly unlikely that in a day or two, Susie could be considered a competent test administrator, especially given the fact that she had previously received no background knowledge or formal training in cognitive tests. Consequently, ethical code E.2.c. would likely have been impacted, particularly if she made scoring errors throughout the administration.

Finally, Armistead, Williams and Jacob's model takes you to Step 5 of the problem-solving model where you *arrive at a conclusion or solution* to the problem. In Case Study 1, Susie had made the decision to administer the WISC-V because it was a "formality" for special education placement. She thought that it was in the client's best interest to receive services sooner rather than later. In making this decision, the team decided that she had clearly violated a number of ethical principles regarding competency and test use. In fact, Susie may have erroneously administered, scored, and interpreted the WISC-V. Consequently, the decisions made for Jayden may not have been made appropriately using the existing data. In this case, for example, IQ tests of 70 +/- (5) are to be further explored in regard to a potential intellectual disability. Therefore, even if Jayden's Full-Scale IQ score was accurate, the team did not complete a follow-up comprehensive assessment. In this example, it is possible that Susie did more damage than good by trying to speed up the special education process for Jayden.

ROLE OF BEHAVIORAL, SOCIAL, AND EMOTIONAL TESTS IN ASSESSMENT

Understanding how children and adolescents process, perceive, and act in their surroundings is an important component in facilitating effective change. Behavioral, social, and emotional test batteries provide insight into a client's beliefs, opinions, feelings, and emotions. When counselors possess both the knowledge and the experience to administer, score, and interpret these batteries, the information that is obtained provides insight that may not otherwise be uncovered in a traditional counseling session. Assessment results, when ethical guidelines are followed, can positively impact the client by providing information that leads to effective treatment decisions.

Administrating, scoring, and interpreting behavioral, social, and emotional tests can be arduous and time consuming. To complicate matters, tests have different administration rules, scoring rubrics, and interpretation steps. In addition to administration, scoring, and interpretive factors, counselors are responsible for integrating results from multiple raters. For example, rating forms are often given to the client, parent, and teacher. Therefore, it is essential for the professional to understand that parent and teacher reports of behavioral, social, and emotional functioning of the child or adolescent is a perspective, which may be quite different from what a child or adolescent self-reports.

Given the complexity of behavioral, social, and emotional assessment, it is vital that counselors follow the ethical guidelines in order to ensure that the information obtained serves to positively affect the children and adolescents they serve. The following case study provides a scenario regarding ethical dilemmas that can surface when using behavioral, social, and emotional tests in the assessment process.

CASE TO CONSIDER

A graduate student enrolled in a personality assessment class was asked to discuss the findings of a battery of tests that she had administered as a class requirement. The participant for this project was selected on a volunteer basis and parental consent was obtained. The parent was informed that the results would not be shared outside of the classroom and that the documents would be destroyed upon grading the

---

assignment. In addition, it was clearly stated on the parent consent form that the results would not be shared with either the parent or the child since the results would be invalid due to the level of competence of the graduate student.

The graduate student presented the case, providing the class with demographics and background history. The participant was described as a 15-year-old Native American female, named Megan, who was in ninth grade in a small rural school. The graduate student reported that Megan was friendly and willing to participate. During rapport building, Megan reported that she liked school, was getting average grades, and had a lot of friends. The battery of tests included two projective tests, one formal personality test, two objective behavioral tests, one objective social test, and one specific depression inventory.

The graduate student reported that the specific tests in the battery indicated overall signs of normalcy with the exception of at-risk scores on a social skills tests completed by the parent and one of the projective tests that revealed signs of aggression, depression, and anxiety. When asked to provide the class with more detail about the findings on the Kinetic Family Drawing, the graduate student reported that in the Kinetic Family Drawing the adolescent drew her family doing something as instructed, but had drawn a gun next to her father. Due to the significance of the weapon, the graduate student wanted to know if she should report this to the parent.

What should the graduate student do? What is the responsibility of the class instructor? Would the decisions be the same or different for a professional counselor?

Understanding the elements needed to ensure sound assessment practice and using the five-step problem-solving model described earlier, the following questions and steps were taken. The first step was to *identify the problem*. The graduate student had already identified this in her conclusion. Do we report the findings to the parent? Is the weapon serious enough to report to the parent even though the parental consent specifically stated that findings would not be reported? In this case, the graduate student, class instructor, parent, and student were *identified as the relevant parties*. The *ethical principles that are most relevant* in this case include

E.8. Multicultural Issues/Diversity in Assessment (p. 12)

Counselors select and use with caution assessment techniques normed on populations other than that of the client. Counselors recognize the effects of age, color, culture disability, ethnic group, gender, race, language preference, religion, spirituality, sexual orientation, and socioeconomic status on test administration and interpretation, and they place test results in proper perspective with other relevant factors.

E.9.a. Reporting (p. 12)

When a counselor report assessment results, they consider the client's personal and cultural background, the level of the client's understanding of the results, and the impact of the results on the client. In reporting assessment results, counselors indicate reservations that exist regarding validity or reliability due to circumstances of the assessment or inappropriateness of the norms for the person tested.

E.6.a Appropriateness of Instruments (p. 11)

Counselors carefully consider the validity, reliability, psychometric limitations, and appropriateness of instruments when selecting assessments and, when possible, use multiple forms of assessment, data, and/or instruments in forming conclusions, diagnoses, or recommendations.

(Reprinted from *ACA Code of Ethics* [ACA, ©2014].
American Counseling Association. Reprinted with permission.
No further reproduction authorized without written
permission from the American Counseling Association.)

Seeking supervision and consultation in this case was already established due to the nature of the graduate student–instructor relationship. By using the problem-solving model and understanding the components needed for best practice, the class asked relevant questions and discussed the ethical principles just listed. When the class discussed reporting and scoring of the assessments, it was suggested that the client's personal and cultural background needed to be taken into consideration. For example, the norms on the social skill test did not represent the adolescent's culture, ethnic group, or race. Therefore, the scores from the parent were invalid. In addition, it became evident that standardization was violated on the projective test because the graduate student did not ask appropriate post-drawing inquiries. The gun was drawn next to the father so the graduate student should have asked, "What is the father doing?" In addition, it was discussed that no single theme on an individual test should be used in isolation and that the psychometrics of projective tests are limited. When asked to go back and follow through on the standardization of the administration, it was revealed that the father was an avid hunter and was drawn as hunting in the Kinetic Family Drawing instrument.

If the problem-solving model is used during ethical dilemmas, it will provide guidance when difficult decisions are presented. Although it wasn't until the class had entered into Step 4 of the problem-solving model that the graduate student had missed an important administration step, nevertheless, it was important that the student process the dilemma that she was facing in order to come up with an appropriate *conclusion or solution* to the situation. Therefore, the decision was made that she would not reveal the results of the test battery to the parent, since there was nothing mandated to report.

SCENARIOS TO DISCUSS

Thus far, you have been presented with two case studies involving a myriad of ethical principles for decision-making purposes. Using the five-step problem-solving model, as presented in the previous case studies, please read through the following scenarios and identify the key components in each step. When you arrive at a conclusion, make sure that the decision is grounded in ACA principles as well as sound practice within the role of assessment. Following those principles and practices can then increase your confidence in the decisions being made for and by the client.

Scenario 1

Steve is a recent graduate from a CACREP program who specialized in school counseling. He earned high marks in his assessment classes and currently is working in a high school setting. An 11th grade student, Amy, who has dreamed of becoming a physician for as long as she can remember has a post-interview with Steve to go through the results of her recent career assessment evaluation. Reviewing Amy's data from the battery of tests, Steve, realizes that Amy's cumulative GPA is below 3.0, her ACT and SAT scores are below average, and her career interest test does not reflect interests in the sciences. Steve is in conflict since Amy has stated her passion to pursue medicine, yet he is confident that the test scores are a valid representation of Amy's abilities and interests. He wants to ensure that the results of the tests help promote Amy's well-being and will serve as a guideline to help facilitate her college/university endeavors.

Scenario 2

Sara, a mental health counselor, has been assigned to work with Devin, a seventh grade boy, who has difficulty maintaining attention to task. His classroom teacher describes him as a student who needs constant reminders, has difficulty with his academics, and exhibits poor social skills. In order for Devin to qualify for Sara's counseling group, he needs a diagnosis of attention-deficit/hyperactivity disorder. She arranges for a comprehensive psychological evaluation. The results indicate that he does not meet the criteria for ADHD and therefore does not qualify for the group. Sara is conflicted in that she wants to promote the well-being of Devin.

FUTURE CONSIDERATIONS REGARDING ETHICAL AND LEGAL ISSUES IN ASSESSMENT

One current topic of discussion within the field of assessment centers on the use of technology in the assessment process. Major test publishers have created online scoring software programs that enable practitioners to input raw data into a database. The software then converts the raw scores to standard scores for interpretative value. Previously, practitioners could purchase a scoring software CD that was only licensed for use on one computer. Typically, practitioners would install the scoring software on their office computer. Given the travel associated with many itinerant professionals, having accessibility to the scoring software presented a challenge. Consequently, the newly created, centrally located database, accessible from any computer appears to make both logical and practical sense. At this time, you may be wondering where the ethical dilemma lies.

In regard to online scoring programs, there are two main ethical issues regarding the use of an online scoring program. The first ethical issue is in regard to the confidentiality of student records. By using the online scoring program, the practitioner is required to enter personally identifiable information into the database. Moreover, at that time, the company supplying the online scoring program has access to the student's educational record. In addition, the testing company has the right to retain the data over an indefinite period of time. That means the practitioner does not have the authority to delete records. What complicates things further is that certain testing companies produce commonly used tests that do not have hand-scoring capabilities. Therefore, if a practitioner wants to use that test, he or she must agree to the terms and conditions of the online scoring program. As you can see, this puts practitioners in an uncomfortable position as they may feel that their hands are tied in such cases.

The second ethical issue relates to parental consent. For example, if you are using online scoring programs, must you be required to gain parental notification and consent for the test publishers to use student data? Additionally, if the student data is to be used by the testing company, do parents have the right to consent or not consent to their child's scores being used for research purposes? One would think that parents would be in control of making such decisions regarding their child. Unfortunately, to date, there are not any definitive answers to the aforementioned questions. Our hope would be that practitioners remain savvy and fully informed regarding the potential ethical and legal challenges that may result from the use of such scoring programs.

CONCLUSION

As mental health professionals, we have had countless clinical experiences that highlight the value gained from a comprehensive psychological assessment. When working with children and adolescents, we have found that there are times when these individuals have difficulty verbally expressing their perspectives. Rather than having this issue thwart the therapeutic relationship, we have relied on assessments to facilitate meaningful communication between parties. Using assessments tends to give the client the individual freedom to express him- or herself in an objective nondefensive way. This method is especially effective when working with children and adolescents at the request of parents rather than seeking out the counseling relationship on their own.

In addition to providing information within the therapeutic relationship, there are various other uses of assessment, including making high-stakes decisions for children and adolescents. Typical high-stakes decisions may include access to special education programming as well as access to community resources via diagnoses. Throughout history, we have seen that when high-stakes decisions do not align with proper practice, legal cases ensue. This is especially evident within cognitive assessment, and our expectation is that this will continue within the realm of social, emotional, and behavioral assessment. To complicate matters further, increased use of technology may factor into ethical and legal decision-making in the coming future. Therefore, as practicing professionals, there is a definite, demonstrated need for us to abide by our ethical standards and remain proactive within the field of assessment rather than reactive to court decisions.

At the end of the day, then, it is imperative to recognize that the assessment tools we use may often result in shaping high-stakes decisions for our clients. Therefore, the overall emphasis of this chapter stresses the need for competency and understanding the variability of the tools that we use. As discussed throughout the case studies, there will be times throughout your professional career that you will have ethical dilemmas that you will have to solve. Through an understanding of theory, development, psychometrics, and competency of the various tools, you will be able to provide valuable treatment for children and adolescents while avoiding potential pitfalls that could lead to ethical and legal ramifications.

DISCUSSION QUESTIONS/PROMPTS

1. Compare and contrast APA, ACA, and NASP codes of ethics.
2. Please discuss a real-life example of an ethical dilemma you encountered and how you solved it. Be sure to include both the positive and negative outcomes of the ethical decision.

3. Please identify the steps that you will take in your practice to ensure that you are proactive in identifying potential ethical dilemmas.

4. In the first case study, how could you have advocated for the child instead of administering the WISC-V incompetently?

5. If the second case study was conducted by a school counselor and the weapon would have been viewed as a possible threat, how would the problem-solving model be different?

THE ETHICAL AND LEGAL BOUNDARIES ALL COUNSELORS MUST UNDERSTAND IN THE PROCESS OF REPORTING ABUSE/NEGLECT AND NOT TAINTING LEGAL INVESTIGATIONS

Brian Peterson

INTRODUCTION

At times, investigating alleged crimes committed against children can be complex, emotional, and overwhelming. In this chapter I will break down the anatomy of working such investigations. This effort invariably utilizes the effective coordination of multiple professionals for a case to be successful. Therefore, having an understanding of the role that each agency, office, and person plays in the case is a basic and extremely essential part of the process.

THE MAKEUP OF THE MULTIDISCIPLINARY TEAM

Most law enforcement agencies throughout the United States have established relationships with child advocacy centers. These relationships enable the formation of the multidisciplinary team, which includes law enforcement, prosecutors, Child Protective Services, forensic interview specialists, forensic medical staff and SANE (Sexual Assault Nurse Examiner), counselors, and victim's assistance workers. Ideally the members of this team effectively serve to both enhance the process of investigating allegations and minimize additional trauma to the victim. Each multidisciplinary team has its own working protocol, rules of confidentiality, agency's policies, and professional codes and standards to guide them. Child Advocacy Centers provide special services for the victims and their nonoffending family members, offering counseling, special classes, and victim assistance.

Roles of Multidisciplinary Team Members

While the makeup of the multidisciplinary team composition may vary from one political jurisdiction to another, a list of usual team members usually includes the following:

Team Member	Role Associated
Forensic Interview	Interview the child or adolescent who has made an outcry of abuse.
Child Protective Services	Screen the child or adolescent to assess for possible physical, emotional, or sexual abuse. Ensure the immediate and physical safety of the child; find alternative emergency placement if necessary.
Law Enforcement	Conduct the criminal investigation, collect evidence, and make arrests when needed.
Prosecutor	Ensure justice is served.
Counselor	Assist the child or adolescent in coping with and processing the trauma or crime against them.

Clearly, there are a number of professionals, serving unique and critical functions in the process of investigating and working with a criminal investigation against a child or teen. While each member serves an important role, the following describes the typical process and associated expectations present in a thorough, professional, and legal/ethical investigation.

BREAKING DOWN THE INVESTIGATIVE PROCESS

A case generally begins with an outcry or allegation that a crime has occurred against a child. The alleged crime may involve neglect, physical or sexual allegations, or combinations of same. Beginning early in the process, law enforcement and Child Protective Services (CPS) combine their efforts, working together discovering and communicating details pertaining to the allegation(s). Law enforcement investigators' primary role at this point is attempting to determine if a criminal act has actually occurred. If such a determination is made, investigators will continue to gather pertinent facts and evidence of the case and forward it to the prosecutor's office for prosecution. If probable cause is established, an arrest may be made prior to the case being submitted to the prosecutor's office.

Child Protective Services investigates the civil aspect. Its primary role at the outset is to assess aspects regarding the safety of the child. If the determination is made that the child's immediate safety is not at risk, CPS will work with the family to reduce the risk of future abuse. If the agency determines the child is at risk of further harm, it will intervene to protect the child by developing a safety plan for placement of the child with a family member or conduct a removal of the child to be placed in foster care or with another family member as an emergency placement. All involved persons need to understand that the eventual (ideal) goal of CPS is to effectively and safely reunite the child with his or her family after counseling and family service programs are received. If counseling services and other interventions are unsuccessful, CPS then develops a plan to seek out an adoptive home for the child.

Important to note here is that while each professional serving on the multidisciplinary team, including the counselor in the case, may have his or her own judgments regarding *if* and *when* the child should be removed from the home, CPS is the agency primarily adjudicated to make the determination of in-home safety.

On the other hand, law enforcement has little direct contact with the alleged victim during the initial interview process. Initially, the alleged victim is taken to a Child Advocacy Center where he or she is interviewed by a forensic interview specialist. The forensic interviewer is specifically trained in asking open-ended questions that will not lead the victim in his or her answers. The interview is monitored on closed-circuit TV by investigation team members who may eventually be prosecuting the case. Counselors should take note that while their role is to be therapeutic, especially in cases where a child or teen is disclosing abuse or neglect, their role *is not* to become the investigator or forensic interviewer.

Upon completing the forensic interview, the CPS worker, and law enforcement investigator usually will meet with the parent(s) or guardian to explain the process of the investigation and will take this time to set appointments for interviews and medical examination of the victim if needed. Child advocacy victim services staff can assist them in filing for victim assistance and services if needed.

Generally speaking, multidisciplinary teams usually meet once a month to staff the new cases and provide updates on the existing cases that have yet to be finalized with a disposition. During this time team members will report what progress has been made on their cases and/or discuss any new developments. It is important to note here that members of the team may not provide all information in detail since they are required to adhere to professional codes related to confidentiality.

The therapist is often instrumental in the multidisciplinary team, for once the child is placed into counseling the therapist may observe behaviors in the child that may indicate the severity of abuse, witness further outcries, or discover involvement of other actors. Additionally, counselors can be of benefit to the team in educating them on the processes of counseling and how the child's developmental level could possible affect the case.

MOTIVATION BEHIND THE OUTCRY

There are several reasons why a child or adolescent may make an outcry of abuse. Possibilities may run the gamut from the abuse actually happening to the fabrication of the event for an unnamed reason. It's our human nature to protect the presumed innocent and potentially weak. When a child makes an allegation, our initial thoughts are to trust rather than consider that he or she may be lying. It's sometimes difficult to accept that a child or adolescent could be dishonest and make a false outcry, but on occasion it does happen.

Depending on the child or adolescent's situation, a recantation or retraction may occur in the aftermath of an outcry. Recantations of abuse occur for various reasons, many of which are centered on feelings toward family members and friends. When a child or adolescent recants a truthful allegation, the chances of revictimization or the continuation of abuse increases (Marx, 1996). Additionally, if the family supported the recantation, chances are they will not take the measures necessary to protect the child in the future. The developmental level of the child often plays a role in the decision to recant a statement. Some of the motivations for recantation include feeling responsible for the abuse that occurred, fearing separations within the family, causing hardships among family members, causing a family member to be removed from the home, and even experiencing undue pressure from authority figures. Cases resulting in recantation can be especially difficult for the multidisciplinary team and cause additional hardship on the child they are desperately trying to protect and help. When a child recants a statement, he or she can easily "fall into the cracks" of the legal system and subsequently not receive the mental health counseling that may be needed. The end result then may be a child or adolescent who becomes an unheard, possibly ongoing, victim of crime.

Under some circumstances, however, children and adolescents may actually make false allegations of abuse. Depending on the child's or adolescent's circumstances, there may be various motivations behind a false outcry. In assessing the purpose behind a false allegation, it is important to acknowledge the motivation and reasoning of the child or adolescent. Some false allegations may be because the child is angry or has a desire to escape the home. Additionally, a certain percentage of the children that we deal with come from dysfunctional homes where they are being reared in unhealthy environments that often lack structure, direction, or moral guidance. These deficiencies are not the fault of the child, but that fact does not make them any less a victim. Children reared in such unhealthy environments often learn manipulative coping skills. In cases in which a child or adolescent is being coached or pressured to make false allegations, it is especially important to remember that younger children, developmentally delayed children, or adolescents will do whatever possible to meet their psychological, physical, and emotional needs. Developmentally speaking, some children may not necessarily understand what it means to lie or the consequence false allegations may have on individuals. In still other situations, false allegations may be strategically planned out to get rewards from parents or even community members.

POINT TO PONDER

In many cases child-friendly agencies often provide gifts and/or rewards when a child visits or comes for services. Rewards received vary from a piece of candy to an expensive prize. While such rewards may provide additional encouragement for some children or adolescents to be truthful, they may provide motivation for others to make false allegations.

THE ROLE OF THE COUNSELOR

Counseling children who have experienced any type of abuse can be a stressful and draining yet rewarding task. In working with children who have made an outcry of abuse, the counselor serves the roles of a healer, support system, confidant, educator, and advocate.

After a child makes an outcry of abuse, the counselor is one of the main people who can assist in ensuring the child feels support enough to not recant a statement of abuse (Marx, 1996). This support is extremely beneficial when the child/adolescent's family or guardian is not supportive or expresses disbelief in his or her allegations or statements. While some individuals struggle with the thought that a parent would not support a child or adolescent in an outcry of abuse, several factors may be included that may not initially come to mind. Reasons why the child may not be fully supported in an outcry of abuse may include factors such as the child's relationship to the offender, his or her parent's relationship to the offender, and/or the familial history of abuse.

In working with the child, the counselor can assess for risk in the child recanting an allegation. Risks for recantation include the child's relationship to the offender, the family's response after the disclosure, the child's placement after disclosure, and evidence of direct pressure. Often, when the offender is a caretaker or guardian, the nonoffending parties pressure the child into recanting the claim by making him or her feel guilty about separating the family or through victim blaming (Marx, 1996).

The counselor plays an important role as the educator in working with all members of the multidisciplinary team. This can include educating prosecutors and investigators on the dynamics of victimization, dynamics of recantation, and how to communicate or interact with a child in a way that is developmentally appropriate (Marx, 1996).

Prior to getting into the specifics on how a therapist can aid and assist in criminal investigation for crimes against children, he or she must first be knowledgeable about the process. The counselor can be either helpful or hurtful to the criminal investigation. Oftentimes if the case is not successful in the court, the child may feel additional hurt; thus, it is important the therapist does not do anything that may taint or make the case more challenging for law enforcement or the prosecutor.

Counselors need to recognize that they do not know all the information pertaining and they may not be privy to case specifics. Law enforcement does have to keep some information confidential to ensure the materials do not get released to family members and the public. *Some of the details of the case can be quite harming if released to individuals.* For example, if a therapist knows some information regarding a case, he or she may be more prone to search for that information during counseling sessions, an action that might eventually lead to the counselor being accused of coaching or leading the child client. Ultimately, then, such actions can work against the defense and cause the perpetrator to get reduced charges or even worse, result in the charges being dismissed completely.

Sometimes a counselor knowing so much information about the case can so greatly affect the counselor's judgment that they begin to "see" the child displaying symptoms that he or she may not actually be having, or the counselor may start identifying themes not necessarily related to the child. When a counselor assumes specifics of the case in this manner, he or she is actually doing a disservice rather than a service to the child. Ultimately, counselors need to keep in mind their goal is to assist the child, not harm the child in the process.

PROFESSIONAL BOUNDARIES

Working as a team often sounds easy, but it can become quite difficult if a teammate crosses the line into someone else's field of expertise. Cases involving crimes against children can often bring about strong and difficult emotions for law enforcement, counselors, child protective service workers, prosecutors, and multidisciplinary team members. All team members must maintain professional boundaries to ensure they do not overstep and cause additional hardships. It should be remembered every team member experiences different emotions, and the emotions are often tied to specific job responsibilities and cognitions.

For example, a law enforcement officer's emotions may be peaked as a result of experiencing the real-life evidence and crime scene, viewing images and videos of the actual crime, witnessing the removal of the child, viewing the autopsy of child death cases, the family requesting updates, interviewing the perpetrator or offender, and/or interviewing witnesses of the crime. A counselor, on the other hand, is more emotionally involved as a result of the continuous emotional engagement with the child or adolescent client and/or the effects that it has on the family.

THERAPIST DOS AND DO NOTS IN WORKING WITH LAW ENFORCEMENT

In navigating the relationship with law enforcement or investigative entities, counselors need to be cognizant of specific guidelines. In working cases in which ongoing investigations are occurring, counselors must be cautions of their interactions with others to ensure the case is not tainted. The following "Do's" and "Do not's" provide an idea of areas in which counselors should be cautious.

Do's	Do not's
Do be respectful.	Do not conduct your own investigation.
Do speak the facts.	Do not promise or speculate a specific outcome.
Do refer all questions regarding investigations to law enforcement or the prosecutor.	Do not assume you know what someone else is doing or the time frame they are working with.
Do understand investigators have heavy caseloads and every case requires details.	Do not solicit confidential information or details from the parents or guardians.
Do understand a good investigation takes time.	Do not hurry the investigative processes.

It is in a person's nature to want to answer someone's specific question and feel as if he or she has helped another person. *However, especially in working crimes against children or adolescents the counselor could jeopardize the integrity of the investigation if he or she reveals confidential case details or make assumptions about the case.* For example, in some cases it is not uncommon for the parent or guardian to solicit information about the case to help the offender or with the intention to leak it to social media.

It is especially important for counselors to understand that investigators have more than one pressing case at a time. If fact, many juggle heavy caseloads and are responsible to many other victims and their families. While the investigator's job sounds relatively easy, counselors need to understand each case may potentially involve the following: working a crime scene; interviewing complainants, suspects, witnesses, and victims; entering evidence; sending evidence out for forensics; gathering and collecting DNA from the crime scene; collecting fingerprints; conducting computer and cell phone forensic findings; reviewing medical records, exams, and autopsies; writing and executing search warrants. The investigation process is time consuming, and the tasks involved require a vast amount of detail to ensure the crime is well investigated.

CASE TO CONSIDER

Timothy is a counselor at an agency that primarily services children affected by crime. The agency Timothy works for is relatively small and has only seven employees who handle all cases against children. A multidisciplinary team is utilized to consolidate the criminal investigation and to prevent additional traumas to the child victim. Because of Timothy's role as a counselor, he and the other counselor often meet individually bimonthly for consultation purposes. During these consultation sessions, Timothy notices that the other counselor often becomes heated and expresses her frustration with law enforcement and other members of the multidisciplinary team for not moving the case as fast as she would prefer. She tells Timothy that she has already talked to the director of the agency and that the director shares her feelings. She continues noting that if the case is not put on the court docket in the next month, she has been instructed to tell the parents to put additional pressure on both the detective leading the criminal investigation and the prosecutor. Additionally, she noted the director, at that point, would also call the supervisors of all multidisciplinary team members involved in the case.

Points to Consider in This Case

A situation such as the preceding case can cause several problems. First, let's consider the situation from the effect it may have on the child or adolescent. As a result of the parent's increased stress levels because charges had not been filed as quickly as they desired, they may feel as if the legal system did not think they are that important. Additionally, the child may feel as if he or she did not do a good enough job explaining what happened or may feel as if the legal system does not consider him or her important. In truth, of course, the safety of the child is of paramount importance in the beginning stages. If the child is judged to be in an unsafe environment, the case will take on more urgency. Conversely, if the child is felt to be in a safe environment, more time can be utilized to ensure the case is properly investigated and justice is served.

Counselors must keep in mind that the investigative practices and prosecution of child offenders is very strategic. It is not an overnight process. In some instances, the desire to save the child or immediately stop the pain of the child can result in the counselor overstepping his or her professional bounds. Therefore, it is critical that when involved in cases such as these, counselors "go slowly" in considering their scope and competence in the case.

CONCLUSION

By building strong, functional relationships within the team wherein each member understands and augments each of the others' differing roles, the chances for a successful outcome are greatly increased. Working together and not against each other is of utmost importance. Effective communication among the members of the multidisciplinary team is an absolute necessity to ensure the investigation and prosecution process runs smoothly. Although the roles of law enforcement, prosecutors, counselors, and others are quite different in terms of the ways they serve children, adolescents, and their families, it should always be remembered that each of these professionals shares as his or her main goal the desire to ensure that the child or adolescent is safe emotionally, physically, and psychologically.

Working cases involving crimes against children can be a long, emotional-draining, and demanding experience. However, this job is *very rewarding* when individuals work together to achieve the ultimate goal of assisting a child though both the emotional aspects and the legal processes.

DISCUSSION QUESTIONS/PROMPTS

1.   Describe and discuss several ways in which a well-meaning counselor might negatively impact the investigation process
2.   Describe the role a professional counselor plays in helping the team successfully complete a thorough and professional investigation.
3.   Describe and discuss the many differing roles and responsibilities of team members.
4.   In considering the list of dos and do nots provided in this chapter, which ones will be the most challenging for you as a therapist?
5.   What will your assumed role be and how will you handle it when you are part of an investigation and you recognize one or more team members not doing what you believe should be done?

WORKING WITH A PSYCHIATRIST WHILE COUNSELING CHILDREN AND ADOLESCENTS

Ethical, Legal, and Practical Considerations

S. Dean Aslinia, Amir Abbassi, and M. Sarfaraz Khan

INTRODUCTION

Counseling children and adolescents is often a challenging endeavor, as it requires multilevel assessments and a vast knowledge base by mental health professionals. In order to be able to work with such a unique population, it is recommended that the mental health professional not only have completed graduate level training and licensure, which is regulated by a state board of examiners for a specific mental health field, but also possess specific training on how to work with the sensitive nature of these types of clients. It is important to note that ethical standards and legal statutes sometimes differ from one another. It is also crucial for a licensed professional mental health worker to be aware of all the potential pitfalls and risks when working with minors.

Counseling and psychotherapy have been broadly defined by many mental health organizations, all of which focus on the process of talk therapy, which results in the psychological well-being of the client. Legally, all licensed mental health professionals, including Licensed Professional Counselors, Licensed Marriage and Family Therapists, Licensed Clinical Social Workers, Licensed Psychiatrists, Licensed Psychiatric Nurses, and Licensed Psychologists, are all allowed by law to facilitate counseling sessions and provide therapy to minors. Each of these categories of mental health professionals, however, has a different and unique definition for their role under the mental health umbrella. Professional counselors, for instance, are defined by the American Counseling Association as having a particular focus on the counseling process with an emphasis on mental health and psychological and human development principles (2014; Remley & Herlihy, 2016).

To obtain licensure as a professional counselor, a minimum of a master's graduate degree, along with the completion of several thousands of hours of direct and indirect counseling internship, a passage of a state specific jurisprudence, and a national board exam are all required. The specific hours and other requirements may vary from state to state. As an example, the state of Texas requires its Licensed Professional Counselor–Interns to complete 3,000 hours of counseling experience under the direct supervision of a board-approved supervisor, prior to obtaining full licensure.

In contrast, licensed psychiatrists are, as defined by the American Psychiatric Association, professionals whose specialty is to focus on mental illness and the chemical stability of their patients (Remley & Herlihy, 2016). To obtain licensure as a psychiatrist, completion of medical school and a four-year intensive residency in psychiatry and/or neurology is required. Children and adolescent psychiatrists must fulfill an additional two-year fellowship after their residency rotation to gain further expertise in working with and treating children and adolescents.

From a collaborative stance, both of these professionals have a unique, yet powerful influence individually, as well as jointly on their clients and patients. The counseling side of the profession, through its major focus on relationship and rapport building with clients, is able to help with overcoming many long-standing behavioral and mental maladjustments for children and adolescent clients who may otherwise be extremely reluctant to open up to anyone. The psychiatry side of the profession, through its highly specialized focus of symptom management and neurotransmitter and chemical regulation quickly stabilizes patients and their emotions so that they may be able to benefit from counseling services.

This chapter will examine the benefits and potential pitfalls of collaboratively working with a psychiatrist to treat a child or adolescent. Additionally, a useful and practical best practice outlined in this chapter allows for creating a better understanding of the similarities and differences between licensed professional counselors and licensed psychiatrists. Lastly, the authors provide clear expectations to follow during a consultation with a psychiatrist for achieving better collaborative outcomes.

When working with children and adolescents, a focused professional clinical assessment is necessary. During such an assessment and information-gathering session, it is important that the counselor collect the relevant information from the client. Oftentimes this includes, but is not limited to, the patient's chief complaint, a thorough psychosocial and family mental health history, and other necessary psychological assessments. It is additionally just as important to be extremely observant with children and adolescents, as sometimes many of their complaints are, in fact, made through nonverbal communication. For instance, an example of these behavioral and/or nonverbal observable acts are healed or healing cut marks, excessive wrist accessories to cover such lacerations resulting from the self-injurious behaviors, or exaggerated makeup or appearance, such as unusual hair color, longer than normal hair length for boys, or unique hair styles. Although these physical appearances could very well be potential self-expressions of a unique personality, often they carry with them deep meanings of symbolism screaming for help.

Once a counselor has completed such detailed information gathering, and has had the opportunity to clinically assess the child through clarifying and processing of information, the counselor can then move into the treatment plan and intervention phase of the counseling process. When extreme symptoms exist, it becomes necessary to make a recommendation for the child to be further assessed by a psychiatrist prior to completing the treatment-planning phase. Psychiatrists are usually able to alleviate many of the symptoms that cause the child to behaviorally and/or physiologically act out. Assessing and making such referrals can potentially make the process of counseling much more effective and efficient, as the symptom management through potential medication treatment may decrease many of the negative cognitive or behavioral maladjustments the child may be experiencing. Such relief may allow the professional counselor to be able to focus on creating long-term coping and/or management strategies for the child instead of having a focus on crisis management, which may be much more short-lived.

To more clearly illustrate the topic covered in this chapter, the authors, who consist of licensed professional counselor–supervisors and a licensed child and adolescent psychiatrist, present the reader with a case study that they have collaboratively worked on that highlights the need for both of these specialties to closely work together in order to achieve definitive results. During this case study, both specialties must remain ethically and legally engaged to achieve the best standard of care for treating the client. In order to protect the identity and ensure confidentiality of the client, the names and some of the information about this client have been changed.

CASE STUDY

Amanda, a 15-year-old Hispanic female, presented herself with her divorced father to a counseling session. Amanda remained very resistant to wanting to talk about her issues or to receiving any help during the initial counseling assessment session. The father was also very hesitant in sharing detailed information, as he labeled most of his chief complaints about Amanda as "attention-seeking behaviors." He reported those behaviors to include the purple hair his daughter had during the initial session, the excessive ear piercings, the "gothic" and "dark" makeup, and the general appearance of the child, which included painted-on and distressed-looking boots, jeans, and T-shirt. Father reported, "She just needs to stop as she is becoming very annoying."

Several minutes into the session, it was clear that all symptoms, and potential issues, were being downplayed by the father, and the child did not feel any sense of safety or comfort to disclose any of her viewpoints. After the counselor completed the psychosocial history information gathering from the father, revealing a history of bipolar disorder on the father's side and depression and suicide on mother's side, appropriate treatment goals were established in order to begin working individually with the child. It was further recommended that additional psychological assessments and a visit to a child and adolescent psychiatrist be made for further evaluation.

Over the next few weeks, the child began to feel more comfortable with the counselor, and she began to disclose much more information throughout the sessions. Her disclosures included reporting several nonsuicidal self-injurious behaviors, where she had begun cutting her thighs and hips several months ago and had now moved to her wrists. She further disclosed several depressive and eating disorder symptoms, including forcing herself to purge her meals as she sought to lose weight to "fit in" with her friends at school.

A family meeting was subsequently called with the divorced parents to inform them of the severity of the child's maladjustments, and to develop a collaborative long-term treatment plan, which called for an increase in both methods of treatment and involving the services of other mental health professionals. This family meeting revealed even more information as both parents were extremely agitated with one another, were very standoffish, and at points even disrespected one another because of their past relationship together. The child even highlighted in the session, "This is why I have issues, because my parents never stop fighting."

The therapist ultimately informed the parents of the dangers that were looming for the safety of their child, as she had now taken to injure herself in an attempt to numb the internal pains she was experiencing in life, hoping to make those perceived internal pains much more tangible and real. Both parents were resistant to the idea of getting a child and adolescent psychiatrist involved as they both reported, "We don't want our child on medication." Nonetheless, the therapist was able to educate them on the severe dangers facing their child and how a child and adolescent psychiatrist would actually be able to assist in alleviating many of the severe symptoms that were being experienced by their daughter. The psycho-educational process was successful and resulted in the parents accepting to schedule an appointment with a child and adolescent psychiatrist.

During their next visit to the counselor's office, both parents presented to the therapy session, and both were extremely agitated with having visited a psychiatrist. One of their complaints was "why their daughter was prescribed antidepressants and antipsychotic medications." Neither was willing to accept the fact that their daughter had reported to the psychiatrist that she was "hearing voices that were telling her to cut herself" and "to just listen to the voice, and the pain would all go away." The parents expressed their unhappiness and reported they would never go back to the psychiatrist and they were only interested in behavioral approaches. From a professional clinical point of view, it was obvious the child was suffering, but the parents had yet to come to terms with their daughter's severe mental health concerns. Ultimately, after many psycho-educational sessions with the parents, they began to accept that it was necessary for their child to be under the care of a psychiatrist. Following a year of treatment, and one suicide attempt, their daughter was finally able to grasp the vague concept of her depressive disorders, began to become more empowered by increasing her self-confidence and self-worth, and began to turn the corner with her new regimen of psychotropic medications.

Certainly, one of the important processes to highlight in this process was the collaborative effort employed by the counselor and psychiatrist to reach the goals set for the child. However, as one may have concluded, several potential obstacles had to be overcome before the client could benefit from this type of a collaborative process. The authors discuss those obstacles in detail next.

First and foremost, it is important to highlight the need for psycho-educational pieces to be included in the counseling process. If a counselor is not well educated about the topics of psychiatry and/or psychopharmacology, it becomes extremely difficult to realize when and where medication can help. As a result, the Council for Accreditation of Counseling and Related Educational Programs (CACREP) has highlighted the following topic under its assessment section of rules in regards to understanding psychopharmacology in its 2009 Standards for accreditation of graduate programs in counseling.

ASSESSMENT G. Knowledge 4

Understands basic classifications, indications, and contraindications of commonly prescribed psychopharmacological medications so that appropriate referrals can be made for medication evaluations and so that the side effects of such medications can be identified.

One of the biggest areas that professional counselors can help with in this collaborative relationship is setting the tone for what their clients can expect from their visits with the psychiatrist. Often that conversation starts with explaining what the initial evaluation of a psychiatrist consists of, and easing the fear of not having any control over what medications the child is prescribed. Once clients realize that a psychiatrist has a much broader scope of practice than just writing a prescription, they become much more comfortable with making such visits.

Here is an example of how this explanation may look: A child and adolescent psychiatric initial evaluation typically lasts anywhere between 45 minutes and an hour depending on the availability of collateral information from the child's parents, teachers, pediatricians, counselors, lab results, psychological assessments, and so on. During the evaluation process, the psychiatrist's main focus is on family, pregnancy and delivery history, initial development milestones of the child, social and educational experiences and hardships, and any abuse or trauma related experiences. After this thorough evaluation is completed, the psychiatrist recommends potential treatment goals, which may include, but are not limited to, counseling or therapy related services as a first line of treatment, and then subsequent medication treatment strategies, as recommended and set forth by the protocols of the American Psychiatric Association and the Federal Drug Administration. It becomes important to highlight to the parents that any such recommendation by the psychiatrist for medication treatment must have the written consent of the child's parents. This entails that the psychiatrist satisfies any and all of the parents' questions when it comes to the potential side effects and benefits of the medication being recommended. If parents are not satisfied with the information they have received, they can simply refuse to consent for the medication, and the psychiatrist will not provide a prescription. When parents do consent to medication treatment of their child, from time to time the psychiatrist may request lab work and tests to be completed, in order to monitor any potential side effects on the child, for example, metabolic syndrome or weight fluctuations.

The second potential obstacle that may need to be overcome is if the parents continue to be resistant or unwilling to share necessary information with the psychiatrist because of the fear that any such disclosure may result in medication recommendations for the child. In the event that this occurs, it becomes necessary for the professional counselor to communicate through legal and ethical channels, and disclose and provide information to the psychiatrist so that the child's best interests are considered. Obviously, such communication would require the consent of the parents under the federal Health Insurance Portability and Accountability Act of 1996 (HIPAA), which protects the confidentiality and medical records of individuals. The use and need of a HIPAA disclosure form depends on several aspects that need to be discussed.

Several of the HIPAA considerations depend on the type of practice that may be treating a certain individual. For instance, if the counselor is in a solo-private-practice setting, before he or she can disclose any information to a third party or unaffiliated provider, a HIPAA release form is required. On the other hand, if both the counselor and psychiatrist work within the same agency, hospital, clinic, or practice, and so long as the client is well aware of the fact that all treating providers in that facility have access to the patient's files (on a need-to-know basis), then additional HIPAA disclosure forms are not necessary to treat the client. It is important to note that several states have passed additional protective measures and legislative statutes to ensure the confidentiality of protected health information. In fact, some of these rules supersede, and are much more restrictive than, HIPAA requirements. A clear example of this is the state of Texas, where effective September 1, 2012, House Bill (HB) 300 amended many of Texas's health, business, commerce, insurance, and government codes to better ensure the security and privacy of Texans' protected health information. HB300 further added many required trainings to be completed by medical and mental health professionals. As a result, it is recommended that the reader research the specific requirements within the state of his or her professional practice to determine if additional requirements are required to be fulfilled in order to ensure confidentiality of clients prior to consulting with a psychiatrist. While it becomes easy to detect the benefits of a collaborative relationship between a counselor and a psychiatrist, it also becomes easy to detect the potential legal and ethical pitfalls of sharing information when proper consents have not been obtained.

The third obstacle that becomes necessary for professional counselors to understand is that the scope and standard of care often practiced by the psychiatrist may be very different from what the counselor is used to providing his or her clients. This topic may become a source of several counseling sessions where one's clients may need the help of their professional counselor to process the treatment differences. As highlighted earlier, psychiatrists are physicians who have completed a residency in psychiatry and obtained specialty training in matters of the brain, which may include the chemical regulation of emotions. As a result, a follow-up visit with a psychiatrist will always be much shorter than the typical counseling session with a professional counselor. This time difference and the perceived lack of caring on behalf of the psychiatrist may become a point of contention by clients, which may additionally require the knowledge and ability to be able to educate the clients about the differences between the specialties.

To quantify time differences, whereas a typical counseling session may last anywhere from 45 minutes to an hour, the typical follow-up session of a psychiatrist may last a maximum of 20 minutes, unless a crisis has ensued and additional treatment options are required. This creates the need for much more succinct communication between the counselor and psychiatrist, so that the psychiatrist is given the necessary pieces of the assessment and intake to be able to make further medicine treatment plans. This time difference often raises many questions about ethical and legal obligations of psychiatrists to professional counselors. This is where a counselor again needs to be educated and knowledgeable about the standards of care and potential differences between treatment approaches to pass along such information to his or her clients. It might have become clear or make perfect sense why a client, after given a full hour to think, speak, process, and reflect, may feel rushed to have to disclose factual information in 10 to 20 minutes and leave with a prescription in hand. It is, however, recommended that professional counselors encourage their clients to share any of their concerns with their psychiatrists firsthand so that the treating psychiatrist may be able to address the concerns firsthand.

The fourth obstacle that needs to be discussed is that professional counselors need to be careful of the ethical and legal traps of making medical or medicine recommendations. Though as mentioned earlier, it is a standard and requirement for professional counselors to obtain training on the topics of psychopharmacology, counselors need to be extremely careful to not make final recommendations on medication types or needs and defer those considerations to medical professionals, in this case the psychiatrist or, when not available, the primary care physician.

Lastly, an obstacle that is much more broad but has implications for all mental health professionals is on a topic (mentioned earlier) in regard to the consent of parents when it comes to medication treatment. It is an ethical and legal requirement for both parents to consent for their child to be medically treated, and the same is true for any other mental health treatment. With any counseling process, both parents must also consent to their child receiving services, unless one of the following exceptions apply: there is a court order signed by a judge giving sole and independent right to one parent to make such determination as to the medical and mental health treatment of their child, or one parent is deceased and/or incarcerated and no access to that parent exists. If any of these conditions exist, it is recommended that the mental health professional obtain a written statement from the client stating this. Failure to obtain consent from both parents or to be deficient in proving due diligence in an attempt to obtain consent may result in disciplinary action for a mental health professional up to forfeiture of licensure.

In the case of Amanda, the coordination of care and the collaborative relationship that was formed between the professional counselor and psychiatrist helped quickly alleviate many of the distressing symptoms Amanda was experiencing. Taking Amanda out of the realm of imminent danger and chronic crisis mode then allowed the counselor to have a client who was much more attentive, focused, and able to follow cognitive, behavioral, or affective techniques to better her life situations. With the help of this collaborative relationship, the psychiatrist was able to help Amanda stop experiencing hallucinations, decrease her depressive episodes, and finally treat her bulimia, which allowed the counselor to work with her to increase her self-worth and confidence. This helped Amanda develop more effective anxiety- and depressive-coping mechanisms, empowered her to appreciate her unique abilities and perceptions in life, and enabled her to help herself in case her symptoms were to return.

DISCUSSION QUESTIONS/PROMPTS

1. What opinions do you hold in regard to medication and treating children?
2. How would you engage and communicate with a psychiatrist?
3. From an ethical perspective, do you believe providing a team approach with a psychiatrist is most beneficial to a client?
4. Have you checked and obtained all necessary Health Protected Information confidentiality laws in your state?
5. How would you handle a case with Amanda? What do you think could have been done differently or better?

NAVIGATING LEGAL ISSUES AND SERVING YOUR CLIENT

Laurel Clement

A portion of my practice is devoted to representing therapists and helping them to navigate the legal system, whether it be in a courtroom or in front of their licensing board. To see his or her way through the jungle, the therapist needs to be armed with a competent attorney and knowledge of the legal and ethical issues that a therapist can encounter.

The courtroom can be a daunting arena. The vocabulary is different, and the professional norms are confusing. At one moment the attorneys are laughing together, and at another moment they are arguing different sides of the same issue. Where does the therapist stand? Whom should she talk to? How long is this hearing going to take?

Legal cases involving children are ripe for the requirement of therapist testimony. In almost all cases it is better to hear the words of the child from an objective professional, such as the child's therapist, than to submit a child to the rigors of the legal system. Therapists can also be helpful in interpreting the meaning behind the words or actions of a child client. In addition, therapists often participate in the legal system for little or no pay. The benefit of their involvement then is threefold: (1) objective professional, (2) trained professional who can speak for the child, and (3) professional who doesn't cost much. No wonder so many therapists are called to testify!

Instead of waiting until you receive a subpoena to discuss courtroom testimony with your client, there are ways to communicate to your client your preferences regarding your testimony in court in your intake forms.

You can let your client know that if you are subpoenaed to testify regarding your counseling relationship with your client that you will expect reasonable compensation. You can certainly give dollar figures, which should normally be in line with your hourly rates. You should specify all items that you expect to be paid for, including the following: preparation for court; review of the client's file; travel to the courthouse or other location; time spent in a deposition; time spent waiting to testify; and/or time actually testifying.

It is suggested that the provision in your intake be broadly worded regarding your participation in the court case. You do not know who will be requiring you to come to court. It could be your client, your client's spouse, or a governmental body such as Child Protective Services. Be clear that, no matter who is subpoenaing you, the client is expected to pay.

It is important that you know that, generally, the court is not going to take into consideration your arrangement with your client in determining if you were properly subpoenaed. However, if remuneration is ordered by the court, the hourly rate that you and your client agreed to will be used as evidence as to what constitutes reasonable rate of compensation.

In Texas, a subpoena in a civil case is *properly served* if placed in the hands of the therapist by a private process server or constable. A subpoena is *not valid* if it is served on the therapist by fax or certified mail or handed to a receptionist or an office coworker. In addition, *your staff or coworkers should be instructed that they are not to agree to accept a subpoena for you.* Unfortunately, such acceptances often occur in many community agencies and may pose a risk to the confidentiality of the client.

In a criminal case, there are more options for serving a subpoena. This may be due to the fact that the district attorney's office or other governmental body carries much of the cost of criminal subpoenas, so lower cost options are created. *The option of sending the subpoena by certified mail is available if the therapist signs the green card, signifying receipt. Another option is transmitting the subpoena by "electronic address," if the receipt of the subpoena is acknowledged.*

It is strongly suggested that you contact an attorney upon the receipt of a subpoena. The attorney may be able to give you information such as whether the subpoena was properly served, what the subpoena actually requires you to do, the pros and cons of complying with the subpoena, and options for legally avoiding the subpoena.

Working with an attorney can be a costly and confusing partnership. This is a list of dos and do nots when meeting with your attorney:

1. *Do* be honest with your attorney.
2. *Do* ask your attorney to specify who his client is and what the limits of his representation are. You may be the client . . . but if you work for a counseling group or an agency, it may be the agency. The "client" is the person or entity to whom the attorney owes a duty to vigilantly represent. If the client is the agency, then the attorney is focused on representing the interests of the agency. If the therapist works for the agency, the interests of the agency and the therapist will, most likely, be aligned. However, for whatever reason, if the interests are not aligned, then the attorney's duty is owed to the agency.

3. *Do not* give your attorney advice about his marriage or raising his children. (Yes, this has happened to me more than once!)

4. *Do not* tell your attorney what details he needs to know. Let your attorney be the attorney.

5. *Do not* tell your attorney what another attorney suggested that you should do. If you prefer the first attorney's advice—go hire him!

6. *Do* listen to your attorney's questions. *Do not* give your attorney details that he doesn't ask about. This takes up meeting time with the lawyer (of which you will probably be billed) and creates an obstacle to a productive meeting. Most likely, the therapist is trying to be helpful. Allow the attorney to be the professional and direct the meeting. This is my *biggest* frustration when working with therapists!

What are some tips for testifying? What should the therapist say and not say while on the witness stand?

1. *One of the most important things to remember when testifying is that the therapist should not have an emotional stake in the outcome of the court case.* What that means is recognizing that you play a small part in a complicated process. The therapist is only one variable. There are numerous other persons who also have an effect on the court case, and their involvement may not be seen by the therapist. Having a stake in the outcome of the case is the same as having expectations about people you have never met.

2. *The therapist needs to answer the questions that are asked.* It is difficult for me to emphasize how important this tip is. If the attorney asks you if you are wearing pants or a skirt, do not explain your dry cleaning bill to the court!

3. *The therapist needs to remain neutral.* If the therapist decides to testify while trying to promote her own agenda, she will be doing a disservice to herself. The court will see the therapist as uncooperative and/or biased and may be less likely to give weight to her testimony. All too often, counselors tend to try to "help" their way out of their appropriate role!

4. *Don't be afraid to introduce yourself to both attorneys before testifying.* It may help you to "get a feel" for their personal style, and it may allow them to personalize you and to understand that you are trying to be helpful to the process.

5. *Recognize your limited involvement in the case.* Remember that your experience with your client has been in the clinical setting. You have no assurance that what your client has been telling you is true. And the truth that your client has been recounting is the truth according to his or her perspective. You were not out with the police the night that the domestic violence occurred. You were not in the courtroom during the other hearings. And you have not heard from every other witness.

Recently, the legislature enacted Texas Family Code 104.008, which prohibits certain testimony. This provision makes clear that a therapist shall not make any recommendation or suggestion to the court regarding the conservatorship, possession, or access of a child unless the therapist has conducted a child custody evaluation or, as more commonly known, a social study. That means that the therapist can't suggest who the child should live with, how much time the child should spend with each parent, or whether the visitation with the parent should be supervised. A therapist practicing outside of Texas should check state statutes to determine the limits of her role when testifying.

I often get asked to discuss, from a legal perspective, the essentials of therapist documentation. It is understandable that therapists are seeking the "best" way to avoid a confrontation with an attorney while the therapist is on the witness stand. I do not dispute the position that very general note taking may be advantageous when persons are examining your notes or cross-examining you in court. However, I am clear on the fact that the more detailed your notes are, the better your case is when trying to defend against an unfounded accusation in front of the licensing board.

There are several items that are important to document. This is a list of suggestions from the legal standpoint; however, it is not an exhaustive list:

1.   Note the name and/or relationship of other persons who are joining the session.
2.   Note any visible injury that is present on a person in your session; ask the individual about it, and document the response. This documentation may prove important with any future issue of domestic violence.
3.   Note any physical altercation that you witness between the clients, such as shoving, slapping, or hitting.
4.   Note in your client's chart when your client does not appear for a session.
5.   Note any discussion of suicidality and the questions that were asked by the therapist to determine the extent of a plan.

If you receive a complaint from your licensing board, your first step should be to consult with your attorney. The attorney can give you information regarding the timelines of the process and your options for responding. I have been appearing before the Texas boards on behalf of therapists for several years now. Although daunting, an attorney can break down the process for you and make it more manageable.

POINT TO PONDER

I would, generally, say that the complaints before the board can be divided into three subject areas:

1.   Dual relationships;
2.   Confidentiality issues; and
3.   Persons who perceive the therapist to be biased or to not have heard them.

Please note that I said "persons" and not "clients." In the state of Texas, and probably in other states, the licensing board hears complaints from any member of the public, not just clients. What this means is that the arena for persons who make a complaint about your therapeutic license can be the boyfriend, mother, roommate, or anyone having a relationship with the client.

I have heard complaints in the past that the licensing board is not helpful enough to the licensed therapist. Please remember that the board is a governmental body and is operating on a shoestring budget. The board is made up of good people who do recognize and accept their difficult mission of protecting the public from unethical therapists. It is important to recognize that the licensing board does not exist to help the licensed therapists under the auspices of the board. The board exists to protect the public.

What steps can you take to minimize your chances for getting a complaint before your licensing board? With dual relationship and confidentiality issues, knowledge of the umbrella of ethical rules and regulations for your profession is paramount. Consultation with your office mates and peer consultation groups is also a great way to network with other therapists and create a nonjudgmental forum for asking questions about your harder cases. Involvement with a state or local counseling organization can be beneficial in several ways. The organization will often have legal assistance for members, and the organization conducts important and effective advocacy work for their members. The Texas Counseling Association, for instance, provides numerous benefits for its members for a nominal yearly fee.

What is the definition of "dual relationship"?

Because we live in a society where persons wear several hats during the day, the concept of a dual relationship can be a slippery slope. It is important to remember that the counseling relationship is a confidential, therapeutic relationship. If anything is occurring that is other than confidential and other than therapeutic, then the relationship has veered from its original intention. For instance, if you visit your client in the hospital, the questions would be whether the visit was confidential and/or therapeutic. It could be argued that the visit is confidential because your role as a therapist is never disclosed. However, the larger question remains of whether the visit would be therapeutic.

Clients are oftentimes not aware of our ethical duty to remain in a single relationship with the client. Their "waiver" or desire to have a relationship with us other than therapeutic is not a factor that is considered when appropriately defining the relationship.

What can be done to minimize having "persons who perceive the therapist to be biased or to not have heard them"? A few suggestions are the following:

1. *Discuss expectations.* When you are seeing a child client of divorce, ask the parents what their expectations are of you. Are they expecting an update

after every session, or do they only expect an update when asked? When your female client brings her boyfriend in for a session, does he understand that he is not your client? Does he understand that he is a collateral source of information for you to help your client and that you are not focused on his issues?

2. *Reflect your role as a professional.* Whatever you say and do needs to reflect the fact that you are a professional with boundaries. How do you sign your e-mails to your clients? Are you more of a friend than a professional with your client? Do you discuss your own family and friends with your client?

3. *Remember that the person paying the bill is going to feel that he or she has a vested interest in your counseling experience.* If that person is not the client, figure out ways to acknowledge his or her participation within the framework of your ethical guidelines. Can you get a release from your adult client to discuss only the financial portion of your case with the person paying the bill? If your client is a teenager, can you get an agreement in writing between the parents, the teenager, and the therapist about what can be discussed between sessions? This written agreement will help to instill in your client the fact that you respect his or her privacy and reassure the parents that you will disclose, for example, harmful behavior.

4. *If your client is the minor child of divorce, be careful not to show favoritism to one parent or another.* Even if you think one parent is a better parent than the other, remember that your client loves them both and needs both of them to be interested in his or her counseling. Perhaps a good way to minimize the appearance of favoritism is to send joint e-mails. Offer them individual sessions to discuss their child. Try not to have one parent and the child as clients, and one parent as a collateral source for the child. The odd man out is going to find a way to even the playing field.

5. *If the child is the subject to a custody or court order be sure to have a copy of the order in your files.* Be clear about which parent has what rights and discuss those rights with the parents. Let the parents know how those rights affect your role, if at all. If the child is in the legal custody of the state, such as with Child Protective Services, there will be a document signed by the judge that allows the state to direct the rights of the child.

6. *Discuss your role and* **your** *expectations of the client in your intake paperwork.* The intake paperwork is a good place to begin the conversation about your professional role with your client, especially for a person who has not been in a counseling relationship before.

What are some ways to ensure that you do not get a complaint on the basis of confidentiality?

First, be clear about the times and the reasons that you will break confidentiality with your client. Make sure to include that information in your informed consent.

Second, make sure that you keep up with changes in the laws and ethics that pertain to confidentiality. At this time, Texas law requires that when a client requests a copy in writing of his or her counseling file, the request must be fulfilled within 15 days. The only provision for not giving the client timely access to the file is if the professional determines that release of that portion would be harmful to the patient's physical, mental, or emotional health. This is a strict standard and should be reviewed with your attorney or other knowledgeable person within the counseling profession. Counselors in other jurisdictions would be wise to check their state statute to ensure that they are responding appropriately to a request for records.

How does the role of advocate fit into the counseling model? One of the best ways that a therapist can be an advocate for her client is to communicate effectively the diagnosis and needs of her client. Although a counselor may not be able to state to the court which parent should have custody of the minor client, the counselor can describe for the court the child's demeanor when discussing each of his or her parents. The counselor can outline for the court the perception that the child has of the time spent with each of the parents.

While communicating with a minor client's parents, the therapist has an opportunity to describe the activities/methods/experiences that the child has found meaningful and the way to motivate the child.

In addition, teaching self-advocacy skills to clients is viewed as an important role for counselors. Working on the building of self-esteem is a way to empower a client to make needed changes in his or her life. And discussing the client's life from a systems perspective may give him or her information about the specific areas that need to be revised.

The important thing to remember about the counselor's role as an advocate is that the advocacy needs to be congruent with the therapeutic relationship that exists between the counselor and the client. If the activity is not solely within the therapeutic role, then the counselor needs to reconsider the action to be taken. In fact, the American Counseling Association (ACA, 2014) wisely includes the following provision in its code of ethics:

A.7.b. Confidentiality and Advocacy

Counselors obtain client consent prior to engaging in advocacy efforts on behalf of an identifiable client to improve the provision of services and to work toward removal of systemic barriers or obstacles that inhibit client access, growth, and development.

The role of advocate can be congruent or incongruent to the best interests of the clients that we serve.

What about the role of a supervisor? I am occasionally asked to clearly define the role of a person that supervises a Licensed Professional Counselor–Intern (LPC–Intern). As defined in Title 22, Texas Administrative Code 681.93(e), "The full professional responsibility for the counseling activities of an LPC-Intern shall rest with the intern's board-approved supervisor(s)."

What, actually, does that mean? What is the role of the supervisor, and what is the supervisor's legal responsibility concerning his or her intern?

Since the rules of Texas and other states provide a provision whereby the intern and the supervisor are not seeing clients at the same location, the expectation of the supervisor having daily contact with the intern is not delineated. What, then, can the supervisor define as her role? My suggestion is the following: "I am the intern's off-site supervisor who oversees her clinical work to ensure that she is in compliance with the Board rules and ethics." It appears that the legal test of "known or should have known" is applicable in this case. Since the supervisor is not on-site, the information that the supervisor receives comes from limited sources: the intern or, possibly, the site supervisor for the intern. Was the supervisor aware that there were concerns about the performance of the intern? Should the supervisor have seen indications that the supervisor needed to take remedial measures? Did the supervisor communicate sufficiently with the site to determine the effectiveness of the intern?

What is clear are the following guidelines for the role of the supervisor:

1. *The supervisor is not the personal therapist for the intern.*

Certainly, the intern and supervisor can discuss how the intern's issues affect her ability to be a competent therapist. Transference and countertransference are appropriate topics for supervision. However, the supervisor and intern need to be mindful of the line between appropriate topics for supervision and the practice of individual counseling methods between the parties. Part of being an effective supervisor may be in suggesting to the intern that individual counseling for her may be needed.

2. *A supervisor may not be an employee of an LPC–Intern.*

My suggestion, in the same vein, is that the intern should also not be the landlord for the supervisor.

3. *The supervisor is not a "friend" of the intern.*

The avoidance of a dual relationship exists also in the supervision role. Please consult your state's ethics on the requirements of the supervisor. In 2009 the Texas Board held that engaging in "multiple episodes of drinking socially with LPC intern" is reason to discipline the supervisor for having a dual relationship.

4. *A relationship between the supervisor and the LPC–Intern that impairs the supervisor's objective, professional judgment shall be avoided.*

What this guideline means is that a dual relationship should be avoided. For example, the intern should probably not be a previous counseling client of the supervisor. The power differential between the past client and the therapist is fertile ground for a conflict within the new roles of intern and supervisor. Also to be considered is whether there is a preexisting friendship that impairs one party's ability to be objective about the supervision relationship.

5. *The contact between the supervisor and intern should clearly outline the expectations between the two roles.*

Besides the state guidelines, what are the expectations between the parties? Is it anticipated that the sessions will all be individual sessions? Or is the supervisor foreseeing that group supervisions will be included? Perhaps it is best that the fee structure be in writing. In addition, it is probably best to come to an agreement concerning communication with the off-site location and the off-site supervisor. The more that is discussed in the beginning, the less area there is for disagreement in the long run.

POINT TO PONDER

We have seen a fabulous expansion of the methodologies available to the wellness community, including Eye Movement Desensitization and Reprocessing (EMDR), coaching, expressive arts, sand tray, brain spotting, and emotional transformation therapy. The results from these techniques have often been impactful and long lasting. The important thing to remember, however, is that if the therapist holds him- or herself out as a licensed counselor, then the therapist must abide by the rules and regulations of the licensing board. The guidelines of dual relationship, record keeping, and the role of the supervisor must be followed.

It is always important to be familiar with the code of ethics of your licensing board. The code of ethics of your state or national counseling association may differ slightly from the code of your state licensing board. For instance, the *ACA Code of Ethics* (ACA, 2014) allows for limited bartering, whereas the Texas State Board of Examiners of Professional Counselors does not. Please examine below:

A.10.d. Bartering

Counselors may barter only if the relationship is not exploitive or harmful and does not place the counselor in an unfair advantage, if the client requests it, and if such arrangements are an accepted practice among professionals in the community. Counselors consider the cultural implications of bartering and discuss relevant concerns with clients and document such agreements in a clear written contract.

The Texas State Board of Examiners of Professional Counselors, however, prohibits bartering. The wording of their prohibition is as follows:

Texas Administrative Code 681.41(m).

Except as provided by this subchapter, non-therapeutic relationships with clients are prohibited.

(1) A non-therapeutic relationship is any non-counseling activity initiated by either the licensee or client that results in a relationship unrelated to therapy.

Having a relationship that includes customer or consumer clearly is not within the purview of the statute.

With respect to distance counseling, there, again, exists a schism between the code of ethics of the American Counseling Association and that of the Texas licensing board. For instance, the ACA has an entire section of its code devoted to distance counseling. Section H is entitled "Distance Counseling, Technology, and Social Media." It includes the provision that "clients have the freedom to choose whether to use distance counseling, social media, and/or technology within the counseling process." In the code of ethics for the Texas State Board of Examiners of Professional Counselors, distance counseling is defined as follows: "Where the client is a resident of or within the State of Texas and the counselor is licensed by the State of Texas." In other words, the definition encompasses only persons who live in Texas or are within the state of Texas at the time of counseling. It is my understanding that distance counseling can be utilized when either the client is out of state for business or a personal trip and/or when the counselor may be out of the state for business or a personal trip. The statute does not encompass those persons who reside outside of the state. Please check your state statutes and ethics to find out what is permissible with your license.

As technology improves and becomes more commonplace, the profession is likely to encounter even more ethical issues regarding the efficacy and practicality of new technology. For instance, many consumers see distance counseling as a way to increase their choices and decrease their travel. However, the counselor should be mindful of the limitations that distance counseling presents. As counselors we rely a great deal upon our face-to-face contact to reliably evaluate our client: their affect, truthfulness, and presentation. Distance counseling impedes that contact. It is important to consider whether that hurdle will allow you to be an effective counselor for any particular client.

Another factor is the issue of confidentiality. Although the online site may be secure, it is clearly challenging to ensure that the client is in an environment where he or she will not be overheard. One of the largest issues, in terms of liability, is the counselor's ability to be responsive to a crisis of the client when distance counseling is employed. The living situation and knowledge of local resources and law enforcement is much easier when the counselor and the client are in the same area. It would seem that marshaling a crisis plan for an out-of-town client would be very challenging when the resources and landscape are unknown.

DISCUSSION QUESTIONS/PROMPTS

1. As was discussed earlier in this book, counselors are likely to receive a subpoena to appear in court during their career; most likely more than just one. What professional advice was offered in this chapter that will aid you in testifying in court?

2. There were three major issues that seem to get clients and/or other persons calling the licensing board. Discuss these issues and how you can best protect yourself from such concerns.

3. What things should be discussed and communicated with your client up front in order to stave off misunderstandings and potential problems later?

4. The field of counseling relies heavily on the use of supervision. In what ways can the supervisor ensure successful and professional obligations are being met in this process? What is the supervisee's role in this process?

5. This chapter provided examples of what to say/do and what not to say/do when consulting with an attorney. Discuss these issues and describe why they are so important.

TECHNOLOGY

Relevance to Ethics With Minors

Kathryn C. MacCluskie, Stephanie S. J. Drcar, and Darnell L. Robinson

INTRODUCTION

Technology and minors seem to go together as naturally as a hand in a glove. The people who are now minors (digital natives) are experiencing a level of societal technological sophistication, with all the associated benefits and vulnerabilities, never before seen in human history. It's not surprising that the professional and legal standards have been unable to keep pace with the rapid developments in technology. That said, this chapter discussion will focus primarily on two prominent aspects of technology and their relevance to working with children and adults.

The 2014 *ACA Code of Ethics* (American Counseling Association [ACA], 2014) features an entire section devoted to technology, and there are three distinct sections that cover distance counseling, technology in general, and social media. Consistent with the incredible expansion and increased sophistication of electronic devices that enable a variety of forms of communication, the current code offers increased specificity compared to previous versions particularly regarding the technology interface. In preparing this chapter, we became aware of the fact that while the use of technology, and the variety of ways it is being used, is continuing to expand (mental health apps for the personal devices, for example), there is, as yet, relatively scant empirical information about efficacy, and even less information about potential liabilities or case law pertaining specifically to violations of the ethics code.

In this chapter, we will present some operational definitions, provide a little bit of discussion about the ways technology is used in counseling, and then focus on the kinds of information and potential issues a counselor needs to be aware of when using technology in a counseling role. We have divided the technology chapter into two sections: social media and distance counseling (synchronous and asynchronous).

SOCIAL MEDIA

More current social media trends include (but aren't limited to) Facebook, Habbo, Nexopia, Twitter, MySpace, Second Life, Yahoo Chat, IMVD, Snapchat and other virtual formats, personal blogs, podcasts, video share sites, and wikis (Eid & Ward, 2009). Social media has inadvertently created an interactive culture within human relations unknown to previous generations (Belkofer & McNutt, 2011). Social networking has evolved into an everyday trend not to be overlooked (Kessler, 2010).

Anyone who has any contact with people under the age of 25 probably has observed that social media appears to have become a prevalent aspect of contemporary adolescent development. Individuals who are postmillennial are considered to be "digital natives," and they are extremely comfortable and familiar with navigating and remaining current with changes in the popular social media sites. Perhaps the most recent, and pressing, characteristics of counseling work with children and minors is navigating the challenges and dilemmas around social media.

Many of us (authors included) have active lives online on a variety of social media sites. The *ACA Code of Ethics* (ACA, 2014) makes specific recommendations about privacy and boundaries. The concern about online boundaries is bidirectional. Clients might be highly interested in the personal web page and other possible personal information of their therapist. Maintenance of appropriate professional boundaries takes on an even more complex level of diligence and awareness when one has an online presence. Although a counselor may have had a very fun weekend socializing with friends, it is unacceptable for that personal information to be available to that counselor's clients, especially minors. Being "tagged" in pictures of social events, perhaps in compromising situations, is unprofessional and in some cases could be poor modeling. Thus, awareness of things like privacy settings, or use of an alias, takes great importance.

Regardless of our own level of participation in social media, knowledge of common social media sites and applications is often necessary for understanding the world of child and adolescent clients. Child and adolescent clients may discuss social media sites and applications far beyond the familiar Facebook, for example, Snapchat, Tumblr, ask.fm, and Vine. These sites and applications contain a language unique to each, and they bring subtleties to the concerns in our clients' lives. If a teenage client shared with you during her intake session that she spends hours on Instagram looking through "#promia" posts, would you have any understanding of the clinical implications of this? (The # symbol before words denote a "hashtag," which is a way to categorize the content of a social media post so that others interested in that content can easily find posts with similar content. The "promia" hashtag stands for "pro-bulimia" and allows users to find posts related to the endorsement of behaviors associated with bulimia.) If a client lacks a degree of other-awareness, he or she may fail to understand that you may or may not be familiar with the subtleties of his or her social media experiences. Your own familiarity with navigation among the social media sites will be not only helpful, but perhaps even necessary, in your effort to establish credibility and rapport with this teen.

Moving beyond our cursory discussion about social media sites, we must emphasize that general knowledge of the existence of various social media sites and setting one's own social media presence to that of "private" hardly constitutes an adequate effort to understand the changing nature of social media in relation to clinical work. Social media platforms play a critical support role in the lives of child and adolescent clients, especially clients of oppressed status who are able to find connection, support, and information through the Internet. Adolescents who are members of a sexual minority group are frequently the victims of discrimination and bullying; social media sites and groups may be a critical lifeline. Consider, for example, a 14-year-old teenager who is transgender, lives in a small and rural town, and "subscribes" to several channels of transgender teenagers on YouTube. This teen learns about the process and impact of hormone therapies and also utilizes the comments section of the video to ask questions and build friendships with other transgender teens; this could prove to be a life-saving connection for an isolated teenager who has never knowingly met another transgender teen in his or her small town. Connections via social media sites and other Internet sites can provide crucial support and information for child and adolescent clients who otherwise would not have easy access to people who have similar experiences or can provide information related to their lives. The converse is also equally true though; social media websites can provide broader opportunities for the types of harassment and abuse that our clients may experiences in person. The height of harassment and abuse is cyberbullying and sexploitation.

Cyberbullying

We would be remiss in a discussion of technology, ethics, and minors if we did not look at frequently occurring forms of abuse online. Tokunaga (2010) noted that more than 97% of youth are connected to the Internet, and that 20% to 40% of all youths have been victims of cyberbullying at least once in their lives. Moreover, there is evidence that victimization is associated with significant psychosocial, academic, and emotional problems; Hinduja and Patchin (2015) report one of every five middle school or high school students experiences impact from cyberbullying. Some authors (Murray, 2014) contend that therapists need to be especially vigilant for abuses through technology. Radhika (2014) explained that cyberbullying can take the form of gossip, exclusion, impersonation, harassment, cyberstalking, flaming, outing and trickery, and cyberthreats; furthermore, over 150 children have taken their own lives as a direct result of cyberbullying (*bullycide* is the term that has been used to describe this).

Hinduja and Patchin (2015) offer readers the following identifiable warning signs that could indicate either victimization or perpetration of cyberbullying. Warning signs of victimization include a child who

- unexpectedly stops using his or her device
- appears jumpy or nervous while using a device
- appears uneasy about going to school or outside in general
- is oversleeping or not sleeping enough
- appears to be angry, depressed, or frustrated after going online
- becomes abnormally withdrawn from usual friends and family members
- avoids discussions about what they are doing online
- frequently calls or texts from school asking to go home ill
- becomes unusually secretive

In contrast, perpetration of cyberbullying might be occurring if the child

- quickly switches screens or hides the device when adults are nearby
- uses his or her devices at unusual hours of the evening
- gets significantly upset if he or she cannot use a device
- laughs while using a device but refuses to show adults what is funny
- avoids discussions about what he or she is doing online
- is exhibiting more behavioral problems or disciplinary actions at school
- appears to be overly concerned with popularity or continued presence in a particular social circle or status
- is increasingly withdrawn or isolated from the family
        (http://www.cyberbullying.us/cyberbullying-warning-signs.pdf;
        reprinted with permission from the Cyberbullying Research Center)

Because the incidence of cyberbullying is so high, we believe counselors working with minors are ethically bound to have awareness of these warning signs as well as awareness about when and how to intervene.

The relevance of this discussion to the current chapter is to emphasize the reasonable likelihood that adolescent clients will have some exposure to cyberbullying, and counselors need to have some awareness about the legal parameters in their jurisdictions. In terms of the ethical call for technological competence, it is obviously of great importance to know about the myriad forms cyberbullying can take and what the warning signs are, for which counselors, teachers, and parents need to be vigilant.

Online Sexual Exploitation

The online platform is an easily accessible avenue for pedophiles to seduce and victimize children and teens. The National Center for Missing and Exploited Children cites an incidence of one in seven Internet users between the ages of 10 and 17 who fall victim to unwanted online sexual solicitation (Wolak, Mitchell, & Finkelhor, 2006). Unfortunately, this data about online sexual victimization may be a significant underestimate of the true incidence, due to the reluctance children may have to admit they have experienced it, out of either embarrassment or fear that they will be restricted from further Internet usage. Additionally, those authors state that responses to a 2005 survey administered by the National Center for Missing and Exploited Children indicated that 65% of adults and 82% of children had no idea of where or how to report an unwanted online sexual encounter.

There are multiple ways a minor can experience online sexual exploitation; some exploitation will ultimately result in direct contact, while other times it remains indirect and virtual. The fact that a contact is virtual, as opposed to in person, doesn't necessarily make an abusive event less traumatic. Numerous authors (O'Leary & D'Ovidio, 2010; Suler, 2004) referred to online disinhibition; the "facelessness" of cyberspace serving to increase one's perception of anonymity and subsequently reduced inhibitions of previously restrained behavior. Another problem endemic to online exploitation is the fact that it can happen literally anywhere there is a device connected to the Internet.

Murray stated that some clients have a heightened vulnerability for online abuse, especially noting that some sex offenders are very highly skilled at targeting. We found disagreement among authors as to what characteristics would make a child most vulnerable; Murray posited that exploitation victims tend to be kids who struggle to make friends and experience lonesomeness. In contrast, O'Leary and D'Ovidio stated that children who are extroverted and adventurous are far more likely than others to use the Internet as a way to meet new people. This suggests that the specter of potential victimhood is not necessarily easy to discern, and that a great deal more information is needed about the variables of vulnerability and the relationship to the process by which children become victims.

Regardless of those vulnerability factors, the outcome of abuse and exploitation can have long-term psychological effects. When a pedophile is able to obtain contact and then subsequently images of a minor, not only is the minor being abused in that moment, but those images may be circulated to many other sex offenders. Those images may well persist indefinitely, resulting in a child experiencing the abuse as ongoing. The guilt and shame associated with this circumstance has potential to be very highly emotionally, psychologically, and developmentally detrimental to a client.

So what should a counselor do upon discovering that a minor client has experienced sexual abuse online? As mandated reporters, counselors are always advised to first file a report with the children's welfare agency for their state. Additionally, the National Center for Missing and Exploited Children has a website for filing reports at http://www.missingkids.com/cybertipline/.

DISTANCE COUNSELING

Introduction and Definition of Terms

The broad term *distance counseling* is used synonymously with a variety of other terms that appear in the professional literature such as web-counseling, cybercounseling, Internet counseling, e-therapy, e-mail counseling, telehealth, cyberpractice, and life coaching, just to name a few. With the creation of the Internet, computers became capable of sharing information, which then made it possible for users to directly communicate on a global level (Myrick & Sabella, 1995). Such developments within the World Wide Web evolved concurrently with a newfound interest in cyberpractice; hence there emerged the evolution of websites such as PsychNET, Psych Central, Cyber-Psyche, Shrink Link, and On-line Psych (Hannon, 1996). Mental health services have been available online in the form of support groups as early as 1982 (Ainsworth, 2004), but it is impossible to accurately date the inception of distance counseling due to confidentiality.

The term *cybercounseling* in our context refers to a licensed counselor who utilizes technology tools and/or social media to provide therapeutic services with clients who are communicating from remote locations versus traditional face-to-face interactions. These therapeutic services are usually fee based. Distance counseling can be either synchronous (occurring in real time) or asynchronous (delayed time between interactions, e.g., e-mail). Continuous and rapid growth in technology and the consumer computer market has sparked a lot of curiosity toward the practice of cybercounseling. But, that's not to say that all of this newly directed attention has been in celebration of this modality. Critics of this practice have raised some major ethical, legal, and moral issues pertaining to the application, effectiveness, validity, regulation, and standardization (or lack thereof) regarding cybercounseling. This section of the chapter will examine some of the clinical and professional issues being discussed in the profession literature regarding cybercounseling, and we will conclude the section with a presentation of the actual ethics code that pertains to technology.

Many counselors have websites to introduce themselves to the public. On their websites they may provide consumers with any number of different types of information, that range from information on their background, training, and qualifications to information about their treatment strategies, the types of clients they serve, and sometimes links to other information about particular types of concerns or disorders. There is a qualitative difference between the already mentioned static websites that merely provide information for people to consume, and websites that allow for, and encourage, interaction between two individuals. Some practitioners offer professional services (cybercounseling) directly online. The bulk of our discussion on cybercounseling focuses on the provision of interactive professional service.

The *ACA Code of Ethics* (ACA, 2014) is explicit about clear competence in technology being essential to perform ethically in a distance counseling context. Beyond the necessity of technological competence, for example, counselors providing distance counseling are responsible for working with clients in their own jurisdiction. Kraus, Stricker, and Speyer (2010) noted that most malpractice policies only cover liability for services provided in states where the therapist is licensed to practice.

Asynchronous and Synchronous Service Provision

As a basis for comparison, traditional face-to-face counseling is synchronous in nature, that is, the dialogue and interactions occur in real time. Asynchronous interaction, as the name implies, is correspondence between a client and clinician that does not necessarily occur in a simultaneous fashion, that is, there is a delay of time between interactions. Technology readily facilitates asynchronous interaction with the use of computers and personal devices; common forms of asynchronous communication include e-mail and texting. Text messaging (i.e., texting) using mobile phones or other software systems blurs the lines between synchronous and asynchronous clinical services because the recipient can choose to respond in real time or wait between responses and extend a string of conversation over hours and days.

One variable in this form of integrated technology and counseling is whether the asynchronous services are the sole form of communication between client and counselor or if they are an adjunct to in-person clinical services. Grohol (1997) describes *e-therapy* as incorporating the strength and convenience of the Internet to deliver both synchronous *and* asynchronous communication between the client and the counselor. It's important to note, however, that the modality of cybercounseling is neither the same as psychotherapy or psychological counseling to the degree that there's no presumption stated to diagnose and or treat medical or mental disorders (Grohol, 1999). One obvious advantage to cybercounseling is that it can fill a gap in service if a client lives in a geographically remote area or has a specific clinical need for which there are no therapists with that skill set in a reasonable driving distance.

The actual services provided via cybercounseling, regardless of whether they are synchronous or asynchronous, can be separated into two functional categories:

1. *Advice*: The therapist gives one or a few responses to the client regarding a specific inquiry, mainly via e-mail. This format is not a good fit for a client

who suffers from extreme distress or is presenting with extreme problems, for example, suicidal ideations, PTSD, or schizophrenia.

2. *E-therapy*: The therapist and the client develop a relationship that's continuous in nature, that's more in-depth than brief "advice," and that tends to have a longer duration of therapeutic services offered. The communications between the therapist and client tend to be synchronous, because both parties are communicating with each other in real time. There are five major options for conducting e-therapy: e-mail, secure web-based message systems, real-time text exchange (chat), videoconferencing, and voice over Internet providers (Ainsworth, 2000; eTherapy.com, 2001; Sussman, 1998)

E-mail is considered to be the most commonly used method for therapists (in cybercounseling) to communicate with clients (Ainsworth, 2000; Sussman, 1998). E-mail, as well as the other aforementioned electronic and/or web-based communication formats, presents huge confidentiality problems for the client as well as the therapist. Such threats to confidentiality include encryption issues; technical failures, delays, and/or breaks that interrupt or end service; verification of the proper "consenting" parties involved (therapist and client); inability to maintain password protected privacy on one's computer; and the issue of verifying the legitimacy of a consenting parent/guardian in treatment of a minor or a disabled client who has a legal guardian.

If the asynchronous interaction is in fact the only form of communication, there are subsequent questions that must be considered and addressed to ensure ethical practice by the counselor. These issues include the following:

1. What steps have been taken to ensure confidentiality? For example, is e-mail encrypted?
2. Has it been unquestionably verified that the legal guardian has granted informed consent for treatment?

The Internet affords a great degree of anonymity, and in fact for some users, the facelessness of it is very appealing. People might be more disinhibited and disclose things they typically would not disclose in a face-to-face conversation (Suler, 2002). Unfortunately, though, the Internet also makes it more challenging for a therapist to verify the identity of the person with whom they are speaking. The legal implications of this problem become even more magnified when the person is a minor because minors are not permitted to independently consent to treatment. Thus, there are at least two individuals whose true identities should be verified prior to proceeding with counseling. Suler (2001) offered the recommendation of either face-to-face or telephone interviews in the assessment stages of relationship development in a distance counseling arrangement.

3. What is the planned procedure for reporting abuse, neglect, or danger to self or others in the absence of verified accuracy of data? Clearly ensuring safety when your client is not physically in an office is more difficult. Even though it is difficult, however, you are still accountable for these arrangements.

The most glaring example of an ethical concern involving asynchronous service would be a client disclosing imminent threat for harm to him- or herself, and the potential delay in response from the counselor. If a minor e-mailed or texted to a counselor that he was going to head to a bridge to jump in the next hour, it is critically important for the counselor to immediately respond. More to the point, if that client did inflict self-harm or successfully completed a suicide, the counselor could be held at least partially responsible if there was evidence that the client had attempted to reach the counselor.

Clinical Impact Is Also an Aspect of Ethics to Be Considered

If you are offering distance counseling, the *ACA Code of Ethics* (ACA, 2014) identifies the components of your Professional Disclosure and Informed Consent forms that are required, which include your contact information, the wait time clients can expect (if asynchronous), emergency procedures to follow if you are unavailable, and your back-up plan if the planned technology is not feasible at your scheduled time (e.g., power outage, computer malfunction).

There is ample evidence that in face-to-face communication, the preponderance of information is transmitted nonverbally (MacCluskie, 2010). In a counseling session, observing nonverbal behavior (and thus information) might be even more important since the therapist is listening and watching intently for nonverbal clues as the client speaks about emotionally charged topics (Kraus et al., 2010). Thus, from the perspective of process dynamics, one of the biggest disadvantages I (KM) have observed in electronic communication, regardless of whether it is synchronous, is the absence of paraverbal and nonverbal data inherent in the other person's communication, unless the speaker is using emoticons. In a face-to-face counseling session, clients often demonstrate a mismatch between their verbal and nonverbal messages, and a counselor can choose to use a supportive challenge, thereby attempting to bring that discrepancy to the client's attention. With text messaging or e-mails, it can be extremely difficult to discern a mismatch from the other person unless the speaker overtly says he or she feels ambivalent. Unfortunately, the most effective supportive challenges occur when the client appears to be mostly unaware of a mismatch, in which cases the client rarely overtly verbalizes the ambivalent feelings. Those inconsistencies are far more evident in vocal qualities and other nonverbal behaviors. While this is more of a clinical issue than a legal and ethical one, it nevertheless poses a limitation in your ability to effectively implement your clinical skills and as such should be listed as a limitation on a professional disclosure statement.

Relationship development and therapeutic alliance are *always* important in counseling, but perhaps nowhere is it more of a critical concern than in working with adolescents who, by definition, can be disempowered, disenfranchised, and distrustful of adults, particularly adults in authority. Counselors who work regularly with teens and young adults are often aware of the challenges around establishing rapport that can be highly evident, especially in the early stages of counseling. While absence of nonverbal data places a counselor at a disadvantage, this detriment needs to be weighed against the potential benefit to rapport that could be gained by using a modality of interaction with which the adolescent is most comfortable. Hanley (2009) examined the impact of distance counseling upon therapeutic alliance among participants between 11 and 19 years of age in the United Kingdom. The majority of those participants (57%) reported a "medium" amount of rapport, while a minority (17%) experienced "high" rapport, and 23% experienced "low." What remains unclear is the extent to which the online platform is the reason for their perceived alliances; perhaps those participants would have had a "medium" amount of rapport if the counseling were face-to-face.

There are particular clinical indicators with which a client might present that should be considered to be disqualifying characteristics in considering candidacy for online counseling. These indicators include active suicidal ideation; thoughts of harming others; emergency situations in their living arrangements; recent history of suicidal, violent, or abusive behavior; delusions; hallucinations; or active, current substance abuse (Kraus et al., 2010). Again, these indicators take on even greater implications when we consider working with minors. Think about the potential complication of needing to contact a parent or guardian in a traditional emergency, and the possibility of other barriers to getting help when all three individuals (therapist, client, adult) are in separate remote locations.

Professional Organizations and Cybercounseling Standards

Kraus et al. (2010) recommends that in order to competently provide distance counseling, a counselor needs to know the potential, recognize the limits, and inform the clients. Due to the fairly recent emergence of cybercounseling, as well as its national/international growth within the field, the profession of counseling (as a whole) and, more specifically, the organizations that mandate, advocate, and validate ethics, standards, and norms for counselors, are presently playing "catch up" to address the developing concerns/issues related to cybercounseling. There are three major professional organizations specific to the "counseling" mental health profession:

1. The National Board for Certified Counselors (NBCC)
2. The American Counseling Association (ACA)
3. The International Society for Mental Health Online (ISMHO).

ISMHO has led the charge to produce case study research that is stored in a database only accessible to dues-paying members of their organization (accessible at http://www.ismho.org). ISMHO (2000) has also developed the most extensive list of guidelines for cyberpractitioners to date. Further, under the leadership of Martha Ainsworth, an independent web-based guide was developed for consumers known as "Metanoia" (Ainsworth, 1999) to help them more effectively navigate the world of cybercounseling. By logging on to http://www.metanoia.com consumers are able to research practitioner credentials, service fees, options for payment, and credential checks. This option gives clients education and choice of their therapist. Both the NBCC and the ACA, as well, have created guidelines to educate and encourage professional competence and responsibility among cyberpractitioners. The only problem is that while the official *ACA Code of Ethics* (ACA, 2014) standards are legally binding for "licensed counselors," compliance with the ACA, NBCC, and/or ISMHO standards is optional. What that means to the profession of counseling (specifically cybercounseling) is that patient care could be helped or damaged, because the professional standards and ethical guidelines are not in alignment.

It should be noted that there are many providers who have opted to offer their therapeutic services online simply because there is an online demand for their services. Along with the reality of such an acknowledgement lies the fact that some qualified cyberpractitioners have the best therapeutic intentions for their clients, while other cyberpractitioners, exploiters, and unscrupulous individuals place profit and/or personal gain over the therapeutic well-being of their clients. Therefore, it's imperative that we consider the ethical, legal, and moral considerations of cybercounseling.

Ethics and Legalities Related to Cybercounseling

The *ACA Code of Ethics* (ACA, 2014) gives us a comprehensive look at ethical and legal concerns related to the practice of cybercounseling and encompasses similar ethical and legal concerns reflected in the standards of both the National Board of Certified Counselors NBCC (2012) and the International Society for Mental Health Online (1997) as they relate to cybercounseling. Up to this point in the chapter we have discussed, in general, issues related to social media and distance counseling with an eye toward working with minors. As a final section of the chapter, we will look at the *ACA Code of Ethics* (ACA, 2014), Section H: Distance Counseling, Technology and Social Media, and offer some clarifying thoughts to help consolidate your understanding of the legal and ethical concerns related to cybercounseling.

The *ACA Code of Ethics* (ACA, 2014) clearly addresses the following professional list of concerns:

- Legal competency
- Legal statutes

- Consent
- Confidentiality
- Security of records
- Client verification
- Counseling relationships and boundaries
- Client fitness for technology
- Effectiveness of services
- Client access to services
- Communication barriers, that is, face-to-face versus electronic verbal and nonverbal communication cues
- Records security
- Client rights
- Multicultural considerations
- Professional versus private social media usage of the counselor and client social media privacy

It is important to note that the *ACA Code of Ethics* is legally binding for professionally licensed counselors, whereas, standards published for the profession are not legally binding.

H.1. Knowledge and Legal Considerations

H.1.a. Knowledge and Competency: Counselors need to acquire a knowledge of technical and legal issues as they relate to technological usage, and ethical and legal aspects relevant to the usage of social media.

- It's imperative that the counselor in question develops technical understanding of the cyber medium that he or she chooses to utilize, as well as, legal matters related to such usage via training, classes, and so on.

H.1.b. Laws and Statutes: Counselors who engage in cybercounseling may be liable to laws and regulations of both the counselor's practicing location and the residential location of the client. Counselors also are responsible for informing their clients of such laws and how they differ state to state and or internationally.

- Simply put, cybercounselors are responsible to be aware of the laws that govern their practicing states, and the state or international laws or their cyberclients locale.

H.2. Informed Consent and Security

H.2.a. Informed Consent and Disclosure: Clients have "choice" in regards to the use of cybercounseling and or social media/technology. In addition to normal face-to-face client consent procedures; clients should also be informed of the following:

- Credentials of the cybercounselor and the cybercounselor's physical practice location and contact info
- Risks and benefits related to cybercounseling, technology, and or the use of social media
- The vulnerability of technological and or social media failures/malfunctions
- Response times to be expected
- Emergency protocol when the counselor isn't accessible
- Time zone variances
- Language/cultural boundaries that may impact the receipt of services
- Possible denial of insurance coverage/benefits
- Policies social media (e.g., Facebook terms and conditions)

H.2.b. Confidentiality Maintained by the Counselor: Counselors identify limitations of confidentiality as they relate to electronic records and transmissions. And clients are informed of possible authorized/unauthorized access to their records (e.g., colleagues, supervisors, other employees, and/ or IT (information technology employees).

H.2.c. Acknowledgement of Limitations: Counselors inform clients of the potential risks related to confidentiality and the use of technology.

H.2.d. Security: Counselors implement modern/up-to-date encryption standards for their websites and or technological/social media to engage with clients.

H.3. Client Verification: Counselors take steps to verify client identity at the onset and throughout the counseling session.

H.4. Distance Counseling Relationship

H.4.a. Benefits and Limitations: Counselors inform clients of the pros and cons of using cybercounseling, technology, and or social media mediums, for example (but not limited to), IT hardware, telephones, other social media and Internet-based vehicles.

H.4.b. Professional Boundaries in Distance Counseling: Professional relationships between counselors and their clients are emphasized. Boundaries and/or relationship appropriateness regarding the use of technology and social media forms.

H.4.c. Technology-Assisted Services: Counselors make reasonable efforts to ensure clients are technologically competent and capable of using and engaging in social media vehicles relevant to the cybercounseling encounter.

H.4.d. Effectiveness of Services: If and when counseling services are considered to be ineffective by either the counselor or the client, face-to-face counseling options are considered. If geographical boundaries pose an issue, the cybercounselor will help the client to find appropriate services.

H.4.e. Access: Counselors equip clients with info regarding reasonable access to important apps for tech-related services.

H.4.f. Communication Differences in Electronic Media: Counselors acknowledge the differences of face-to-face versus electronic communications of both verbal and nonverbal cues.

H.5. Records and Web Maintenance

H.5.a. Records: Counselors maintain digital records in accordance with governing laws and statutes, and inform clients on the manner in which such data is stored and preserved digitally, including, but not limited to encryption method, and security measures in place.

H.5.b. Client Rights: Counselors who provide a professional website also provide links to professional credential boards to promote client rights and address ethical matters.

H.5.c. Electronic Links: Counselors routinely check electronic links and ensure their appropriateness.

H.5.d. Multicultural and Disability Considerations: Counselors with active websites offer accessibility to those clients with disabilities, and offer translation capabilities to those clients who speak a different primary language (when possible).

H.6. Social Media

H.6.a. Virtual Professional Presence: When counselors opt to have professional and personal existence on social media use, the professional and personal social activity should be clearly separate and distinguishable.

Hw.6.b. Social Media as Part of Informed Consent: Clients are clearly informed of the pros, cons and boundaries of using social media; by the counselor during the informed consent procedure.

H.6.c. Client Virtual Presence: Counselors acknowledge the privacy of their clients' social media activity, except if permission is granted to view such social media activity.

H.6.d. Use of Public Social Media: Counselors exercise caution to avoid displaying personal info via public social media.

(Based on the ACA Code of Ethics [ACA, ©2014].
American Counseling Association. Reprinted with permission.
No further reproduction authorized without written permission
from the American Counseling Association.)

CONCLUSION

This chapter has covered the aspects of counseling with minors as technology pertains to that work. Like so many other aspects of technological development, social media, cybercounseling, and hybridized forms of service delivery using technology offer an elegant solution to challenges in service delivery while simultaneously clearly presenting a minefield of liabilities and highly complex concerns around boundaries and professional responsibility. In this chapter, we have tried to give readers both an overview of the state of affairs in the field with regard to professional standards and an awareness of the types of issues with which they need be concerned as they embark on their infusion of technology in the context of clinical work with minors. Because technology is continuing to develop and unfold at an exponential rate, it is critically important that counselors make every effort to remain current with regard to how standards and laws are evolving in this realm.

DISCUSSION QUESTIONS/PROMPTS

1. What proactive steps should counselors take to ensure that cybersecurity measures are reasonably implemented to secure client confidentiality?
2. What types of "client" presenting issues could potentially be too hazardous for the scope of cybercounseling? What ethical and legal issues might the counselor face in this type of scenario? Could the counselor in question be potentially legally liable?
3. Cyberbullying may "look different" than traditional bullying that occurs in real-life interactions; however, it can be just as harmful to children and youth. As a counselor, how might you respond if you learned that your 13-year-old client was receiving upwards of 50 harassing text messages a day from classmates that contained messages that called your client a variety of upsetting names? How might your response differ if this harassment was only occurring in real life (i.e., in the hallways between classes, before and after school)?
4. Imagine that you are working with a teen client whose friend has informed you that the client is talking about suicide on his Facebook page. When you ask him about it in your session, he flatly denies it. You could easily go on his Facebook page in session in order to challenge his denial. What should you do?
5. Do you agree that cybercounseling is a good option for people seeking services? Considering limits of confidentiality, particularly with minors, how would you structure and screen potential minor clients and their parents before taking them as clients?
6. The 2014 *ACA Code of Ethics* (ACA, 2014) provides increased specificity and guidance related to technological ethical concerns; however, given that

advances in technology will outpace the future revisions to the code, it will likely be more difficult to apply current guidelines to future technological concerns. What future technological advances do you anticipate will provide ethical challenges with your clinical work with children/adolescents and how do current code guidelines apply to these future challenges?

7.   The *ACA Code of Ethics* is very explicit about the necessity of staying current with technology. When a counselor either has a heavy caseload of children and adolescents, or has children of his or her own, this currency is somewhat easier to maintain. What suggestions would you give to a colleague who only sees minors occasionally and does not have children or regular contact with minors outside of work?

THE IMPORTANCE OF NETWORKING/WEBBING

Salene J. Cowher

INTRODUCTION

The role of the school counselor, which revolves around providing services for an underage population within the school setting, is unique and can be somewhat daunting. Since the United States constitution gives significant control to states, each state constitution in turn plays a pivotal part in determining job roles and functions for school counselors. The American School Counselor Association (ASCA) has established standards for best practice among school counselors. This effort by school counselors' professional organization has helped to ensure consistency across school settings; but ultimate jurisdiction rests with state and local governments (as primarily represented through school boards).

Within this unique role, the school counselor must work to fulfill the needs of students at the school. Although a plethora of materials dealing with the "fundamentals" associated with various developmental frameworks exist, special challenges emerge that confound developmental schemata, such as those stemming from *DSM (Diagnostic and Statistical Manual)* diagnoses; abuse and neglect; ethnic, racial, gender, and diversity issues. As an ethical professional, the school counselor must recognize his or her professional limitations and refer, as appropriate, within the parameters established by the context in which he or she functions—school-wise, board-wise, state-wise, and so on. Of paramount importance, of course, are the needs of the students.

"Networking" with agencies (example: protective services), professional organizations (example: American Counseling Association), special interest organizations (example: National Alliance for the Mentally Ill), professional specialists (example: psychiatrists), and other professionals in and outside the field of school counseling can provide a stronger foundation for addressing the challenges that student issues present. A significant challenge, however, may lie in determining which contacts to use under what circumstances. The more appropriate pathway for referral may involve "webbing" with various resources.

For example, established protocols may mandate reporting suspected child abuse and neglect to a protective service and/or law enforcement agency, depending upon prescribed dictates. The school counselor should still be aware of service limitations and seek guidance, refer, and/or mentor from a strongly established "web." Rather than describe this process as "networking," a more appropriate depiction may be "webbing" since the primary challenge is to address the unique needs of the individual child.

Counselors working within clinical settings should also be aware of resources available to them. Again, established protocols are vital; however, no one agency can provide for every potential need. For example, I have frequently responded to queries from potential clients and mentored clinicians in my work with eating disorders and image disturbances. One agency, in particular, often refers clients to my practice, even though the nature of their work is fairly comprehensive in scope.

WEBBING RESOURCES: SKILLS, COMPETENCE, SCOPE, COMMUNITY, WILLINGNESS TO HELP

Counselors should weave a web of resources—and be willing to feel caught up in that web—in order to address student/client needs. Factors to be considered in developing a resource web include availability of services, skill levels within the resource, competence, scope of practice, community politics and expectations, and (very importantly) the willingness to help. I have found it useful to occasionally consult with professional organizations and advocacy-inspired groups at the national level when trying to determine how to effectively utilize my resources. Their responses have often caused me to reexamine and refine my "web."

Several years ago, I reported/supported other reports to protective services for a young girl. Information I had received from her school and other professionals who had provided assessments and counseled her left it unclear to me how I should respond to a gut feeling I had about sexual abuse and follow-up with legal advocacy. Protective services had provided an immediate response, but I was concerned about her ongoing safety.

Finally, I telephoned RAINN (Rape, Abuse and Incest National Network). Speaking to an advocate there about details of the case further underscored the importance of legal advocacy for the child as the victim of a crime. My resource web included one victims' advocacy group in my office area. They provided me with helpful information and counsel beyond what I had anticipated. The webbing with RAINN and victims' advocacy proved helpful in determining how to proceed.

In regard to this case, the girl's home was located in an underserviced area. There were no victims' advocacy groups in her community; but through the advice and counsel of victims' advocacy in my own locale, I was able to appropriately link with the court system in her area. The lack of services in a child's immediate jurisdictional area should not prohibit the counselor from continuing to seek appropriate support and advocacy.

Professional organizations (American Counseling Association, American Mental Health Counselors Association, American School Counselor Association, etc.), credentialing boards, and even professional liability insurance carriers can provide assistance. These groups typically mentor and guide members. Accessing information through these entities can assist in determining skills and competence levels, scope of practice, and expertise of professionals within agencies and those who practice privately. Even so, the counselor needs to personally familiarize himself or herself with resources.

Although there are many examples from my own experience, one that comes to mind involved a highly publicized case involving sexual abuse. Without providing too much identifying detail, I had been asked to assist in determining the perpetrator of sexual abuse involving a pre-language child. Since I did not have direct access to the child, I interviewed service providers who had worked with her. All of the providers had been technically "qualified" to conduct critical assessments with potential assailants; however, a review of their reports proved too superficial to be of assistance.

After leafing through reams of case history, buried within the first few allegations with another child, I found an exceptionally thoughtful assessment and well-written synopsis. This professional became entangled in my resource web.

Although an agency may have a list of professionals who seem equally well qualified, that is typically not the case. This psychologist specializes in working with children and adolescents. Presumably, her expertise would not lie solely with dynamics/issues related to sexual abuse. On the other hand, I haven't reviewed other assessments she has conducted. If I were seeking someone who could screen for opioid addiction, for example, enlisting the assistance of a drug and alcohol professional might be considered. There are also assessments I could conduct but would prefer at least one other opinion to further substantiate or detract from my findings.

Critical resources within a resource web should include those who can assist in reinforcing/challenging one's own work, as well as professionals who can mentor and provide a "sounding board." In addition to providing feedback and professional support, these resources can also prove to be vital to our self-care. Compassion/caregiver fatigue (née "burnout") is a very real dilemma for counselors.

When the term *burnout* was popular, I facilitated workshops on burnout prevention. The adage we used was: You can't burn out unless you've been on fire. Many counselors begin their careers wanting to make a real difference in the world—a noble goal; that gung-ho spirit is energizing. When the day-to-day frustrations of working within the helping professions begin to mount, however, it is easy to experience an energy loss and increasing sense of hopelessness. If you find a supportive resource person who empathizes and lifts your spirits when the going gets tough, definitely adhere them to your web.

In discussing resources to assist with self-care, there are others who can help: clergy, life coaches, family, and friends. Having cheerleader types is fine. My experience is that—however well intended—those who can't relate to my profession are less helpful for self-care needs emerging from my role as a counselor. Luckily, these folks never seem to get tired of me when I begin to whine (and I can whine a lot)!

As a former counselor educator and graduate professor emeritus, I sometimes find myself cast as an "expert." Even so, having resource professionals who function as sounding boards for me is crucial. A counselor may find himself or herself in a similar position because of expertise or circumstance. For example, school counselors in remote rural areas may find community members expecting a broader skill set and scope of expertise than they (counselors) can legitimately provide. On the other hand, counselors want to be responsive to the need for services.

WORKING WITH UNDERSERVICED POPULATIONS

Reaching out to others via organizational involvement can be helpful. Soliciting the guidance of former professors from the field can also help. Because of remote isolation and the scarcity of service providers close to a rural school, appropriate referral and subsequent compliance may be more challenging for the school counselor. Developing trust and rapport with members of the community is vital to successful service provision and referral. Depending upon the area, linking with pastors and pastoral counselors may be useful. If there is an active agricultural community, connecting with groups such as 4-H and fair/carnival committees may provide a way to normalize and allay concerns, especially regarding referral.

As example, I directed a grant-funded program for rural high school students for several years. The primary goal of this effort was to encourage rural youth to finish high school and continue their education at the postsecondary level. Several other professors, graduate students, and undergraduate students, and a myriad of other university personnel, community members, and special guests contributed to making this a highly successful endeavor. Initially, however, only schools in a handful of rural counties were targeted—primarily through contacts with school counselors and their principals. Once our planning team began publicizing the effort at fairs and carnivals (I can't remember who suggested this, but it was a great idea), we were receiving telephone inquiries from school counselors in other outlying counties. We were also hearing from parents and students, as well, asking if they could participate.

Another observation from this initiative in regard to "normalizing" the idea of referral emerged during work with students in theme-focused groups. Although the theme might have been linked to career planning, once trust and rapport developed, students readily suggested that we include more sensitive topics, such as family violence, homelessness, and spirituality. Unfortunately, our time frame did not allow for more extensive processing with many of the students who wanted to share deeply personal concerns. We did, however, relay these concerns and issues to their school counselors, who—hopefully—welcomed this unique opportunity for direct service and referral. Thus, the web expands.

From this example, there is an allusion to the importance of recognizing when an opportunity exists and a subsequent willingness to respond or help. Obviously, the counselor must have the desire to create a resource web, or the point is moot. Even with such a desire, though, some potential resources may simply be unwilling to respond—or, to respond in a helpful manner.

There may be a number of reasons that a potential resource is unwilling to respond or is not helpful in response. Unless the counselor must analyze and dissect those reasons (i.e., because of a mandate or protocol), I recommend exclusion of the resource. Determining that the resource should be excluded, of course, can be difficult. For example, let's say that you start a new job and are immediately approached by an overly friendly person who is ready to "spill the beans" on your coworkers. It can be tempting to "jump aboard the gossip train." Being new—and vulnerable—connecting with such an "in-the-know" person can seem reassuring. But is it? The person may truly have information about everyone, but is it helpful information for you—at least, at this point—as a newbie? One of the mottoes that I embrace is that "forewarned is forearmed"; but, in this context, I'm not so sure that the intent of the resource is really to help.

Sometimes, an initial effort at contacting a potential resource proves fruitless. Perhaps the person was unavailable or unfriendly. First impressions are important, but second chances may be vital, too. My first impression of the professor who became my doctoral (and dissertation) adviser was negative. He seemed large and a little pompous (if you are reading this, Joe, remember that my impression changed!). As a newbie who felt small and vulnerable, my own anxieties had initially strongly influenced my impression. After taking a (required) individualized study on a theoretical topic of my choice (existentialism/death and dying), I experienced him very differently; he entered my resource web.

A final example comes from having worked with those who have rich experiences and a wealth of expertise but simply won't help. Maybe they are victims of caregiver fatigue or maybe they feel like victims, in general. Maybe there's another reason. In the end, it may not matter for my resource web because they won't be included.

I have worked with people in situations where I tried desperately to siphon off some of what I knew to be their strong knowledge base—to no avail. In one case, the closest I got to developing rapport with a learning support expert was that I got him to talk about his model train collection. In another situation with a vocational counseling expert, she talked about her postretirement interest in starting a housecleaning service. An expert in Asperger's disorder talked incessantly about his golf game. Need I say more? None of these individuals jumped into my web.

Although I have provided recommendations for developing a resource web, it is not to imply that a mistake was made if a resource proves to be ineffectual. In my opinion, as long as the counselor follows prescribed/mandated protocols, there can be no real mistakes when developing a resource web. In fact, the likelihood of actually making a mistake is greatly enhanced when a counselor acts without the foundation of having a strong web of resources.

MANAGING RISK

In regard to making mistakes that may be problematic, counselors should not rely solely upon liability protection from the agency/institution where they work. Legal counsel provides protection for the agency, rather than the individual employee. If there is a unionized environment, legal/ethical counsel may be available through that means. Professional counselors should always consider purchasing professional liability insurance of their own in order to manage potential risk. As members of professional organizations, such as ACA (American Counseling Association) and ASCA, and through credentialing boards, such as NBCC (National Board of Certified Counselors), liability insurance can be procured at a reasonable cost. There are also private insurers that provide liability insurance for counselors.

The insurance group through which I have my policy publishes regular online and print newsletters and updates that include real cases with ethical and legal issues outlined. Outcomes from these areas are also provided. In a recent issue, for example, the counselor's liability stemmed from an ethical dilemma regarding confidentiality and informed consent. The counselor was being sued for $175,000 with legal costs in excess of $15,000. Luckily, he had liability insurance as part of his risk management plan.

Risk management when counseling underage populations can, of course, be complicated. For example, counselors may be aware of the need for parental/guardian consent, but if the parents are not living together, accessing the most recent custody agreement is crucial. In cases where the child has been in and out of the home—maybe even with parental rights at issue—the counselor may want to consult with resources involved in those processes. Protective services contact in this situation is obvious; however, there may also be a group, such as CASA (Court-Appointed Special Advocates), working with the child, protective services, and the courts. CASA works independently as an advocate in the best interests of the child, which can result in dissolution of parental rights and adoption. In this instance, then, in addition to dealing with child protective services personnel, contact with CASA resources might prove helpful. The school counselor especially needs to be aware of any changes in family structure; the more resources within the web, the more likely that information will be thorough and up-to-date. Thus, the counselor can react appropriately.

Contemporary life can present complex challenges, and counselors function within that increasingly litigious world. Even when discussing a child's case with a resource professional, there may be dilemmas about technological means for communication. For example, should the counselor use the telephone (landline, cell; text, talk), Internet (e-mail, social network, Skype), etc. Ethical guidelines continue to evolve in regard to the rapid growth of internet and subsequent issues. When seeking advice from my own resources, I frequently use e-mail with generic inquiries. If I am delving into specific details, I definitely prefer landline telephone communications because of the legal protections afforded that modality. I also find the personal dialogue helpful for my own processing. My strong recommendation regarding communications, documentation, and so on is to remain abreast of constantly evolving ethical (i.e., ACA) and legal (i.e., Health Insurance Portability and Accountability Act) guidelines. Review samples provided online and in print when developing or updating material you are using. Remember that you are expected to know what to do because you are the professional!

WORKING WITH DUAL RELATIONSHIPS

A former student, now in private practice, became active in an advocacy group. (To protect the former student's identity, I have changed some details.) He was married to an attorney who practiced in the same locality. He had been advocating for dissolution of parental rights in a case through this organization. Before the case was resolved, he discovered that his wife was representing the parents in court. In order to avoid any ethical/legal complications (and fearing repercussion from his wife), he opted to separate completely from the case and even exited his membership in the advocacy group. The case was turned over to another advocate. Thus, his "solution" to an ethical dilemma was avoidance (escape?).

What if an event occurs with someone you know or who is close to you? Because counselors typically have a broad scope of involvement and personal lives of their own, they can find themselves needing to contact resources for personal reasons that involve children. Dual relationship issues and conflicts of interest are delineated in the ethics code, and counselors are often advised to avoid these situations. In real life, however, abstinence isn't always possible.

For example, a counselor is mandated to report suspected child abuse and neglect. The counselor attends a family function and witnesses harm to a child to whom he or she is related. That relationship may even be a loving one. Clearly, the counselor must report the abuse. But, does he or she report as a mandated reporter? Loving relative? When case follow-up ensues and counselor/resource professionals meet face-to-face, how does their exchange impact professional perceptions then and potentially with other cases, later on?

I discussed this issue with ethics and legal representatives from ACA a few years ago and found that this scenario actually represented a common dilemma for counselors. Although ACA did not pretend to posit a global, easy answer, their reply underscored the following:

• The counselor does not absent his or her role as a mandated reporter because a victim is known.
• Morally, if not ethically, a victim known to the counselor is entitled to the same services and consideration as anyone else (maybe more so, morally).
• Because of ties to the victim's family, the counselor may want to report with anonymity.
• Subsequent meetings with professional resources regarding this victimization should be kept completely separate from any other case involvement.
• As members of ACA, counselors are entitled to free consultation with ethics and legal experts employed by ACA, as well as support and mentorship.

What I found to be most helpful and reassuring during this exchange was the organization's willingness to support and mentor. Representatives did not simply parrot back language from the ethics code; rather, they really wanted to help. We don't always view professional organizations from this perspective.

WORKING WITH YOUR WEB AND REMEMBERING YOUR ETHICS

Of course, the information I have presented here is not intended to be all-inclusive and set in stone. Clearly recognize that the counselor's resource web should be constantly changing—expanding and contracting—depending upon client needs and as resources are added and deleted. A child coming from another culture may necessitate a very specialized resource being added to your web, and an accompanying change in how you provide direct service. Even provision of a fairly "typical" topic may necessitate consultation and change in counselor service delivery, for example, responding to a parent's concern that you are practicing white magic when you use progressive relaxation tapes (yes, this happened to me). Be open to possibilities and seek out those who can help.

Ethical principles provide a framework for professional counselors to attain and maintain consistent and (ideally) high standards of practice. These standards are developed through professional organizations, such as the American Counseling Association and American School Counselors Association. Through the effective incorporation of ethical standards, children across schools, settings, and communities can all receive equally high-level service. In order to optimize effort in an ethically sound manner, a counselor needs to engage resources that augment and support his or her efforts. That engagement should be as thorough and comprehensive as possible.

Working with underage populations presents special challenges to counselors who must focus primarily on client needs, while also constantly and professionally honoring the legal rights and responsibilities of parents and guardians under whose care those clients reside. Ideally, a collaborative relationship exists with parents and guardians; however, the counselor must also be cognizant of exceptions and advocate in the best interests of the children.

School counselors, in particular, may be expected to serve from a broader community perspective, especially in underserviced areas. These counselors may need to broaden their resource webs to include community members who can assist, especially with appropriate referral. Maintaining a community presence is vital.

Counselors should refer to ethical principles regularly, making sure that they understand and recognize the intent of these standards and potential legal/practice implications. Procuring and using professional resources to assist, clarify, and support their efforts will maximize success and minimize problematic "mistakes."

Counselors function in the world, which necessitates awareness of a greater complexity. As a result, they should be prepared for risk at both the professional (i.e., carrying professional liability insurance) and personal (i.e., exercising adequate self-care) levels. Maintaining high ethical standards will not guarantee that the counselor will never face a challenge, but it will evidence best practice for the children we serve. Doesn't every child deserve that effort?

DISCUSSION QUESTIONS/PROMPTS

1. What resources might need to be included in a school counselor's web when a group of non-English-speaking children arrive at school from another country?
2. What resources might be needed when working with a child who recently lost a military parent who had been fighting overseas?
3. What resources have you used to assist with your own self-care? Have these been adequate? Explain.

4. What resources should I have utilized in dealing with the parent who thought I was practicing white magic with her child when using relaxation tapes? In your opinion, should I have continued to use the tapes? Explain.

5. There are certainly examples of resources beyond those I have provided. What are some examples? How might your examples be used by an ethical counselor?

RESOURCES FOR WHICH PREVIOUS CITATIONS MAY NOT HAVE BEEN PROVIDED

RAINN: www.rainn.org; 1-800-656-HOPE; 1220 L Street NW, Suite 505, Washington, DC 20005

CASA: www.casaforchildren.org; 1-800-628-3233; 529 14th Street NW, Suite 420, Washington, DC 20045

CHALLENGING CASES

Teri Ann Sartor

INTRODUCTION

Counselors who work with children face many ethical dilemmas with a multitude of possible actions. The purpose of this chapter is to apply information presented in previous chapters and determine what may be possible courses of action for situations a counselor may encounter when working with child or adolescent clients. A case scenario will be described for analysis; it should be noted the scenario is based off previous cases and case law. Following the scenario, questions for consideration and the findings and/or rulings of the actual case will be discussed. As you read the case scenarios, be sure to utilize Sartor and McHenry's (unpublished) Ethical Decision Making Model for Children and Adolescents and the virtue ethics of veracity, fidelity, authenticity, justice, and non-maleficence to determine what you as a counselor should do differently.

For your reference, Sartor and McHenry's Ethical Decision Making Model for Children and Adolescents is outlined next:

1. Determine the ethical dilemma
2. Evaluate how the dilemma can impact the child–parent relationship.
3. Evaluate how the dilemma can impact the child–therapist relationship.
4. Consider and determine how relevant ethical codes and theories (especially developmental) impact the possible directions.
5. Review similar court cases and rulings in your state and nationally.
6. Consult with other professional counselors.
7. Create a plan.

8. Follow through with the plan and continuously reevaluate potential relationship concerns.
9. Revise plan when needed, and repeat Step 8.

Counselors must note that not every possible situation a child and adolescent counselor may face is included in this chapter, and the cases provided are more related to recent trends in counseling. If you are struggling or contemplating the best possible action for a particular case, it is suggested you search for relevant cases that closely fit the current ethical dilemma. Counselors and other professionals do have free resources available for searches, for example, http://law.justia.com and http://caselaw.findlaw.com. Because a search must be used to find relevant cases relating to counseling children and adolescents, counselors should be mindful that attorneys are also sometimes referred to as "counselor" in the documents. Thus, mental health counselors should pay attention to detail and the context in which the counselor is being referred.

CASE 1: THE ELEMENTARY COUNSELOR

Mrs. James has been employed as an elementary counselor for approximately six years. The school is in a neighborhood of higher socioeconomic status. Mrs. James loves her job and helping children. She prides herself on being seen as approachable and fun loving by her students. Mr. Smith, the high school counselor, is considered the lead counselor for the school district; he has been employed with the school district for approximately 20 years. When Mrs. James experiences difficulties with students or is unsure of how to help a student she contacts Mr. Smith for consultation and supervision.

At the beginning of the school year, a third grader, Sally Ruth, approached Mrs. James. Sally Ruth comes from a well-known and model family in the community. She informed Mrs. James that her father would often walk around the house after showers without a towel. Previous to this disclosure, many teachers had told Mrs. James that Sally Ruth had often lied about happenings at school and been known to fabricate outrageous stories, so Mrs. James was hesitant to believe Sally Ruth's statement. This story was reported to Mrs. James three additional times. Additionally, not long after the fourth time, Sally Ruth reported inappropriate touching had occurred during a playful wrestling match between her father and other sibling. Mrs. James remained hesitant to believe these stories due to the previously mentioned experiences of other teachers with Sally Ruth and because the family was prominent in the community. On many levels for Mrs. James, the story just simply did not fit.

After winter break when Sally Ruth returned to school, she informed Mrs. James of an additional incident in which she walked in on her father masturbating where he subsequently asked her to participate in this activity. Through additional interactions with Sally Ruth, Mrs. James had noticed she had a tendency to "stretch the truth," so she decided to give Sally Ruth some advice on what to do about this situation. Mrs. James informed Sally Ruth, to speak to her mother about this event and ask her father to cover up and be more discrete about his activities.

Because of Sally Ruth's frequent claims, Mrs. James decided to consult with Mr. Smith; both agreed that Sally Ruth had fabricated the accusation reported after winter break and decided Mrs. James should speak with the parents to discuss the allegations she had made. During the conversation with her parents, they noted the allegations reported prior to winter break were true, and steps were taken to remedy the situation. Both parents denied the incident that was reported after winter break.

To ensure the situation was corrected, Mrs. James monitored the situation closely by speaking to Sally Ruth on a daily basis. Sally Ruth began reporting daily her father was now wearing a robe around the house.

Questions:

1. What is the ethical dilemma and what would the ethical decision making model look like?
2. What steps did Mrs. James/Mr. Smith take to ensure the safety of Sally Ruth? Should Mrs. James have done something in addition to what she did? If so, what should she have done?
3. If anything, what did Mrs. James do correctly/incorrectly?
4. If you were Mrs. James what would you see as the potential outcomes of this situation?
5. If you were Mr. Smith, how would you supervise Mrs. James?

Analysis of the Elementary School Counselor

The preceding case scenario mirrors the beginnings of *Hughes v. Stanley County School District* (Supreme Court of South Dakota, 2001). While this case was not finalized until 2001, the situation in this case began to take shape in the fall of 1994.

The ethical issue in this case is the failure of the school counselor (Hughes) to report child abuse. In South Dakota and throughout the rest of the United States, counselors and other professionals must report when abuse is suspected. Remember, this law does not indicate abuse must be reported when it is *confirmed*—it must be reported when *suspected*. Despite the possibility of abuse occurring in the home, the school counselor failed to report the possible abuse! In this specific case, the school district also had a policy about reporting abuse—thus, Hughes could be terminated as a result of the failure to report along with being prosecuted for failure to report. Hughes did choose to consult with one other counselor, but the concern that exists with this case lies with the person Hughes chose to consult with. This is a prime example of why it is necessary to *always* consult with one or more trusted counselors.

Afterthoughts

Hindsight is usually 20/20. As counselors, we have a small window of time to report suspected cases of child abuse. In this case, the child reported the abuse on several occasions, but it was dismissed due to her tendency to exaggerate or stretch the truth. Remember, it is not the counselor's job to do the investigation nor does the counselor have the credentials to decide if the incident occurred or did not occur. All claims of child abuse, verbal or nonverbal, must be taken seriously.

CASE 2: AN ADOLESCENT COUNSELOR AND CONFLICTS WITH CLIENTS/EMPLOYER

John is a licensed marriage and family therapist with approximately seven years of experience postgraduation from the local theological seminary. After he obtained full licensure as a marriage and family therapist, he accepted a position as an adolescent counselor at the local medical center.

The medical center provided many opportunities and a wide variety of experiences, specialty areas, and promotion opportunities for counselors. Counselors employed by the center could work with young children, adolescents, families, Employee Assistance Programs (EAP), pastoral services, and so on. After 2 years of working with adolescents, John was excited when he was given the opportunity to become the lead counselor of the adolescent unit.

John enjoyed this additional responsibility and felt as if he could build a strong rapport with the vast majority of his clients, and his training provided him with the necessary knowledge and skills to assist them in coping and resolving their difficulties. Everything was going well for John until he became extremely uncomfortable with the disclosure a 16-year-old female made in one of his counseling sessions. During the fifth session, his client, Tammy, informed him she was experiencing problems in her relationship with her girlfriend. Initially John thought this was a typical friendship, but upon further exploration, he was informed that it was a romantic relationship. Tammy also told John that she had not yet informed her parents about her girlfriend and would like his support, insight, and help in how to "come out" to her parents. John informed Tammy that he could not assist her in this area because he does not support homosexuality and was "not trained" in working with homosexuals. He continued by stating that he would be willing to work with Tammy on all other areas of her life with the exceptions of her choice of being homosexual and telling her parents. At the end of this session, a sixth session was scheduled, but Tammy failed to attend. Feeling hurt by John's statements, Tammy decided she would not go back to counseling. Weeks later, Tammy's parents called John, noting she had begun participating in self-injurious behaviors and "acting depressed." At that time, John informed her parents Tammy did not show up for her sixth session. Her parents became inquisitive at this time as to possible reasons, and John informed them he could not and would not provide counseling for homosexual issues.

Questions:

1. What are the ethical concerns of this case (abandonment, discrimination, inappropriate self-disclosure, maleficence, non-maleficence, lack of seeking supervision, imposing values, etc.)?
2. Instead of immediately telling Tammy he could not counsel her on this topic, what should John have done?
3. What implications does this situation have for the counseling profession?

Analysis of the Adolescent Counselor and Conflicts

The case of the adolescent counselor and conflicts has a plethora of ethical issues. Some of utmost significance include those surrounding value judgments, issues related to counselor struggles—not client struggles—and confidentiality. Prior to looking at the related case law, it is important to address the specifics of this case scenario. In this case, the counselor, John, felt uncomfortable due to *his own personal* belief systems and as a result told his client he did not support homosexuality. Developmentally speaking, the client in this case may have felt quite confused and surprised that John was not supporting her because he did not support homosexuality. Additionally, John informed Tammy he would not assist her with her primary concerns prior to seeking supervision, and ultimately this could have contributed to the emotional distress Tammy began to experience (depression and self-injurious behaviors). Lastly, John did break confidentiality. While the parents do have a right to know what goes on in counseling, John disrespected Tammy by telling her parents about her sexual orientation prior to her being ready. If John would have evaluated his own values and beliefs further and sought supervision, he could have worked with Tammy to eventually help her disclose this information to her parents when she felt comfortable.

In taking a closer look the scenario in this case is actually connected to several cases. While there are quite a few court documents specifically relating to the preceding scenario, caution was exercised as a result of state licensing boards not sanctioning licensed holders in some cases. In recent years these cases have become extremely relevant in regard to discrimination, counselor education, practicum and internship experiences, and even within state laws and ethical codes. The main ethical concerns of this case and similar cases are based off sections A.4.b. Personal Values and C.5. Nondiscrimination of the *ACA Code of Ethics*. These sections are as follows:

A.4.b. Personal Values

Counselors are aware of—and avoid imposing—their own values, attitudes, beliefs, and behaviors. Counselors respect the diversity of clients, trainees, and research participants and seek training in areas in which they are at risk of imposing their values onto clients, especially when the counselor's values are inconsistent with the client's goals or are discriminatory in nature.

C.5. Nondiscrimination

Counselors do not condone or engage in discrimination against prospective or current clients, students, employees, supervisees, or research participants based on age, culture, disability, ethnicity, race, religion/spirituality, gender, gender identity, sexual orientation, marital/partnership status, language preference, socioeconomic status, immigration status, or any basis proscribed by law.

(Reprinted from *ACA Code of Ethics* [ACA, ©2014].
American Counseling Association. Reprinted with permission.
No further reproduction authorized without written
permission from the American Counseling Association.)

The case of *Keeton v. Anderson-Wiley* (2011b) identifies a counselor-in-training who filed suit against the faculty (and university) after she was required to complete a remediation plan specifically related to LGBTQIA (lesbian, gay, bisexual, transgendered, queer, intersex, and allies) populations prior to completing her clinical experiences. In this case, the primary concerns of faculty were related to Keeton's statements that she had intent to impose her religious beliefs on clients and refer them to conversion therapy, a therapy that is not supported by the American Counseling Association. Additionally, she had also made references that it would be difficult for her to work with LGBTQIA populations and separate her beliefs from those of her clients. Keeton did agree to the remediation plan and indicated she would "learn to separate [her] personal values and beliefs from those of the client so that she may attend to any need of future clients in an ethical manner" (United States Court of Appeals, 2011, p. 10). The remediate plan consisted of her reading selected articles and attending events and workshops.

Because of good faith and Keeton's written agreement to improve in this area, the faculty agreed to allow her to enroll in her clinical experience while completing the remediation. After her agreement to complete the remediation plan, Keeton changed her mind and claimed she was not going to agree to do something she knew she was not going to complete successfully. Keeton questioned the remediation plan suggesting she was singled out because of the time requirement of reading articles and attending events and workshops others students would not have to attend. Overall, the university's desire to have students comply with the *ACA Code of Ethics* when they work with students in clinical experiences with actual clients who could be harmed from a student counselor's actions. This statement provided an adequate explanation and need for the remediation plan. Ultimately it was decided by the courts, Keeton was not treated unfairly because of her religious beliefs and university officials were "motivated by a legitimate pedagogical interest in cultivating a professional demeanor and concern that she might prove unreceptive to certain issues and openly judge her client" (The United States District Court for the Southern District of Georgia Augusta Division, 2012, p. 65). Despite Keeton's claims, the court sided with the university based on its policies being applicable to all students not just Keeton.

The case of *Ward v. Wilbanks* has become one of the most notable and most important cases to have an impact on the counseling profession and its ability to promote nondiscrimination (Kaplan, 2014). It is specifically tied to a graduate student refusing to counsel clients who identify themselves as homosexual due to a conflict in religious beliefs.

Ward was a counseling student who was working in an in-house counseling clinic operated by her current university. During the intake form review of one of her assigned clients, Ward noted the client indicated he wanted assistance with feelings of depression and issues related to his same-sex relationship. When Ward discovered this information she contacted her supervisor and sought to refer this particular client to another practicum student based on her religious beliefs that individuals are capable of refraining from engaging in homosexual conduct (*Ward v. Wilbanks*, 2009 as cited in Kaplan, 2014). More specifically it was noted Ward asked her supervisor if she should meet the client and refer them to another counselor if she was asked to affirm the client's same-sex relationship or if the university should reassign the client at the onset.

This conversation lead to an informal review of Ward, which was seen as a way to assist students in discovering ways to improve their performance or encourage voluntary removal from the program (*Ward v. Polite et al.*, 2012). The review committee decided a remediation plan was not applicable in this case; thus, Ward was given the options of voluntarily withdrawing from the program or seek a formal review. Ward sought the formal review.

During the formal review faculty members and the student representative informed Ward of their concerns and shared the opinion that her behaviors violated the *ACA Code of Ethics*. Despite their concerns, Ward claimed she did not discriminate against anyone, and she had no problems counseling gay or lesbian populations so long as she did not have to affirm their beliefs. Two days after the formal review, the university sent Ward a letter dismissing her from the program. Ward's appeal was later denied by the dean of the College of Education, and Ward chose to file suit on the faculty and university.

While the court in this specific case sided with the student, there are some valuable lessoned to be learned. This case has led to much-needed changes in the *Code of Ethics* and further attention to details within the gatekeeping process of counselor trainees. The most significant claim that Ward made in this case was she did not discriminate against this client because the individual was never her client (she had not met with him), and the client did not know of the referral so was not harmed in the process. Perhaps this is why the difference between the C.5 in the 2005 and 2014 *ACA Code of Ethics*. The 2014 *Code of Ethics* is clear to include "discrimination against perspective or current clients, students" (ACA, 2014, p. 9).

Court documents indicate that Ward was known for expressing her religious views in class and would often get into debates with counseling faculty; however, despite these debates Ward did well academically (Ward v. Wilbanks, 2012). Should the faculty have documented and remediated this sooner and prior to the practicum experience, perhaps the case outcome would have turned out differently.

Afterthoughts

The preceding cases could have easily been avoided. As mental health professionals we must remember we are not in this profession for us; we are here to help the client. Helping the client means working from the client's frame of reference, not imposing our own views or beliefs on the client, and being nonjudgmental. If a counselor struggles with accepting the client or potential client for who he or she is and where he or she is, it is not the client's problem—it is the counselor's problem. The codes of ethics are very clear in these areas. As stated in Chapter 6, counselors need to remember there is a difference between comfort and competence.

These cases also amplify the need for counselor education programs to communicate expectations, evaluate progress, and assess students as they matriculate. Special attention should be paid to the potential areas of concern shown by students in working with specific populations. As gatekeepers for the field, and therefore protectors of future clients, counselor educators should consider formal mechanisms in their programs to educate counseling students on legal and ethical mandates related to denial of services based on counselor beliefs.

CASE 3: THE CHILD COUNSELOR AND PROTECTING A CHILD'S RIGHT TO CONFIDENTIALITY

Mr. Rogers is a counselor in private practice in a large metropolitan area. He has maintained a lucrative practice for 15 years and specializes in counseling young children. Mr. Rogers has been seeing Charlie, an 11-year-old male, for approximately four months. Charlie's mother initially requested counseling as a result of his recent anger outbursts, continuous worrying, and difficulty sleeping at night. At the beginning of the counseling, Charlie was very hesitant about the process. He sat in the counselor's office and communicated he was scared to discuss certain things with Mr. Rogers.

Concerned about what Charlie was scared of discussing, Mr. Rogers promised Charlie all information he revealed would be kept in confidence (within the limits of confidentiality) and details of their conversations would not be revealed to his parents. Shortly after this promise was made, Charlie began to become more open and explore reasoning behind his anger, worry, and difficulties sleeping.

Charlie indicated he was concerned that he might have to choose a parent to live with when he turned 12. He claimed his stepmother (previous nanny) told him this would create additional problems between his parents, and this worried him. Deep down Charlie blamed himself a little for his parents separating, and he didn't want to make things worse by choosing one over the other. After a couple of months of counseling, Charlie seemed much better. As a result of Charlie's progress, Mr. Rogers and Charlie decided to terminate their counseling relationship. In their last session Charlie reiterated his desire for the promise to be kept. Additionally, a couple weeks prior to his 12th birthday, Charlie wrote a letter to Mr. Rogers, which was delivered by his mother, requesting the promise to continue. Approximately one month after the delivery of the letter, Mr. Rogers received a properly delivered subpoena that requested a court appearance from Mr. Rogers and Charlie's counseling records.

Questions:

1. What is the ethical dilemma?
2. What might Sartor and McHenry's ethical decision making model look like?
3. If you were Mr. Rogers, what would you do in this situation? Would you agree to release the records or testify based on the parents'/guardians' right to the information?

Analysis of the Child Counselor and Protecting the Child's Right to Confidentiality

This case scenario is based on the Texas case of *Abrams v. Jones* (Supreme Court of Texas, 1999). In this particular case, Abrams, the mental health professional, refused to release records because of the malicious intent of use by the parents. In efforts to ensure the child was comfortable within the sessions, Abrams did promise information presented would remain confidential; thus, if Abrams would have released records, the ethical principal of fidelity would be violated. Additionally, Abrams claimed it would not be appropriate to release the child's records because the parents were not acting in the best interests of the child and their motivations would harm the child. Abrams was advocating for the child, and in doing so he was able to protect the child's right to confidentiality. Ultimately, Abrams chose to act on behalf of the child reflecting in beneficence and non-maleficence.

The outcome of the *Abrams v. Jones* case favored the mental health professional and his decision not to release the records. Thus, in cases like this one it is wise for counselors to know how their state defines the parental rights and the boundaries of those rights when it comes to children.

In the event Abrams did not act on behalf of the child, the child may have experienced extreme stress and may have viewed the counseling profession in a negative light. If the information would have been released, additional distress may have been experienced by the child due to the perceived power of choosing one parent over the other. Additionally, the child might have begun to feel that counseling was not personally safe, a conclusion that might then close off a clear area of help should additional emotional disturbances occur in the future.

Afterthoughts

While parents do have the right to information presented in counseling sessions with their children, counselors must remember parents are not privy to all information. The child or adolescent is first priority, and he or she also has the right to confidentiality. While some counselors may have faltered under the pressure of parents, he kept his promise to the child and was true to his word. This counselor was very wise and thoughtful; his actions show a true sense of counselor advocacy on behalf of a child client.

CASE 4: THE BOSS'S REQUEST

Janette is a counselor at a community counseling center. She has recently become fully licensed as a professional counselor and has worked for the center for approximately six months. One day while working on her case notes, Janette's boss, Charles, enters his office with a serious look on his face. Charles informs Janette that his daughter is experiencing difficulties in school, is having trouble sleeping at night, and has been having anger outburst. He tells Janette he would like her to provide counseling for his daughter. Charles then informs Janette that she is the best counselor in the area and makes many positive statements about the services she provides. Hesitant about this request, Janette informs Charles she needs to think about whether she has the time to devote to another client.

Questions:

1. How should Janette respond to Charles?
2. What might the ethical decision making process look like?
3. Does this violate any codes listed in the *ACA Code of Ethics?* If Janette was a school counselor would this violate the ASCA *Ethical Standards for School Counselors?*
4. Regardless of her response to Charles's request, Janette may experience professional consequences. What are the possible consequences if she agrees/disagrees to Charles's request?

Analysis of the Boss's Requests

While there may not be a specific case regarding this situation, this case scenario could lead to action being taking against a counselor by the state licensing board. Dual relationships are one of the top violations counselors make. To see specifics regarding each state, counselors are encouraged to go to their state licensing board's website.

CASE 5: THE "COACHING" PARENT AND THE COUNSELOR

Sarah is a child counselor at a community agency that works with children who have been allegedly abused. Prior to receiving services from the agency in which Sarah works, the child must go through the process of a forensic interview. Christina, a 5-year-old, was referred to the community agency as a result of her mother's various reports to Child Protective Services claiming that Christina was abused by her father.

Prior to the forensic interview, the director of the community agency, the investigator from Child Protective Services, and the law enforcement investigator inform Sarah that they would like her to counsel the child as a result of some of the concerns of this case. Sarah agreed she would see Christina due to the request of the multidisciplinary team. In reviewing the case records, it was noted that Christina did not make an outcry of abuse during the forensic interview, and her mother had made three claims of abuse against the child's father and has taken Christina to numerous doctors in efforts to confirm her suspicion. The file also indicated that Christina's mother and father have been divorced since Christina was approximately two years of age and currently have shared custody.

During the intake interview with Christina's mother, she was easily distracted and had difficulty answer questions pertaining to her daughter. Despite Sarah's attempts to redirect her, Christina's mother would often rant about her disappointment that no one is taking her claims seriously including medical doctors, Child Protective Services, and law enforcement. She continued and stated the only one she trusts is the director of the agency because she has heard she will make sure something will happen to individuals like her ex-husband. Her mother also noted that other children's counseling clinics did not take her seriously, and medical doctors claimed that despite her comments, physical evidence was not observed during examinations. Christina's mother begs Sarah to make a report on her behalf on several occasions during the interview; at these times Sarah was able to put the focus back on the intake questions.

The next week Sarah began providing play therapy services to Christina. Immediately after the session, Christina's mother became inquisitive about the session and "wanted to know everything." Sarah reminded her that she would inform her of Christina's progress when needed. Despite, the mother's disappointment in Sarah's answer, she continued to bring Christian back for the next four sessions, each session trying to get detailed information from Sarah about the play sessions.

Prior to the sixth play session Christina's mother came in for a parent-consult session. During the session, Christina's mother noted she has been having more difficulty than normal controlling Christina's behaviors, and this frequently occurs after the now-supervised visitations with her father. Her mother informs Sarah that she would like her to make another report to Child Protective Services because visits with her father seem to be making Christina act out. Sarah informed the mother she would not make a report on this matter because there is not cause. As a result, the mother stormed out of the consultation session and immediately spoke to the director of the agency. At this time the director of the agency told the mother the same thing Sarah did. At this time Christina's mother left the agency and informed all workers she would not be bringing her child back, ordered or otherwise.

Questions:

1. What are the possible ethical dilemmas in this case?
2. As a counselor, do you feel this situation should be reported in some form or fashion?
3. If so, what should be reported?
4. Do you feel the child is being harmed in anyway?

Analysis of the Coach and the Counselor

Child counselors may be occasionally faced with parents who make false allegations of their child being abused. In situations such as these, the counselor must keep in mind that the child is always the first priority. While there are specific court cases tied to this case study, the specific cases will not be named here to further protect the children and adolescents named in the case.

In the specific case described here, the mother's claims were not found to be true. Additionally, it was found the child was harmed in the process due to the exposure to unnecessary medical examinations, home videotaping conversations with the child describing alleged claims, and falsifying statements about her father that could potentially jeopardize the relationship between him and his daughter.

While counselors need to take all cases of abuse seriously, the counselors in both the case scenario and the actual cases were wise to not buckle under the mother's pressure to make a report due to the possibility of fabrication and further harm being placed on the child. As a result of the continuous reports by the mother, the court eventually gave full custody to the father with the child only having supervised visits with the mother. Court documents suggested significant impairment of the mother and indicated the mother struggled in certain areas of parenting including the lack of boundaries, disciplinary practices, controllability, and the lack of consistency of schedule with the child and failure to comply with the courts requests. On the other end, the court noted an extreme difference in the handling of the child between the father and mother, with the father having a sense of boundaries and his ability to better handle bad behaviors of the child.

Afterthoughts

Situations in which children are coached into making outcries of abuse should be taken just as seriously as true outcries of abuse. Counselors should continuously be aware of familial and environmental factors that may influence a child's development and the healing process. While the alleged abuse may not have truly occurred, counselors must consider what the child may be experiencing emotionally, physically, or psychologically as a result of the untrue allegation. Because of the lasting effects of these allegations on the child, counselors who work with children and adolescents should request prior counseling documents to ensure needed areas are processed. As mentioned in Chapter 9, there are occasions when recanted and coached or false outcries of abuse are made and later a true allegation is filed on a separate incident.

Additionally, counselors have another responsibility in this area in regard to appropriate communication with law enforcement. If a child is being coached by a parent or caregiver, it is not helpful to apply pressure to law enforcement or other investigative entities. Counselors must remember that law enforcement are trained in their specialty as we are trained in ours; applying pressure to these individuals in situations of true or false allegations may lead to an incomplete investigation and additional hardship on the child or adolescent.

RELEVANCE AND COLLECTIVE THOUGHTS
OF CHALLENGING CASES

As counselors, counselor educators, and counselor supervisors, we have the privilege of sharing in the journey of growth with children and adolescents. This privilege is not something to be taken lightly and requires respect toward children and adolescents. Counselors who are faced with ethical dilemmas should always keep the child or adolescent as their top priority in making decisions based on thought. This extends to choosing to work for a particular agency/school, with a certain group, or even being an advocate. Counselors should be cognizant of how actions and the *ACA Code of Ethics* (ACA, 2014), section D.1.g. Employer Policies, relates to this privilege. Section D.1.g. Employer Policies indicates,

> The acceptance of employment in an agency or institution implies that counselors are in agreement with its general policies and principles. Counselors strive to reach agreement with employers regarding acceptable standards of client care and professional conduct that allow for changes in institutional policy conducive to the growth and development of clients.

Notice it references the growth and development of the client (child or adolescent) not the company or counselor.

Additionally, should counselors face an ethical dilemma or a situation that may call for reference to previous court cases, counselors must be thorough in their research. It should be remembered that language or verbiage differs in accordance to profession (for example, mental health counselor versus legal counsel). These terms must not be brushed over or skimmed lightly, as the child or adolescent client, their families, and the counselor may be put in a compromising situation if assessment of the situation is not done properly.

CONCLUDING THOUGHTS

Jim McHenry

When I began my career as a counselor educator (1969), I remember Dr. William Groves, our department chair, commenting that he could get all the professional journals for the department through our departmental membership in the American Personnel and Guidance Association. Things were much simpler (and cheaper!) in those early days of the profession.

Flash forward to today, and we are members of a profession that has expanded almost geometrically. Such growth, of course, clearly has been driven by the recognition of the worth and value counselors have come to possess in today's society. And, over those years, of course, the profession has spawned many counseling specialties, subspecialties, and the like in the attempt to meet the ever-expanding need for counselors. Indeed, one size does not fit all. Modern-day professional counseling practitioners now complete expanded degree programs and extensive internships, follow up with ongoing in-service requirements, and along the way, must learn to develop and effectively utilize a diverse (to borrow Dr. Cowher's frame) web of resources. And, in working with those webs and those networks, understanding, recognizing, and augmenting the professional roles of the many helping professionals with whom counselors rub shoulders is absolutely essential.

Of course, several very basic ideas form the cornerstone of our professional role and should be ever-present in the practitioner's mind.

1. The client, whether he or she is 2 or 15 or even 77, comes first.
2. As professionals, we need to do everything within our professional power to aid and assist the client.
3. In performing that service, we must be aware of and adhere to ethical practices.

4.   Such awareness and adherence necessitates *not only* to initially learn ethical and legal mandates, but also to keep up with changes within the profession (e.g., online counseling issues) and utilizing available resources (e.g., fellow counselors, in-service).

5.   And in order to most effectively and successfully meet the needs of the client, we must be aware of the complementary roles that other helping professionals play, and the ethical boundaries of their practices.

This book serves as just one piece of the puzzle in the process of practicing legally and ethically throughout your career. As counselors, we are constantly learning from every client, every article, and every book we read. Counseling is a profession of continuous learning.

MULTIPLE CHOICE QUESTIONS

1. Informed consent is
   A. Good practice
   B. Legal
   C. Important to the counselor/client relationship
   D. All of the above

2. If the child or teen cannot provide legal consent, the counselor should most likely
   A. Get consent only from the parents/guardians
   B. Move past consent as it will not matter anyway
   C. Get the legal consent from parents/guardians but also work with the client to understand as best he or she can the limitations of consent to the degree possible
   D. All of the above are correct

3. Informed consent is
   A. Always needed to provide any type of therapy
   B. Never needed until the counselor determines there may be a big issue in the case
   C. Typically required/mandated except for certain circumstances such as crisis or emergency therapy
   D. Necessary primarily to avoid legal situations

4. Reporting potential abuse is
   A. Mandated by law only after the counselor has clear proof
   B. Required by professional standards and legal mandates
   C. Always done first to the parents/guardians

D. A situation in which the counselor must never go back over the informed consent

5. The first step in the ethical decision making model offered by the authors is
   A. Determine the dilemma
   B. Develop a plan
   C. Consult with other professionals
   D. Evaluate the impact of the dilemma on the relationship between the parents and client

6. Regardless of the model you use for the ethical decision making process, in regard to consulting with other professionals, you should
   A. Only do this as a last resort
   B. Do this as the very first step
   C. Consult after you have determined the dilemma
   D. Consult with a minimum of three other professionals

7. When you get a subpoena, according to the American Counseling Association, you should
   A. Obtain written consent (or other form) to allow only the minimum amount of information to be shared with others
   B. Immediately turn over your records
   C. Follow the rules of the subpoena
   D. Consult with others

8. Regardless of the ethical decision making model employed, the final step should be
   A. Documentation of why you did what you did
   B. Analysis of the impact of your decision, including revising the plan as needed
   C. Consulting with others
   D. Determining the true dilemma

9. When the parent/guardian is the one providing consent, he or she has
   A. All access to all records and information from sessions, including details of who and what was discussed
   B. Only very limited access because the counselor should protect confidentiality as much as possible
   C. The right to listen in on the session
   D. None of the above are correct

10. Issues like confidentiality, informed consent, and reporting potential abuse are
    A. In place to protect the client and offer the best care
    B. Considered necessary to provide professional care
    C. Challenging at times, but well worth the effort to help develop the counseling process
    D. All of the above

11. The legal parallel of the ethical term *confidentiality* is which of the following?
    A. Informed consent
    B. Privacy
    C. Duty to protect
    D. Duty to warn

12. Professional school counselors are exempt from adhering to which of the following practices?
    A. Case note documentation and record keeping
    B. Informed consent
    C. Outcomes measurement and accountability
    D. None of the above

13. Counselors must consider only the chronological age of the child or adolescent client when making a determination about disclosing confidential information to a parent or guardian.
    A. True
    B. False

14. Clinical mental health counselors and professional school counselors must always breach confidentiality and report non-suicidal self-injurious behavior of a child or adolescent to a third party (administrator, parent, guardian, etc.).
    A. True
    B. False

15. Which of the following is not generally required of case documentation and record-keeping practices for clinical mental health counselors working with children and adolescents?
    A. Parent or guardian informed consent to treatment
    B. Diagnosis and treatment plan
    C. Most recent divorce or custody orders (as applicable)
    D. Written or verbal permission by the child or adolescent client to breach confidentiality when it is both necessary and reasonable to do so.

16. Professional school counselors are advised to document which of the following for each counseling-related interaction with a child or adolescent:
    A. Date of the counseling interaction
    B. Main topic or focus of the counseling interaction
    C. Progress toward relevant goals and objectives (academic, personal, social, career developmental domains)
    D. All of the above

17. For both clinical mental health counselors and professional school counselors, the primary obligation of *confidentiality* is to the _____?
    A. Child or adolescent client
    B. Parent or guardian

C. School or agency administrator/supervisor
D. None of the above

18. When explaining *confidentiality* (and exceptions to confidentiality) to a child or adolescent client, counselors are advised to consider all of the following *except*
    A. Specific examples of when a breach is necessary or mandatory
    B. The setting in which counseling occurs
    C. The presenting concern of the child or adolescent client
    D. Developmental factors and chronological age of the child or adolescent client
    E. All of these should be considered and discussed (as applicable)

19. Counselors who work with children or adolescents have no further ethical duty to the minor client upon informing a parent or other third party of any behavior that evidences potential for serious and foreseeable harm.
    A. False
    B. True

20. Documentation and record keeping is an ethical responsibility to the _____ that promotes _____.
    A. Counselor; the counselor's right to practice
    B. Public; public trust in the profession
    C. Client; the client's well-being
    D. Third-party payer; integrity and fidelity in claims processing and utilization review

21. LGBTQ youth are _____ times more likely than their heterosexual peers to attempt suicide.
    A. 2
    B. 5
    C. 12
    D. 18

22. PFLAG is an organization that represents which of the following?
    A. People Fighting to Liberate All Gays
    B. Partners Focusing on Loving All Gays
    C. Parents, Family and Friends of Lesbians and Gays
    D. None of the above

23. Counselors can refer their clients to other counselors when there are
    A. Value differences between client and counselor
    B. Ethnic differences between client and counselor
    C. Counselor cultural incompetence
    D. Counselor competence deficiencies

24. _____% of LGBTQ students reported experiencing harassment at school in the past year (GLSEN, 2009).
   A. 20
   B. 40
   C. 60
   D. 80

25. During the coming-out process, LGBTQ youth experience _____ in self-esteem, life satisfaction, and happiness.
   A. Increase
   B. Decrease
   C. No change
   D. No difference from heterosexual teens

26. Assuming that a client is heterosexual is an example of
   A. Heterosexual privilege
   B. Homophobia
   C. Microaggression
   D. All of the above
   E. A and C only

27. Your client is in the process of coming-out as lesbian. In your sessions you find that she has an embedded belief that same-sex attraction is a sin and that she can change to become heterosexual. As a result, she is participating in self-harm behaviors such as cutting. It is likely that your client is experiencing
   A. Internalized homosexuality
   B. Internalized homophobia and heterosexism
   C. Internalized heterosexism
   D. Internalized transsexualism

28. Which of these is appropriate from an ethical counseling perspective?
   A. Focusing on sexual orientation only when it is relevant
   B. Attempting to have clients renounce or change their sexual orientation
   C. Attributing a client's problem to sexual orientation without evidence that this is the case
   D. Transferring LGBTQ clients to another therapist based solely on sexual orientation

29. The sexual orientation of a transgender individual can be
   A. Bisexual
   B. Heterosexual
   C. Same sex
   D. All of the above

30. If a parent requests to know if his or her child/teen has disclosed same-sex attraction to you as the counselor, it is your obligation to
    A. Let the parent know the child's sexual orientation based on the fact that your client is a minor
    B. Let the child/teen make the decision to tell the parent based on the ethical principles of respect for autonomy and confidentiality established at the beginning of the counseling relationship
    C. Let the parent know their child's sexual orientation based on the fact that the child may be in danger legally and ethically as a result of being LGBTQ
    D. Let a third party decide whether you should tell the parent his or her child's sexual orientation

31. Counselors are ethically obligated to use only tests that they are/have
    A. Familiar with
    B. Trained and competent with
    C. Access to
    D. Qualitative methodologies

32. If standardization is breached during administration, counselors have the ethical duty to
    A. Interpret the results regardless
    B. Report the incidence and interpret the findings
    C. Note the condition and question the validity
    D. Not report the findings

33. Which of the following steps should be allotted the most time?
    A. Identify the problem
    B. Identify all relevant parties
    C. Describe the ethical principles
    D. Seek supervision and consultation

34. Counselors administer, score, and interpret tests for all the purposes *except*
    A. Educational
    B. Psychological
    C. Career assessment
    D. Sexual identity

35. The underlying theme of the landmark cases *Larry P. v. Riles, Diana v. Board of Education*, and *Guadalupe v. Tempe Elementary School District* is
    A. Cultural competence in assessment
    B. Informed consent
    C. Instrumentation with insufficient empirical data
    D. Proper diagnosis

36. Section E of the *ACA Code of Ethics* focuses on
    A. Supervision, training, and teaching
    B. Evaluation, assessment, and interpretation
    C. The counseling relationship
    D. Professional responsibility

37. The main ethical dilemma presented in Susie's case was
    A. Inexperience
    B. Administrative pressure
    C. Lack of follow-through from school psychologist
    D. Limits of competence

38. The main ethical dilemma presented in Megan's case was
    A. Cultural competence
    B. Informed consent
    C. Scoring and interpretation
    D. Working with minors

39. In the scenario of Steve, what would be the identifying problem?
    A. The results of the assessment are in conflict with the client's interests
    B. Amy's results are considered invalid
    C. Amy cannot get into medical school with her GPA
    D. Career assessments were not appropriately used

40. In the scenario of Devin, how should Sara handle the situation?
    A. Give him a diagnosis of ADHD
    B. Use the results of the assessment to promote the well-being of Devin
    C. Administer another ADHD rating scale
    D. Refuse to allow Devin to participate in the counseling group

41. When it comes to professional counselors and their understanding and knowledge base of psychotropic medications, which of the following statements is true?
    A. Professional counselors focus their efforts on the therapeutic relationship and refer to psychiatrists anytime questions about medication are raised.
    B. Professional counselors cannot legally or ethically provide any information on medication and therefore need to defer all such questions to a trained professional.
    C. Professional counselors are required to have an understanding of basic classifications, indications, and contraindications of commonly prescribed psychopharmacological medications.

D. Professional counselors are aware of when the need for a referral comes up and without giving any recommendations refer the client to a psychiatrist.

42. When working with children and adolescents, a professional counselor has an ethical obligation to

A. Assess the client thoroughly and make referrals to other professionals as necessary

B. Look for more than just verbal statements and behaviors, as nonverbal cues may be much more telling

C. Educate clients and their families about the potential benefits or disadvantages of different treatment modalities

D. All of the above

43. When it comes to disclosing treatment or medical records to other third-party providers, which of the following statements is correct?

A. HIPAA allows such disclosures as long as they are for treatment or billing purposes.

B. HIPAA may be good with certain disclosures; however state laws should also be consulted before releasing any information.

C. HIPAA is a federal act that was placed in 1996, and thus as long HIPAA standards are met, a provider is protected by law.

D. All of the above.

44. As discussed in the book, the typical follow-up psychiatry appointment may be

A. 45–50 minutes

B. 15–20 minutes

C. 25–30 minutes

D. 5–10 minutes

45. If a child discloses nonsuicidal self-injurious behavior,

A. Professional counselors should keep that information confidential to continue to build rapport with the client

B. Professional counselors should inform parents or guardians promptly

C. Professional counselors should call the police immediately

D. Professional counselors should send the child to an inpatient facility promptly

46. Legally, all of the following mental health professionals are able to provide counseling services *except*

A. Licensed Psychiatric Nurses

B. Licensed Professional Counselors

C. Licensed Psychiatrists

D. Licensed Certified Mental Health Diagnosticians

E. Licensed Psychologist

47. Psychiatrists have specialized training through the _____ model, which allows them to _____ rebalance a patient.
   A. Physiological; emotionally
   B. Behavioral; practically
   C. Medical; chemically
   D. Anatomical; emotionally
   E. None of the above

48. The collaborative relationship between a psychiatrist and a professional counselor can allow them to
   A. Develop and treat patients much more efficiently
   B. Communicate all the necessary information without the need for consent
   C. Alleviate extreme symptoms quickly
   D. Allow counselor to focus on cognitive and emotional aspects more quickly
   E. All but B

49. The best way to determine if HIPAA rules and regulations are the most stringent regulations within your state is to
   A. Contact the board of examiners for your particular licensure
   B. Contact the national HIPAA office in Washington DC
   C. Obtain yearly continuing education units on HIPAA regulations
   D. All of the above

50. When treating minors, it is imperative that
   A. Both parents be present during each therapy session
   B. Both parents be willing to take the child to a psychiatrist
   C. The child sign an assent to the counseling forms
   D. One of the parents be present when visiting with a psychiatrist
   E. None of the above

51. The 2014 *ACA Code of Ethics* provides guidance on which of the following topics?
   A. Distance Counseling and Technology
   B. Social Media, Technology, and Reporting Issues Regarding Technology
   C. Distance Counseling, Technology, and Social Media
   D. Technology and Social Media

52. Which of the following statements regarding Internet access and cyber-bullying is most accurate?
   A. The majority of youth have access to the Internet, but a negligible portion of them report experiencing cyberbullying in their lifetime.

B. The majority of youth have access to the Internet, and a notable portion (i.e., 20% to 40%) report experiencing cyberbullying in their lifetime.

C. Roughly more than half of youth have access to the Internet, and a negligible portion of them report experiencing cyberbullying in their lifetime.

D. Roughly more than half of youth have access to the Internet, and a notable portion (i.e., 20% to 40%) report experiencing cyberbullying in their lifetime.

53. Research has found what type of children to be more vulnerable to online exploitation from sex offenders?
A. Socially inhibited and lonely children
B. Extroverted and adventurous children
C. Both socially inhibited and extroverted children, suggesting a range of potential victimhood
D. No firm conclusions can be made based on literature at this time

54. Which of the following is *not* an example of asynchronous counseling?
A. Video chatting
B. E-mail
C. Text messages
D. Online message boards

55. What are the main professional agencies that have done the most extensive work in producing codes of ethics/professional standards for the practice of cybercounseling?
A. The National Board of Certified Counselors (NBCC), the American Counselor Association (ACA), and the National Association of Social Workers (NASW)
B. The American School Counseling Association (ASCA), the American Psychological Association (APA), and the National Board of Certified Counselors (NBCC)
C. The National Board of Certified Counselors (NBCC), the American Counseling Association (ACA), and the International Society for Mental Health Online (ISMHO)
D. The *Practitioners Guide to Ethical Decision Making (PGEDM)*; the *Diagnostic and Statistical Manual*, fifth edition (*DSM-5*); and the American Counseling Association (ACA)

56. What's the most commonly used method for cybercounselors to communicate with their clients?
A. Instagram
B. Webcam

C. Videoconferencing

D. E-mail

57. Cybercounseling mainly operates under two broad categories of e-mail delivery for its clients. What are the two broad categories, and what method of communication exchange best serves each category?

A. Advice—synchronous; e-mail—asynchronous

B. Advice—e-mail; e-mail—synchronous

C. E-mail—asynchronous; advice—synchronous

D. Advice—asynchronous; e-mail—synchronous

58. Which standard from the 2014 *ACA Code of Ethics* (ACA, 2014) specifically addresses the potential of communication misinterpretations (between counselor and client) when using technology for the purpose of delivering counseling services?

A. H.2.a

B. G.5.h

C. H.5.d

D. H.4.f

59. The proliferation of social media trends has resulted in

A. Those trends becoming a prevalent influence on adolescent development

B. The emergence of a new interactive culture

C. Shifts in acceptable interpersonal behavior

D. All of the above

60. Which of the following is not mentioned as an identifiable warning sign of a child being cyberbullied?

A. Oversleeping or not sleeping enough

B. Increased absenteeism from school

C. Interest in anime

D. Becoming unusually secretive

61. Which of the following resources would be considered a (counseling) professional organization?

A. ACA

B. NBCC

C. ASCA

D. State licensing board

62. Which of the following resources would be considered a credentialing board?

A. CASA

B. NBCC

C. ACA

D. RAINN

63. Which of the following resources would be most likely to draft a professional code of ethics for counselors?
    A. CASA
    B. NBCC
    C. ACA
    D. NAMI

64. In most states, counselors play what role in responding to child abuse and neglect?
    A. Citizen's arrest
    B. Mandated reporter
    C. Sympathetic witness
    D. Journalist

65. Which of the following is *not* a challenge typically faced by school counselors in remote locations?
    A. Scarcity of services close to the school
    B. Parental insecurity about complying with referral
    C. Population density making a commute more difficult
    D. Community expectations beyond the counselor's expertise

66. An ethical dilemma for the counselor who witnesses the child of a close friend being abused by the friend would most likely be
    A. Informed consent
    B. Scope of practice
    C. Level of expertise
    D. Dual relationship

67. Which of the following is *not* a good reason for having a code of ethics?
    A. Ensuring consistent professional standards
    B. Promoting professional integrity
    C. Ensuring high pay standards for counselors
    D. Building a foundation for the services that counselors provide

68. A professional organization that specifically responds to school counselors is
    A. CASA
    B. ASCA
    C. NBCC
    D. State licensing board

69. Which of the following is *not* a reason why counselors who work in agency settings need resource webs?
    A. One agency cannot respond to every potential need
    B. Agencies are typically deficient in employing well-qualified personnel
    C. It can be challenging for one professional resource to conduct all possible assessments
    D. Outsourcing is often necessary when clients present unique challenges

70. Which of the following is *not* a reason why counselors should procure their own professional liability insurance?

A. The cost of legal representation can be high

B. Working with underage populations (and their parents/guardians) can present special ethical and legal challenges

C. Legal counsel representing the counselor's place of employment will also represent the counselor, as long as the counselor remits part of his or her salary as payment

D. Counselors function within a litigious and complex world

1. D	2. C	3. C	4. B	5. A	6. C	7. A	8. B	9. B	10. D
11. B	12. D	13. B	14. B	15. D	16. D	17. A	18. E	19. A	20. C
21. B	22. C	23. D	24. D	25. B	26. E	27. B	28. A	29. D	30. B
31. B	32. C	33. A	34. D	35. A	36. B	37. D	38. C	39. A	40. B
41. C	42. D	43. B	44. D	45. B	46. D	47. C	48. E	49. A	50. B
51. C	52. B	53. C	54. A	55. C	56. D	57. D	58. D	59. D	60. C
61. A	62. B	63. C	64. B	65. C	66. D	67. C	68. B	69. B	70. C

REFERENCES

Abrams v. Jones. 99-0184 (Supreme Court of Texas 1999). Retrieved from http://caselaw.findlaw.com/tx-supreme-court/1171932.html

Acker, G. M. (2010). The challenges in providing services to clients with mental illness: Managed care, burnout, and somatic symptoms among social workers. *Community Mental Health Journal, 46*, 591–600.

Ainsworth, M. (1999). *Introductions to online counseling: Metanoia guide to Internet mental health services.* Retrieved August 1, 2015 from http://www.metanoia.org

Ainsworth, M. (2000). *Metanoia: The ABC's of Internet counseling* [Online]. Retrieved August 1, 2015 from http://www.metanoia.org/imhs

Ainsworth, M. (2004). E-therapy: History and survey. Retrieved from http://www.metanoia.org/imhs/history.htm#top

American Academy of Pediatrics. (2013). Homosexuality and adolescence. *Pediatrics, 92*, 631–634.

American Art Therapy Association (AATA). (2013). *Ethical principles for art therapists.* Alexandria, VA: Author.

American Art Therapy Association. (2015). What is art therapy? Retrieved from http://www.arttherapy.org/upload/whatisarttherapy.pdf

American Counseling Association. (2013). Ethical issues related to conversion or reparative therapy. Retrieved from http://www.counseling.org/news/updates/2013/01/16/ethical-issues-related-to-conversion-or-reparative-therapy

American Counseling Association. (2014). *ACA code of ethics.* Alexandria, VA: Author. Retrieved from http://www.counseling.org/docs/ethics/2014-aca-code-of-ethics.pdf?sfvrsn=4

American Educational Research Association (AERA), American Psychological Association (APA), & National Council on Measurement in Education

(NCME). (2014). *Standards for educational and psychological testing*. Washington, DC: Author.

American Mental Health Counselors Association (AMHCA). (2010). AMHCA code of ethics. Alexandria, VA: Author.

American Music Therapy Association. (2015). Retrieved from: http://www.musictherapy.org/about/musictherapy.

American Psychiatric Association. (2000). *Position statement on therapies focused on attempts to change sexual orientation (reparative or conversion therapies)*. Retrieved from http://web.archive.org/web/20110407082738/http://www.psych.org/Departments/EDU/Library/APAOfficialDocumentsand Related/PositionStatements/200001.aspx

American Psychological Association (APA). (2009). *Report of the American Psychological Association task force on appropriate therapeutic responses to sexual orientation*. Retrieved from http://www.apa.org/pi/lgbt/resources/sexual-orientation.aspx

American Psychological Association. (2010). *Ethical principles of psychologists and code of conduct*. Washington, DC: Author.

American School Counselor Association. (2005a). *About ASCA*. Retrieved from http://www.schoolcounselor.org/content.asp?contentid=127

American School Counselor Association. (2005b). *The ASCA national model: A framework for school counseling programs* (2nd ed.). Alexandria, VA: Author.

American School Counselor Association. (2007). *The professional school counselor and LGBTQ youth*. Retrieved from http://asca2.timberlakepublishing.com//files/PS_LGBTQ.pdf

American School Counselor Association. (2010). *Ethical standards for school counselors*. Alexandria, VA: Author.

American School Counselor Association. (2015). *Legal and ethical FAQ*. Retrieved from www.schoolcounselor.org

Armistead, L., Williams, B. B., & Jacob, S. (2011). *Professional ethics for school psychologists: A problem-solving model casebook* (2nd ed.). Bethesda, MD: National Association of School Psychologists.

Arredondo, P., Toporek, R., Brown, S. P., Jones, J., Locke, D., Sanchez, J., & Stadler, H. A. (1996). Operationalization of the multicultural counseling competencies. *Journal of Multicultural Counseling and Development, 24*, 42–78.

Association of Lesbian, Gay, Bisexual, and Transgender Issues in Counseling. (2009). *Competencies for counseling with transgender clients*. Alexandria, VA: Author.

Association of Lesbian, Gay, Bisexual, and Transgender Issues in Counseling. (2012). *ALGBTIC Competencies for counseling LGBQQIA individuals*. Alexandria, VA: Author.

Association of Play Therapy. (n.d.). Retrieved from www. a4pt.org

Baumerind, D. (1991, February). The influence of parenting style on adolescent competence and substance use. *The Journal of Early Adolescence, 11*, 56–95.

Belkofer, C. M., & McNutt, J. V. (2011). Understanding social media culture and its ethical challenges for art therapists. *Journal of the American Art Therapy Association, 28*, 159–164.

Bell, H., Kulkarni, S., & Dalton, L. (2003). Organizational prevention of vicarious trauma. *Families in Society: The Journal of Contemporary Human Services, 84*(4), 463–470.

Bernal, A. T., & Coolhart, D. (2005). Learning from sexual minorities: Adolescents and the coming out process. *Guidance & Counseling, 20*, 128–138.

Bober, T., & Regehr, C. (2005). Strategies for reducing secondary or vicarious trauma: Do they work? *Brief Treatment and Crisis Intervention, 6*, 1–9. doi: 10.1093/brief treatment/mhj001

Bodenhorn, N. (2006). Exploratory study of common and challenging ethical dilemmas experienced by professional school counselors. *Professional School Counseling, 10*, 195–202.

Bruff v. North Mississippi Health Services, Inc., 244 F.3d 495 (5th Cir. 2001).

Carrion, V., & Lock, J. (1997). The coming-out process: Developmental stages for sexual minority youth. *Clinical Child Psychology and Psychiatry, 2*, 369–377.

CASA. (2016). Retrieved from www.casaforchildren.org

Cass, V. (1979). Homosexual identity formation: A theoretical model. *Journal of Homosexuality, 4*, 219–235.

Cass, V. (1984). Homosexual identity formation: Testing a theoretical model. *The Journal of Sex Research, 20*, 143–167.

Chutter, K. (2007). Opening our awareness to heterosexist and homophobic attitudes in society. *Relational Child and Youth Care Practice, 20*, 22–27.

Crisp, C., & McCave, E. L. (2007). Gay affirmative practice: A model for social work practice with gay, lesbian, and bisexual youth. *Child and Adolescent Social Work Journal, 24*, 403–421. doi: 10.1007/S10560–007–0091-z

D'Augelli, A. (2002). Mental health problems among lesbian, gay and bisexual youths ages 14 to 21. *Clinical Child Psychology and Psychiatry, 7*, 433–456.

Davis, W., Geller, K., & Thaut, M. (2008) *An introduction to music therapy: Theory and practice* (3rd ed.). Silver Spring, MD: American Music Therapy Association.

Drescher, J., & Leli, U. (2004). *Transgender subjectivities: A clinician's guide.* Binghamton, NY: The Haworth Medical Press.

Dugger, S. M., & Carlson, L. A. (2012). Sexual minority youth: The case of Donald Wilson. In S. H. Dworkin & M. Pope (Eds.), *Casebook for counseling lesbian, gay, bisexual, and transgender persons and their families* (pp. 7–22). Alexandria, VA: American Counseling Association.

Dworkin, S. H., & Pope, M. (2012). *Casebook for counseling lesbian, gay, bisexual, and transgender persons and their families.* Alexandria, VA: American Counseling Association.

Eid, M., & Ward, S. J. A. (2009). Ethics, new media and social networks. *Global Media Journal Canadian Edition, 2*, 1–4.

Eliason, M. J. (1996). Beyond a minoritizing view. *Journal of Homosexuality, 30*(3), 31–56.

Erford, B. T. (2011). *Transforming the school counseling profession* (3rd ed.). Upper Saddle River, NJ: Pearson Education Inc.

Erikson, E. (1959). *Identity and the life cycle.* New York, NY: International Universities Press, Inc.

Espelage, D., & Swearer, S. (2008). Addressing research gaps in the intersection between homophobia and bullying. *Social Psychology Review, 37,* 155–159.

eTherapy.com. (2001). *eTherapy.com* [Online]. Retrieved January 22, 2001 from http://www.etherapy.com

Family Educational Rights and Privacy Act (FERPA). 20 U.S.C. § 1232g (1974).

Field, J. E., & Baker, S. (2004). Defining and examining school counselor advocacy. *Professional School Counseling, 8*(1), 56–63.

Ford, M. P., & Hendrick, S. S. (2003). Therapists' sexual values for self and clients: Implications for practice and training. *Professional Psychology: Research and Practice, 34*(1), 80–87.

Fowler, J. (1981). *Stages of faith.* New York, NY: Harper & Row.

Francis, P. C., & Dugger, S. M. (2014). Professionalism, ethics, and value-based conflicts in counseling: An introduction to the special section. *Journal of Counseling & Development, 92,* 131–134.

Freeman, S. (2000). *Ethics: An introduction to philosophy and practice.* Belmont, CA: Wadsworth.

Gates, G. J., Ost, J., & Birch E. (2004). *Gay & lesbian atlas.* Baltimore, MD: Urban Institute Press.

Geldard, K., Geldard, D., & Yin Foo, R. (2013). *Counselling children* (4th ed.). Thousand Oaks, CA: Sage Publications Ltd.

Gilligan, C., Ward, J. V., & Taylor, J. M. (Eds.). (1988). *Mapping the moral domain.* Cambridge, MA: Harvard University Press.

Glasser, W. (2008). Personal communication. Atlanta, GA.

Glosoff, H. L., & Pate, R. H. (2002). Privacy and confidentiality in school counseling. *Professional School Counseling, 6,* 20–27.

Granello, D. H., & Young, M. E. (2012). *Counseling today: Foundations of professional identity.* Boston, MA: Pearson.

Gray, L. A., Ancis, J. R., Ladany, N., & Walker, J. A. (2001). Psychotherapy trainees' experience of counterproductive events in supervision. *Journal of Counseling Psychology, 48,* 371–383.

Green, R. (2003). When therapists do not want their clients to be homosexual: A response to Rosik's article. *Journal of Marital and Family Therapy, 29,* 29–38.

Greene, B. (1994). Lesbian women of color: Triple jeopardy. In L. Comas-Diaz & B. Greene (Eds.), *Women of color: Integrating ethnic and gender identities in psychotherapy* (pp. 109–147). New York, NY: The Guilford Press.

Grohol, J. (1997). *Why online psychotherapy? Because there is a need* [Online]. Retrieved January 22, 2001 from http://sucjcemtra:/cp./archives/n102297. htm

Grohol, J. (1999). *Best practices in e-therapy: Definition and scope of e-therapy* [Online]. Retrieved January 22, 2001 from http://psych-central.com/best/ best4.htm

Grossman A., & D'Augelli, A. (2006). Transgender youth: Invisible and vulnerable. *Journal of Homosexuality, 51*, 111–128.

Grov, C., Bimbi, D. S., Nanin, J. E., & Parsons, J. T. (2006). Race, ethnicity, gender, and generational factors associated with the coming-out process among gay, lesbian, and bisexual individuals. *The Journal of Sex Research, 43*, 115–121.

Gussak, D., & Orr, P. (2005). Ethical responsibilities: Preparing students for the real art therapy world. *Art Therapy Journal of the American Art Therapy Association, 22*(2), 101–104.

Hanley, T. (2009). The working alliance in online therapy with young people: Preliminary findings. *British Journal of Guidance & Counselling, 37* (3), 257–269.

Hannon, K. (1996). Upset? Try cybertherapy. *U.S. News and World Report, 120*, 81–83.

Hays, P. A. (2001). *Addressing cultural complexities in practice: A framework for clinicians and counselors.* Washington, DC: American Psychological Association.

Helminiak, D. A. (2000). *What the Bible really says about homosexuality.* Estancia, NM: Alamo Square Press.

Herek, G., Cogan, J., Gillis, J., & Glunt, E. (1997). Correlates of internalized homophobia in a community sample of lesbians and gay men. *Journal of the Gay and Lesbian Medical Association, 2*, 17–25.

Herlihy, B., & Corey, G. (2015). *ACA ethical standards casebook.* Alexandria, VA: American Counseling Association.

Hernstein, R. J., & Murray, C. (1994). *The bell curve: Intelligence and class structure in American life.* New York, NY: Free Press.

Hess, R. S., Magnuson, S., & Beeler, L. (2012). *Counseling children and adolescents in schools.* Thousand Oaks, CA: Sage Publications Ltd.

Hesse, A. R. (2002). Secondary trauma: How working with trauma survivors affects therapists. *Clinical Social Work Journal, 30*(3), 293–309.

Hinduja, S., & Patchin, J. W. (2015). *Cyberbullying warning signs: Red flags that a child is involved in cyberbullying.* Retrieved August 15, 2015 from http://www.cyberbullying.us/cyberbullying-warning-signs.pdf

Hinz, L. (2013). The life cycle of images: Revisiting the ethical treatment of the art therapy image. *Art Therapy: Journal of the American Art Therapy Association, 30*(1), 46–49.

Hollander, G. (2000). Questioning youths: Challenges to working with youths forming identities. *School Psychology Review, 29*, 173–179.

Hughes v. Stanley County School District. Supreme Court of South Dakota (2001). Retrieved from http://caselaw.findlaw.com

Huss, S. N., Bryant, A., & Mulet, S. (2008). Managing the quagmire in a school: Bringing the parents on board. *Professional School Counseling, 11*, 362–367.

Iliffe, G., & Steed, L. G. (2000). Exploring the counselor's experience of working with perpetrators and survivors of domestic violence. *Journal of International Violence, 15*(4), 393–412.

Ingersoll, R. E., Bauer, A., & Burns, L. (2004). Children and psychotropic medication: What role should advocacy counseling play? *Journal of Counseling and Development, 82*(3), 337–343.

International Society of Mental Health. (1997). Retrieved from http://www.ismho.org

International Society for Mental Health Online. (2000). *ISMHO/PSI suggested principles for the online provision of mental health services* [Online]. Retrieved January 22, 2001 from http://www.ismho.org/suggestions.html as cited in Childress, C. A. (2000). Ethical issues in providing online psychotherapeutic interventions. *Journal of Medical Internet Research, 2*.

Isaacs, M. L. (1997). The duty to warn and protect: Tarasoff and the elementary school counselor. *Elementary School Guidance and Counseling, 31*, 326–342.

Isaacs, M. L., & Stone, C. (2001). Confidentiality with minors: Mental health counselors' attitudes toward breaching or preserving confidentiality. *Journal of Mental Health Counseling, 23*, 342–356.

Jennings, S. (1997). *Dramatherapy theory and practice 3*. New York, NY: Routledge.

Junge, M., & Asawa, P. (1994). *A history of art therapy in the United States*. Alexandria, VA: American Art Therapy Association.

Kanyal, M. (2014). *Children's rights 0–8: Promoting participation and education in care*. New York, NY: Routledge.

Kaplan, D. M. (2014). Ethical implications of a critical legal case for the counseling profession: Ward v. Wilbanks. *Journal of Counseling and Development, 92*, 142–146.

Kaufman G., & Raphael, L. (1996). *Coming out of shame*. New York, NY: Doubleday.

Keeton v. Anderson-Wiley. 664 F.3d 865. (2011a). Retrieved from http://www.leagle.com

Keeton v. Anderson-Wiley. U.S. Court of Appeals, 11th circuit.1013935. (2011b). Retrieved from http://www.acluga.org/download_file/view_inline/1405/311/

Keeton v. Anderson-Wiley. U. S. District Court of Georgia Augusta Division, 110099 (2012).

Kessler, S. (2010). *The case for social media in the schools*. Retrieved from http://mashable.com/2010/09/29/social-media-in-school/

King, S. (2008). Exploring the role of counselor support: Gay, lesbian, bisexual, and questioning adolescents struggling with acceptance and disclosure. *Journal of GLB Family Studies, 4*, 361–384.

Kinsey, A. C., Pomeroy, W. B., & Martin, C. E. (1948). *Sexual behavior in the human male.* Philadelphia, PA: W. B. Saunders.

Knowles, L. P. (1996). Art therapists exhibiting children's art: When, where, and why. *Art Therapy: Journal of the American Art Therapy Association, 13*(3), 205–207.

Koocher, G. P. (2003). Ethical issues in psychotherapy with adolescents. *Journal of Clinical Psychology: In Session, 59*(11), 1247–1256. doi: 10.1002/jclp.10215

Kosciw, J. G., Greytak, E. A., Bartkiewicz, M. J., Boesen, M. J., & Palmer, N. A. (2012). *The 2011 National School Climate Survey: The experiences of lesbian, gay, bisexual and transgender youth in our nation's schools.* New York, NY: GLSEN.

Kraus, R., Stricker, G., & Speyer, C. (2010). *Online counseling: A handbook for mental health professionals.* London: Elsevier Academic Press.

Landreth, G. (2012). *Play therapy: The art of the relationship* (3rd ed.). New York, NY: Routledge.

Landsman, M. J., Groza, V., Tyler, M., & Malone, K. (2001). Outcomes of family-centered residential treatment. *Child Welfare, 80*, 351–379.

Lawrence, G., & Robinson Kurpius, S. E. (2000). Legal and ethical issues involved when counseling minors in non-school settings. *Journal of Counseling and Development, 78*(2), 130–136.

Ledyard, P. (1998). Counseling minors: Ethical and legal issues. *Counseling & Values, 42*, 171–177.

Lewis, J., Arnold, M., House, R., & Toporek, R. (2003). *Advocacy competencies.* Retrieved from http://www.counseling.org/Resources

Lewis, J. A., Ratts, M. J., Paladino, D. A., & Toporek, R. L. (2011). Social justice counseling and advocacy: Developing new leadership roles and competencies. *Journal for Social Action in Counseling and Psychology, 3*(1), 5–16.

MacCluskie, K. C. (2010). *Acquiring counseling skills: Integrating microskills, multiculturalism, theory, and self-awareness.* Pearson Merrill Prentice-Hall.

Marcus, E. (2005). *Is it a choice? Answers to the most frequently asked questions about gay & lesbian people* (3rd ed.). San Francisco, CA: HarperOne.

Marx, S. P. (1996). Victim recantation in child sexual abuse cases: The prosecutors role in prevention. *Child Welfare, 75*(3), 219–233.

Maslach, C. (2003). Job Burnout: New directions in research and intervention. *Current Directions in Psychological Science, 12*, 189–192.

Matthews, C., & Salazar, C. (2012). An integrative, empowerment model for helping lesbian, gay, and bisexual youth negotiate the coming-out process. *Journal of LGBT Issues in Counseling, 6*(2), 96–117. doi: 10.1080/15538605.2012.678176

McHenry, B., Sikorski, A., & McHenry, J. (2014). *A counselor's introduction to neuroscience.* New York, NY: Routledge.

McIntosh, P. (1988). *White privilege and male privilege: A personal account of coming to see corresponds through work in women's studies.* Working Paper #189. Wellesley, MA: Wellesley Centers for Women.

Meyer, I. H. (2003). Prejudice, social stress, and mental health in lesbian, gay, and bisexual populations: Conceptual issues and research evidence. *Psychological Bulletin, 129,* 674–697.

Mitchell, C. W., Disque, J. G., & Robertson, P. (2002). When parents want to know: Responding to parental demands for confidential information. *Professional School Counseling, 6,* 156–161.

Moon, B. (2006). *Ethical issues in art therapy* (2nd ed.). Springfield, IL: Charles Thomas Pub. Ltd.

Morrison L. L., & L'Heureux, J. (2001). Suicide and gay/lesbian/bisexual youth: Implications for clinicians. *Journal of Adolescence, 24,* 39–49.

Mosher, C. M. (2001). The social implications of sexual identity formation and the coming-out process: A review of the theoretical and empirical literature. *The Family Journal, 9,* 164–173.

Moyer, M. S., & Sullivan, J. R. (2008). Student risk-taking behaviors: When do school counselors break confidentiality? *Professional School Counseling, 11,* 236–245.

Moyer, M. S., Sullivan, J. R., & Growcock, D. (2012). When is it ethical to inform administrators about student risk-taking behaviors? Perceptions of school counselors. *Professional School Counseling, 15,* 98–109.

Murray, A. (2014). Protecting children and young people—the "online" generation. In P. Weitz (Ed.), *Psychotherapy 2.0: Meeting the challenges and potential of the digital age* (pp. 209–243). London: Karnac.

Myrick, R. D., & Sabella, R. A. (1995). Cyberspace: New place for counselor supervision. *Elementary School Guidance and Counseling, 30,* 35–44.

National Association of School Psychologists (NASP). (2010). *Principles for professional ethics.* Bethesda, MD: Author.

National Board of Certified Counselors. (2012). Retrieved from: http://www.nbcc.org/Assets/Ethics/NBCCPolicyRegardingPracticeofDistanceCounselingBoard.pdf

Noftle, J. W., Cook, S., Leschied, A., St. Pierre, J. Stewart, S. L., & Johnson, A. M. (2011). The trajectory of change for children and youth in residential treatment. *Child Psychiatry and Human Development, 42,* 65–77.

North American Drama Therapy Association. (2016). *Code of ethical principles.* Retrieved February 12, 2016 from http://www.nadta.org/about-nadta/code-of-ethics.html

O'Leary, R. J., & D'Ovidio, R. (2010). Online sexual exploitation of children. *The International Association of Computer Investigative Specialist.* Retrieved August 13, 2015 from http://www.nga.org/files/live/sites/NGA/files/pdf/0703ONLINECHILD.PDF

Pearlman, L. A. (1995). Self-care from trauma therapists: Ameliorating vicarious traumatization. In B. H. Stamm (Ed.), *Secondary traumatic stress: Self-care issues for clinicians, researchers, and educators* (pp. 51–64). Lutherville, MD: Sidran Press.

Pearlman, L. A. (1999). Self-care for trauma therapists. In B. H. Stamm (Ed.), *Secondary traumatic stress: Self-care issues for clinicians, researchers, and educators* (2nd ed., pp. 51–64). Lutherville, MD: Sidran Press.

Peterson, M., & Scanlon, M. (2002). Diagnosis and placement variables affecting the outcome of adolescents with behavioral disorders. *Residential Treatment for Children and Youth, 20*, 15–23.

Piaget, J. (1972). *The psychology of intelligence.* Totowa, NJ: Littlefield.

Radhika, G. (2014). Impact of cyber-bullying—a new outbreak IOSR (International Organization of Scientific Research). *Journal of Humanities and Social Science (IOSR-JHSS), 50*–53. Retrieved from www.iosrjournals.org

RAINN. (2016). www.rainn.org

Ray, D. (2011). *Advanced play therapy: Essential conditions, knowledge, and skills for child practice.* New York, NY: Routledge.

Remley, T. P. (1985). The law and ethical practices in elementary and middle schools. *Elementary School Guidance & Counseling, 19*, 181–189.

Remley, T. P., & Herlihy, B. (2014). *Ethical, legal, and professional issues in counseling* (4th ed.). Upper Saddle River, NJ: Pearson.

Remley, T. P., & Herlihy, B. (2016). *Ethical, legal, and professional issues in counseling* (5th ed.). Upper Saddle River, NJ: Pearson.

Ronnestad, M. H., & Skovholt, T. M. (2003). The journey of the counselor and therapist: Research findings and perspectives on professional development. *Journal of Career Development, 30*, 5–44. doi: 0894–8453/03/09000–0005/0

Rosario, M., Schrimshaw, E. W., & Hunter, J. (2004). Ethnic/racial differences in the coming-out process of lesbian, gay, and bisexual youths: A comparison of sexual identity development over time. *Cultural Diversity and Ethnic Minority Psychology, 10*, 215–228.

Saakvitne, K. W. (2002). Shared trauma: The therapist's increased vulnerability. *Psychoanalytic Dialogues, 12*(3), 443–449.

Sattler, J. M. (2014). *Foundations of behavioral, social, and clinical assessment of children* (6th ed.). San Diego, CA: Author.

Sealander, K. A. (1999). Confidentiality and the law. *Professional School Counseling, 3*, 122–127.

Shiles, M. (2009). Discriminatory referrals: Uncovering a potential ethical dilemma facing practitioners. *Ethics and Behavior, 19*(2), 142–155. doi: 10.1080/105084209027772777

Singh, A. A. (2008). *Counseling queer (LGBT) youth.* American Counseling Association Podcast. Retrieved from http://www.counseling.org/counselors/TP/podcastsmembers/CT2.aspx

Sorensen, R. (1973). *Adolescent sexuality in contemporary society.* New York, NY: World Book.

Souders, T., Strom-Gottfried, K., & DeVito, D. (2009, June). *FAQ on services to minors of divorced parents.* Thiemann Advisory: University of North Carolina School of Social Work. Retrieved from www.ssw.unc.edu

Stamm, B. H. (1995). *Work-related secondary traumatic stress- self-care issues for clinicians, researchers and educators.* Lutherville, MD: Sidran Press.

Stein, R. H. (1990). *Ethical issues in counseling.* Buffalo, NY: Prometheus.

Stone, C. B. (2003). Counselors as advocates for gay, lesbian, and bisexual youth: A call for equity and action. *Journal of Multicultural Counseling and Development, 31,* 143–155.

Studer, J. R. (2015). *The essential school counselor in a changing society.* Thousand Oak, CA: Sage Publications Ltd.

Such, C. (2014). History and development of children's rights. In M. Kanyal (Ed.), *Children's rights 0–8: Promoting participation and education in care* (pp. 7–25). New York, NY: Routledge.

Sue, D., Capodilupo, C., Torino, G., Bucceri, J., Holder, A., Nadal, K., & Esquilin, M. (2007). Racial microaggressions in everyday life: Implications for clinical practice. *American Psychologist, 62*(4), 271–286.

Sue, D. W., & Sue, D. (2013). *Counseling the culturally diverse: Theory and practice* (6th ed.). New York, NY: Wiley.

Suler, J. R. (2001). Assessing a persons' suitability for online therapy. *Cyberpsychology and Behavior, 4,* 675–679.

Suler, J. (2002). Identity management in cyberspace. *Journal of Applied Psychoanalytic Studies, 4*(4), 455–459.

Suler, J. R. (2004). The online disinhibition effect. *Cyberpsychology and Behavior, 7,* 321–326.

Sussman, R. J. (1998). Counseling online. *CTOnline* [Online]. Retrieved January 22, 2001 from http://www.orgctonline/sr598counseling./sussman.htm

Tehrani, N. (2007). The cost of caring-the impact of secondary trauma on assumptions, values, and beliefs. *Counseling Psychology Quarterly, 20*(4), 325–339. doi: 10.1080/09515070701690069

Tokunaga, R. S. (2010). Following you home from school: A critical review and synthesis of research on cyberbullying victimization. *Computers in Human Behavior, 26*(3), 277–287.

Troiden, R. (1988). Homosexual identity development. *Journal of Adolescent Health Care, 9,* 105–113.

Tuckman, B. (1965). Developmental sequence in small groups. *Psychological Bulletin, 63*(6), 384–399.

Twist, M., Murphy, M., Green, M., & Palmanteer, D. (2006). Therapists' support of gay and lesbian human rights. *Guidance & Counseling, 21,* 107–113.

Vick, R. (2011). Ethics on exhibit. *Art Therapy: Journal of the American Art Therapy Association, 28*(4), 152–158.

Walden v. Centers for Disease Control and Prevention. No. 1:08-cv-02278-JEC (U. S. District Court from the Northern District of Georgia March 18, 2010).

Ward v. Polite et al. United States Court of Appeals, Sixth Circuit. 102100. 2145 (2012). Retrieved from http://www.ca6.uscourts.gov/opinions.pdf/ 12a0024p-06.pdf

Ward v. Wilbanks. U.S. Court of Appeals 0911237 (E.D. Mich. January 27, 2012).

Ward v. Wilbanks. U.S. Dist. LEXIS 127038 (E.D. Mich., July 26, 2010). Retrieved from http://www.lexisnexis.com

Wehrman, J. D., Williams, R., Field, J., & Schroeder, S. D. (2010). Accountability through documentation: What are best practices for school counselors? *Journal of School Counseling, 8*(38), 1–23.

Wheeler, A. M., & Bertram, B. (2012). *The counselor and the law: A guide to legal and ethical practice* (6th ed.). Alexandria, VA: American Counseling Association.

Whitcomb, S. A., & Merrell, K. W. (2013). *Behavioral, social, and emotional assessment of children and adolescents* (4th ed.). New York, NY: Routledge.

Wicks, R. J., & Buck, T. C. (2014). "Alonetime": Recovering a rich classical resource for counselor self-renewal. *Journal of Mental Health Counseling, 36,* 288–301.

Wilcoxon, S. A. (1990). Protecting the best interest of minors: A new ethical standard for counselors. *Journal of Offender Counseling, 10,* 9–17.

Wilmshurst, I. A. (2002). Treatment programs for youth with emotional and behavioral disorders: An outcome study of two alternative approaches. *Mental Health Services Research, 4,* 85–96.

Wolak, J., Mitchell, K., & Finkelhor, D. (2006). *Online victimization of youth: Five years later.* Washington, DC: National Center for Missing & Exploited Children.

Wright, E. R., & Perry, B. L. (2006). Sexual identity distress, social support, and the health of gay, lesbian, and bisexual youth. *Journal of Homosexuality, 15,* 81–110.

Zinmesiter, K. (2006). Real numbers: Sex in America. *The American Enterprise, 17,* 24–25.

INDEX

Note: Page numbers in *italics* indicate figures.

For Product Safety Concerns and Information please contact our EU
representative GPSR@taylorandfrancis.com
Taylor & Francis Verlag GmbH, Kaufingerstraße 24, 80331 München, Germany

www.ingramcontent.com/pod-product-compliance
Lightning Source LLC
Chambersburg PA
CBHW070407270326
41926CB00014B/2739